The Path

to

War

THE PATH

TO

WAR

HOW THE FIRST WORLD WAR
CREATED MODERN AMERICA

Michael S. Neiberg

OXFORD
UNIVERSITY PRESS

OXFORD
UNIVERSITY PRESS

Oxford University Press is a department of the University of Oxford.
It furthers the University's objective of excellence in research, scholarship,
and education by publishing worldwide. Oxford is a registered trade mark of
Oxford University Press in the UK and certain other countries.

Published in the United States of America by Oxford University Press
198 Madison Avenue, New York, NY 10016, United States of America.

Library of Congress Cataloging-in-Publication Data
Names: Neiberg, Michael S., author.
Title: The path to war : how the First World War created modern America /
Michael S. Neiberg.
Description: New York : Oxford University Press, 2016. |
Includes bibliographical references and index.
Identifiers: LCCN 2016006846 | ISBN 9780190464967
Subjects: LCSH: World War, 1914–1918—United States. |
United States—Politics and government—1913-1921.
Classification: LCC D619 .N45 2016 | DDC 940.3/73—dc23
LC record available at https://lccn.loc.gov/2016006846

1 3 5 7 9 8 6 4 2

Printed by Sheridan Books, Inc., United States of America

CONTENTS

THE PATH

TO

WAR

Introduction

The Road Over There Starts on a Commuter Train

ON APRIL 9, 1917, GEORGE M. COHAN, one of the most celebrated entertainers in America, was reading about his country's declaration of war
against Germany on his usual Monday-morning commute into
Manhattan from his family's weekend house in New Rochelle. Suddenly
swept up in a moment of patriotism, he began to hum chords until
something stuck. Then some lyrics came to him. By the time he had arrived at Grand Central Terminal half an hour later, he thought he might
have something special. Instead of going to his office, Cohan went to see
his friend Joe Humphreys, the ring announcer at Madison Square
Garden, and sang the song for him. "George," the normally hard-to-
please Humphreys told him, "you've got a song."

Although it later became part of entertainment lore, Cohan's family
never liked that version of events. His then-eight-year-old daughter,
Mary, later recalled her father gathering the family together in the
kitchen on Sunday, the day before his commute into Manhattan. Cohan
told them that he had written a new song to support his nation now that
it was at war, and he wanted them to be the first to hear it. Mary remembered her father singing the song for his wife and children in full voice
as if he were on the stage, complete with a pot on his head for a helmet
and a broomstick on his shoulder for a rifle. He performed the song so

3

convincingly that Mary left the kitchen in tears, believing that her father was going off to war that same day.

Whichever version of the story is closer to the truth, the song that Cohan wrote, "Over There," became for a time the most popular song in America. Within a month after its release people across the country were singing it on the streets, in theaters, and in their homes. The first nationally distributed production of the song, sung by Vaudeville star Billy Murray, sold a record-breaking 1.5 million copies. Cohan himself later recorded a version, as did two more of America's most famous entertainers, Cohan's Broadway protégée Nora Bayes and tenor Enrico Caruso.

That Cohan would have written the best-selling and most-performed song of his generation would have come as no surprise to anyone alive in 1917. What might have been a surprise is that Cohan, known for his catchy Tin Pan Alley tunes, would have turned his talents to America's participation in the war in Europe. That he did so reflects the evolution of a larger national journey from impartiality or even indifference in 1914 to an uneasy neutrality in 1915 and 1916 to a determination in 1917 to fight and win "until it's over, Over There." The song's popularity showed how much the country had changed in two years. In 1915, "I Didn't Raise My Boy to Be a Soldier" had been one of the year's biggest hits and had sparked national controversy following a sharp retort from former president Theodore Roosevelt.[1] In addition to "Over There," for which Woodrow Wilson himself sent him a congratulatory note, Cohan wrote and produced a show that raised $700,000 for the American Red Cross.

The three singers who carried the song into every home and theater in America symbolized the country's transition from neutrality to war. Their own stories reflected the wide range of responses to the events in Europe between 1914 and 1917. Billy Murray came from an Irish-American community in Philadelphia that had initially shown little sympathy for the Allied cause. Opposed to the British occupation of Ireland, most Irish-Americans saw rank hypocrisy in French and British claims to be fighting for the rights of poor little Belgium, while the rights of poor little Ireland went ignored. Britain's brutal crushing of the Easter Rising in Dublin in April 1916 led to suspicion and mistrust about the wisdom of using American power to help the British win a war, but, paradoxically, it also drew Irish-Americans into a closer alignment with the beliefs of the American people more generally.

Nora Bayes, raised in a Jewish family in Joliet, Illinois, was born Eleanor Goldberg. The Jewish-Americans in her neighborhood would almost certainly have supported the Central Powers in 1914. Germany and Austria-Hungary had far better reputations as places for Jews to live than the notoriously anti-Semitic Russia, whose pogroms had recently chased hundreds of thousands of Jews from their homes. Still, by the time Bayes performed her version of "Over There," events in both Europe and in the United States had led Jewish-Americans to change their minds about the wisdom, and the purpose, of the war. They were fully in support of America's entry into the war by April 1917.

Enrico Caruso's native Italy had initially stayed out of the war, giving Italian-Americans an incentive to avoid thinking too deeply about it. In the spring of 1915, however, Italy joined the Allies, linking Italians in the United States to the war in Europe. As the war continued over the next two years, the sentiments of most Americans increasingly aligned with those of the Italian-American community. For all three groups, as well as for Protestant Americans like Cohan, both their responses to the war and what they thought it meant for the United States evolved as they came to see their common interests converge in a time of national crisis. Notably, no well-known version of "Over There" was sung by an African-American singer. The war played a critical role in the dual process of uniting white Americans while reinforcing segregation both at home and in the armed forces, even though by 1917 African-Americans shared the general pro-belligerence attitude of white Americans.

At about the same time that Cohan wrote "Over There," the country's most famous director, Cecil B. DeMille, and its best-known actress, Mary Pickford, were finishing a movie they co-produced called *The Little American*. In the movie, Angela (played by Pickford) is wooed by both a French nobleman and Karl, a man of mixed German and American ancestry. There is little subtlety here; Angela symbolizes American neutrality as the two men, standing in for the great warring powers, vie for her affections. When the war begins, Karl returns to Hamburg to serve in the German Army. Angela travels to Europe a few months later and the Germans torpedo her ship. She survives the sinking and makes her way to the French side of the Western Front where she witnesses German soldiers pillaging and raping. Angela finally agrees to abandon her neutrality and help some French soldiers, which she does by means of a secret telephone to which she has access. Soldiers from a German unit find her and attempt to rape her, but one of the soldiers turns out to be Karl, who saves her. (He cannot, however, save the other women in the building whom the Germans presumably rape.)

The incident makes Angela all the more determined to help the French and she tries to use the secret telephone again. Karl discovers what she is doing and decides he must help her escape. Both are captured by the Germans, who prepare to execute them by firing squad. A French shell interrupts the proceedings like a *deus ex machina*, allowing Angela and Karl to escape to the safety of French lines. Both return to the United States, although Karl does so temporarily as a prisoner of war. Angry at Karl, but probably still in love with him, Angela tells him, "I was neutral—till I saw your soldiers destroying women and shooting old men! Then I stopped being 'neutral' and became a human being!"[2] Like Angela, the United States came to see Germany as operating outside the basic boundaries of the civilized world. Nevertheless, most Americans blamed the imperial German system, not individual Germans like Karl who, one presumes, can be rehabilitated by prolonged exposure to the graces of democracy and pluralism in the United States.

America changed dramatically between August 1914 and April 1917. By the latter date the country was ready to fight a war, something that the vast majority of Americans would have found inconceivable just three short years earlier. The road to 1917 involved domestic, international, and transnational themes. Seeing themselves as a burgeoning and exceptional global power, the American people debated the rights and responsibilities that came with power and neutrality in an age of unprecedented warfare. The latter included the obligation to help the victims of the war and to try to bring the warring parties to peace. The former included the ability to profit from wartime trade and perhaps even to reorient the center of the world economy by forcing it to move from London, Paris, and Berlin to New York City. All Americans, not just the great industrialists and financiers of the East, saw the possible benefits from such a transition of economic might across the Atlantic Ocean. Thus the debate about America's role in the First World War involved much more than a debate over the arcane details of international law. It meant nothing less than a chance for Americans to assume a dominant place among the world's great powers.

This book tells the story of how Americans responded to the outbreak of war in Europe in 1914, how they dealt with their nation's era of neutrality from 1914 to 1917, and how they finally saw the inescapable necessity of taking part in, to that point, the most murderous conflict in human history. Until now, scholars have largely told that story through the eyes of the man who made the final decision in 1917, President Woodrow Wilson. This book takes a different approach. While not denying the critical role of the president and his advisors, it seeks to get beyond hackneyed explanations, such as the rights of neutral nations, blockade policy, and Wilson's theories about how to reorganize the community of nations. The real story is far more interesting, with the potential for offering insights into American history as well as the study of societies at war.

This approach can also help to fill in the gap in America's collective amnesia over the First World War. Although largely forgotten today, the war is fundamental to American history. The country's entry into the war marked the end of one era and the start of another, one whose impact we are still feeling, even if we do not always recognize it. The war occurred precisely as Americans were debating the role that a newly powerful United States should play in the world. Some, like Theodore Roosevelt, thought that the outbreak of war in Europe in 1914 proved that the time had come for the country to take a much more prominent place on the world stage. Using its military power for good, he believed, could make both the nation and the world a safer and more just place. Roosevelt had little patience for Wilson's brand of idealism, and from 1914 to 1917 he urged, in increasingly intemperate language, that the president do his job and prepare the nation for a war it would sooner or later have to fight. When he read the Zimmermann Telegram, Roosevelt supposedly said that if Wilson did not declare war, he would go to the White House and skin the president alive. This era is not nearly as dull and colorless as the black-and-white photos in schoolbooks might suggest.[3]

This book analyzes American reactions to the war by looking at how over time Americans understood its causes, its evolution, and their relationship to it. The following chapters also examine key points of transition, such as the sinking of the *Lusitania*, news of the massacres of

Armenians inside the Ottoman Empire, and the collapse of the tsarist regime in Russia. The world changed tremendously in a few short years, and Americans had no choice but to change with it. They did not, of course, always agree on how they should change. A large and diverse society in the process of assimilating new arrivals and adjusting to modernization and urbanization, Americans often preferred not to think about the terrible war in Europe. By 1917, however, US citizens realized that ignoring the war or pretending it had nothing to do with them imperiled their future.

Most important, they realized that they had run out of options. Between 1914 and 1917, Americans had variously hoped that their nation could serve as an arbiter (as it had during the Russo-Japanese War, earning Theodore Roosevelt the country's first Nobel Peace Prize), the leader of a global peace movement, the center of international arbitration, and the advocate of worldwide disarmament. By early 1917, however, the vast majority had come to two conclusions. First, as Charles Fremont Taylor, the editor of a Philadelphia-based magazine articulated, "no nation can be a hermit in these days of steamships, railroads, telegraphs, ocean cables, wireless, etc."[4] They no longer believed, as they had in 1914, that the Atlantic Ocean provided the country with sufficient protection from Europe's wars. Second, they believed that their leaders had tried every option short of war only to find the country in an even more perilous geopolitical position.

In the pages that follow I argue that we need to understand how the American people reacted to these crucial years. Contrary to what many have written or assumed, Americans were neither the unwilling dupes of propaganda, the blind followers of a messianic president, or naive puppets of a millionaire class. Rather, I argue, they chose to fight, even if they did so because they thought they had run out of viable alternatives. To paraphrase Leon Trotsky, Americans may not always have been interested in the war, but the war came to be interested in them. By 1917 they had finally come to that realization. Although they did not all enter into the war with joy, they did enter it as a people united to face common threats and, for a time at least, to celebrate that decision in song. Their country would emerge from the war and the peace it produced a far different place. We need to take a close look at it if we are to have any hope of understanding it.

1

Understanding the Two Germanys

IN 1913, FEW AMERICANS HAD any reason to have heard of the charming but relatively isolated Alsatian garrison town of Zabern. Off the beaten path for wealthy Americans making their summer trips to Europe's capital cities, mountain resorts, and beaches, it had few attractions worthy of inclusion in a tourist's guidebook. Like the towns around it, Zabern had in the previous forty years changed both its spelling and the government to which it answered. In 1871, Zabern (in French, Saverne), like the rest of Alsace and most of Lorraine, had transferred from French control to German control in the wake of France's defeat in the Franco-Prussian War.

In 1911 the imperial German government in Berlin granted Alsace more autonomy to direct its cultural and educational affairs. The region, like Germany's heavily Polish eastern districts, had a diverse population that recognized German political authority, but sought to maintain its distinct traditions and language. Zabern, and Alsace-Lorraine more generally, had a mixed population of relatively disaffected French residents, newly arrived Germans, and a traditional population of Alsatians and Lorrainers trying to adapt to historical and political circumstances as best they could. The German government hoped that the 1911 reforms might placate them all.[1]

Zabern's anonymity ended in November 1913 when the town's name began to appear in American newspaper headlines. Tensions had risen in Alsace in the preceding months over what the French and Alsatians saw as German refusal to abide by the promises of cultural autonomy built into the 1911 reforms. Into this increasingly tense mix stepped a nineteen-year-old baron and army lieutenant named Günther von Forstner. Arrogant even by contemporary Prussian Army standards, Forstner had no sympathy for the residents of Zabern and their desires for more cultural autonomy. He saw in their eyes looks of disapproval and defiance of his, and Germany's, authority to govern them.

In late October 1913, Forstner had publicly referred to the locals as "Wackes," an Alsatian slur both hard to translate ("lazy bums" may come closest) and so deeply insulting to the locals that the German Army had banned its use in a 1903 regulation. Rather than apologize for the hurt he had caused, Forstner instead promised his men ten marks for each local they shot should riots break out. A photograph taken by a local resident from an upper-story window showed Forstner swaggering down the streets of Zabern with an armed guard merely to buy bread. It soon appeared in newspapers in both Europe and the United States. Shortly thereafter, Forstner struck a lame cobbler with the back of his saber for the crime of not properly acknowledging him on the street. With his erect, overly military bearing and his superior attitude, Forstner became the perfect caricature of Prussian arrogance as well as ready-made fodder for political cartoonists like Alsace's own famous folk artist Jean-Jacques Waltz, better known as Hansi. One of Hansi's cartoons showed a teacher in Alsatian dress lecturing a pint-sized Forstner in full dress uniform while standing in front of a row of six portraits of Alsatian generals who had served in the French Army and defeated Prussians in past wars. The text reads, "And now, Monsieur the Baron will permit me to introduce him to some authentic Alsatian Wackes."

Rather than punish Forstner for his adolescent stupidity and force him to apologize to the locals for his offensive behavior, the lieutenant's superior officers defended him and the right of German officers more generally by citing a long since forgotten Prussian siege law passed a century earlier during the Napoleonic Wars. This preposterous overstretch of military authority caused a political scandal inside Germany. Socialists and many non-Prussian delegates in the Reichstag demanded that the government punish the army for overstepping its legal and constitutional bounds. They forced the only vote of no confidence in the history of the Second Reich, demanded the resignation of Chancellor Theobald von Bethmann-Hollweg for his handling of the crisis, and even took the bold step of refusing to stand when Kaiser Wilhelm II came to the Reichstag for ceremonies closing the year's parliamentary session. Nationalists and most Prussian delegates defended the army, with some arguing that it need never answer to civil authority, only to the kaiser himself.

Seeing the risk of a German version of France's Dreyfus Affair resulting from the Zabern incident, Wilhelm forged a shaky political compromise.[2] He knew that the Reichstag had far less power than parliaments in Great Britain or France, but it could still delay or modify important legislation, such as the defense bill then under consideration. A crisis could have consequences for a changing Germany that no one could predict. Wilhelm thus ordered the entire garrison out of Zabern but gave out only the lightest of punishments to the offending officers. Although the compromise satisfied no one, it offered just enough to all parties involved to calm tensions and allow Wilhelm to depict himself as representing all of Germany, not just the army and the extreme nationalists.[3]

Americans followed the Zabern Affair closely; it showed them the German system at its worst. Editorials spoke with one voice about the scandal, ascribing it to the lack of genuine democracy in Germany. The affair, they argued, had shown that the German people were, in the words of a Colorado newspaper, merely "marionettes in a kind of burlesque on constitutional government" and that "the Kaiser and his chancellor were the only real rulers in Germany." The problem, reported the New York *Tribune* "is in every garrison town in Germany, even in [Berlin's] Unter den Linden itself." The German military, they argued, "regard themselves not so much the servants of the state as the overlords of all mere civilians."[4]

American newspapers analyzed the situation through the lens of the "Two Germanys," an idea popular on both sides of the Atlantic and even among many Germans themselves. It posited that the unification of the country completed in the 1870s had imposed a Prussian autocracy on the rest of Germany, stamping out all democratic opposition along the way. The militarist, domineering nature of the Prussian elite had then slowly strangled the humanistic, scientific Germany of years past. Many emigrants from Germany to the United States saw the same problem, often coming to America to avoid the anti-Catholic and overly militarist tone of the new Germany. Americans thus looked at Germany in 1913–14 with ambivalence, admiring Germany's contribution to science, education, medicine, and the arts, but at the same time detesting its militaristic trappings and undemocratic form of government. Consequently, they saw the essentially good and decent German people as victims of their own government, and the excessive militarism of the regime as a product of its retrograde system of autocracy.[5]

The powerful push against the army during the Zabern Affair suggested that perhaps German militarism had begun to lose its grip on society, just as French militarism had during the years of the Dreyfus Affair.[6] The coming years might therefore see the German people assert their right to liberty. As the New York *Times* noted, the Zabern Affair could go down in European history as "one of the most striking victories won by public opinion" should the German people keep up the pressure for further political reform in the years to come.[7] One Alabama newspaper admiringly quoted German politician Matthias Erzberger, who said that the events at Zabern had opened up "a political struggle in Germany in which compromise is scarcely possible."[8] Most Americans watched with sympathetic eyes as Erzberger and others challenged Prussian militarists in the hopes of creating a democratic Germany that would present no threat to its neighbors and thereby become a force for stability in the heart of Europe.

The embers of the Zabern Affair had not yet cooled by the time that Europe suddenly found itself at war in August 1914. When the armies of Europe became locked into a continental war whose causes many Americans found hard to comprehend, they returned to ideas about the Two Germanys and the imposition of Prussian values across the German state. The German system required, in the words of veteran foreign affairs correspondent Frederick Palmer, "obedience to superiors, from bottom to top."[9] Now those autocratic superiors had dragged a pacific people into a war. Early on, many hoped that the German people would rise against their government and repudiate its aggressive foreign policy. As Stanford president David Starr Jordan, a pacifist and an admirer of

German culture and education, wrote in the war's early weeks, "Of all the many issues, good or bad, which may come from this war, none is more important than this, that the German people should take possession of Germany."[10]

These ideas existed both among the elite and the American people more generally. President Wilson's friend and confidant Edward House blamed the German militarist party for the outbreak of the war, but he stopped short of blaming the German people themselves. He had recently toured Europe and found no desire for war in England, France, or among the wider German people. Only among the officials in the German government did he find a worldview encouraging war instead of continued peace. Shortly after attending the *Schrippenfest* ceremony, "a gorgeous presentation of devotional militarism in the Prussian style," on June 1, 1914, House told Wilson that the German system represented "militarism run stark mad."[11] That militarism, more than any other single factor, shocked those who had presumed that democracy would triumph over it in the wake of the Zabern Affair. The American ambassador to Great Britain, Walter Hines Page, agreed, writing to House shortly after the war started that "no power on earth could have prevented it. German militarism, which is *the* crime of the last fifty years, has been working for this for 25 years. It is the logical result of their spirit and enterprise."[12] The fifty years that Page noted marked the start of the three Wars of German Unification in 1864, beginning with Prussia's victory over Denmark.[13]

Newspaper and magazine editors shared these sentiments. The *Living Age* noted in November that its editorial staff had approached the war's first few months with an attitude of strict neutrality. Within a few short months, their position on the outbreak of the war had changed. Even if none of the lurid tales of German atrocities coming out of Belgium proved to be true, they noted, "all that America stands for is the negation of all that Prussia stands for." The Germans (or, in some people's formulations, the Prussians) had gone to war not in self-defense but in order to satisfy the acquisitive desires of a regime that did not represent the wishes of its own people. Germany, it concluded later in the same issue, had abandoned its Christian morals in favor of an atheist ideology that only worshipped empire, army, and militarism.[14] Harvard's former president Charles Eliot, an admirer of German educational and scientific methods, concluded in December 1914 that "Europe now has a chance to make a choice between the German ideal of the State and the Anglo-American ideal. These two ideals are very different; and the present conflict shows that they cannot coexist any longer in modern Europe." Eliot wanted to see the war continue "so long as Germany persists in its policies of world empire, dynastic rule, autocratic bureaucracy, and the use of force in international dealings."[15]

Two prominent American jurists held mock trials and both found Germany guilty of having started an unnecessary war. Tennessee Judge John Allison called the invasion of Belgium "the crime of the century" and concluded that it proved that Germany had planned the war, although he also took great pains to lay the blame on the German elite, not the German people.[16] Philadelphia Judge James M. Beck put the great powers before a fictional "Supreme Court of Civilization," using the words of European leaders as their "testimony." He found the German case not a justification for German actions but "a plea of Guilty at the bar of the world." He, too, absolved the German people, for whom he claimed a "deep affection," saying that his Court of Civilization should "distinguish between the military caste, headed by the Kaiser and the Crown Prince, which precipitated this great calamity, and the German people," whom their own government had "deceived and misled" into starting an unjust war.[17]

These ideas were widespread across the United States. In mid-August, the influential journal *Literary Digest* surveyed the country's newspapers and found that the vast majority blamed Germany for "letting the Austro-Servian crisis precipitate a European war." They judged Germany's response to a situation that posed no real threat to any state in Europe to be extreme and provocative. "American opinion," the magazine stated, "is almost solidly against Germany as the aggressor, ruthlessly plunging Europe into what looks like the bloodiest of wars to satisfy the overwhelming ambition of the emperor." It ended by concluding that "in this country, little fault is found with the course pursued by the French and British governments." Yet the *Literary Digest* did not blame the German people, whom the magazine saw as victims of their own irresponsible and unrepresentative government.[18]

The war confirmed the Zabern image of Germany as a country whose guiding force came from what the editors of *Life* called in August 1914 a

Prussian spirit of "blood and iron tonic" that their leaders fed the German people in lieu of giving them a democratic system of governance that could advance their true interests.[19] The *Living Age* likewise blamed the regime, but not the "guiltless" and "deceived" German people.[20] Journalist and veteran war correspondent Richard Harding Davis described the Prussian system as becoming like Frankenstein's monster whose only purpose had become killing. The monster, Davis told his readers, had grown out of control, until at last it had committed "the crime of the century," a felony that it had been plotting for decades. Eventually, he argued, the German people would see what the monster had done, rise up, and destroy it.[21] *Life* also used the image of Frankenstein's creation to describe the Germans in a cartoon from late August. Similarly, the Chicago *Defender* depicted a gruesome figure called "War" as a skeleton wearing a spike helmet and a German dress uniform.[22]

Until the German people took their great nation away from its repressive regime, their country stood outside the family of civilized nations. Willa Cather captured this zeitgeist in her Pulitzer Prize–winning book, *One of Ours*. The book focuses on a family in a rural Nebraska community. When the "bewildering" war in Europe begins, the matriarch of the Wheeler family rummages through the attic to find a map of Europe and an old set of encyclopedias. Although she sees Paris as a city of sin and wickedness, the pious Mrs. Wheeler nevertheless hangs the map, "a thing for which Nebraska farmers had never had much need," on a wall in her parlor and begins to pray "fervently" for the salvation of France. The Wheelers do not want to see America enter the war—their thoughts are instead on the profits they hope to make if the war causes wheat prices to rise—but they see Germany as having unleashed a "menace" to their "comfortable, established way of thinking." Cather described the Wheelers as thinking that "something new, and certainly evil, was at work among mankind. Nobody was ready with a name for it," although they believed that the blame for it should rest in Berlin.[23]

German behavior seemed so out of character that it was difficult to comprehend. How could a nation that had made so much progress have decided to begin a war on such a scale as this one? The New York *Evening Post*'s Oswald Villard (himself born in Wiesbaden) answered the question by returning to the idea of the Two Germanys. He even used the phrase as a chapter title in his 1915 book, *Germany Embattled*. "America has much in common with the great German nation," Villard wrote in September 1914, "but has little in common with the military caste and the imperial attitude" of the martial state.[24] To Villard and others, the modern, Prussified, Germany no longer stood for the "humanitarian ideals that [have] led all the world in her effort to solve social problems," but instead for the "autocratic Prussian militarism which slashes lame cobblers and bends a nation to its imperious will." *Life* called Germany a "cruel union of the wolf (Prussia) and his prey (the rest of Germany)." The magazine bemoaned the "spectacle of a great people befuddled and misled in this country by one second-rate man, himself misled by a lot of bughouse militants whose trade is destruction."[25]

As all observers did in 1914 and 1915, Villard made a sharp distinction between Germans in Europe and German-Americans, many of whom were republicans who had immigrated to the United States after 1848 when "the Prussian militarists blew to pieces that noble uprising and ended that brave if helpless demand for true democracy."[26] Harvard historian William Roscoe Thayer also made the same distinctions, describing non-Prussian Germans as "not a race of fighters, but thinkers, scholars, visionaries, fed on pig meat and beer, docile peasants and masterful musicians. . . . Not until the Prussian will energized them did the non-Prussians loom up as Moloch worshipers, thirsting for world empire."[27]

The outbreak of the war proved that the German people had lost the struggle for the soul of their nation that the Zabern Affair had set in motion the year before. The war had thereby destroyed whatever chance they had for peaceful democratic development, leaving them trapped inside a warlike regime bent on an ultimately futile quest for global dominance.[28] Judge Beck argued that the German government would now have to continue prosecuting an unjust war in order to keep its own population in check and thereby attempt to hold off the "dreadful reckoning" of social revolution from its own people after decades of lies and oppression.[29] The terrible war in Europe, he feared, might continue less for reasons of foreign policy goals than to keep an illegitimate regime in power.

Similarly, Willa Cather's chief protagonist, Claude Wheeler, reflects that perhaps the American people had been wrong all along about Germany. Although he had admired German culture, education, and music before the war, in 1914 he realizes how badly the German elite has tricked the civilized world. Wheeler soon puts aside all thoughts of traveling to Germany for pleasure and ceases to envy a friend who had gone there for an advanced degree. Suddenly feelings of revulsion replace those of admiration. "It's as if we invited a neighbor over here and showed him our cattle and our barns, and all the time he was planning how he would come at night and club us in our beds."[30]

From these ideas, many Americans concluded that they could best support the German people by opposing their government. As Villard noted, "A German victory would spell the strengthening of absolutism everywhere and of its bond-servant militarism. It would mean the subordination of the nobler Germany to the reactionary. It would mean not a Germany to be beloved and honored of [sic] all thinking men, but a Germany to be feared and dreaded. . . . Against this possibility Americans must protest the louder the more they are indebted to Germany." Although Villard did not argue for America to enter the war, he saw Kaiser Wilhelm's Germany as an existential threat not only to Germany but to freedom and democracy everywhere, even in the United States. Americans thus had a moral obligation to demonstrate their opposition to the "wickedly unnecessary" actions of the Prussians.[31] His viewpoint stressed a growing tension in American attitudes, namely a repulsion at German actions but an unwillingness to commit the United States to play a direct role in stopping them.

Blaming Germany's militarist autocracy for the seemingly inexplicable actions of the Germans in 1914 had the virtue of holding out some hope that the problem rested less with the German people than with their government; removing or changing the latter might make the former perfectly acceptable after the resumption of peace. Muckraking journalist Ray Stannard Baker, who had toured Germany before the war and professed a "warm liking" for its people, also expressed deep suspicions about what he called the German elite's "momentous conception of the totalitarian state." The German government, he believed, had planned this war for years as demonstrated in a military training program "more comprehensive than any, perhaps, ever before devised." The Prussian system, he wrote, was "inimical to our own."[32] Similarly, Henry L. Stimson, secretary of war in the Taft administration, took a pro-Allied position from the start, recalling his father's decision before the war to move his family out of Berlin because of the "martial swagger" of the German ruling class.[33] Changing that ruling class, and the basis of its power, became a key part of American ideas for reforming Europe.

Germany's premeditated attack appeared all the more egregious because of the repeated statements in favor of peace that Kaiser Wilhelm II had made in the years before 1914. House and Andrew Carnegie were among those who had put great faith in him as an agent of stability in European politics in the years before the war. He could certainly act in a bombastic and provocative manner, but he boasted that he had been on the throne since 1888 and had not started a war; his cousins in England and Russia, on the other hand, had fought unpopular wars in South Africa and Manchuria. Journalists before 1914 described Wilhelm as a man of the barracks but not the battlefield, meaning that he enjoyed being with soldiers, but had little thirst for war. His role in defusing the Zabern Affair had apparently proved his willingness to stand up to the militarists and serve, in Carnegie's words, as Europe's "apostle of peace." He had a reputation in 1914 as a moderate, acting against the ultranationalist Junkers and their leader, his own son, the chauvinistic playboy Crown Prince Wilhelm. Even after the war began, House still believed that the kaiser might be the European leader most amenable to forging a compromise peace, given his past pacific behavior; he advised President Wilson to make his first overtures for peace to Wilhelm rather than to the French or British.[34]

The war led many to conclude that the kaiser had been deceiving the world all along. This sense of betrayal helps to explain why Wilhelm became far and away the single most lampooned and ridiculed figure in the American media. Cartoons depicted him as everything from a simpleminded ape to a crazy man to a wicked fiend. His past professions in favor of peace had merely masked Germany's long-term plan to dominate Europe, and maybe the world. In doing so he had even claimed God's blessing as expressed in the German slogan "Gott Mit Uns" (God Is with Us). "What God can this be?" asked *Life*. "Not our Christian God, our benevolent Creator, a God of love and hope and mercy. The god that helps the Kaiser is a god of broken faith, with bloodshot eyes, loose lips, and a dripping sword." The faith that Wilhelm had broken, of course, referred to his prewar promises of a peaceful reign.[35]

Proof of the inherent evil of the German system existed in the words of the Germans themselves. One book in particular stood out, Friedrich von Bernhardi's *Germany and the Next War*, published in America in 1913 around the same time that the Zabern Affair began. According to the *New Republic*, by late 1914 the book could "be found at every railway newsstand and in every hotel [in the United States]. . . . For many an American reader, Bernhardi is the only expositor of German thought."[36] American periodicals discussed Bernhardi, a Prussian general and military theorist, without mentioning his first name or giving him any other identifier, suggesting that he had indeed become a well-known shorthand for German policy. Most articles about him assumed that the American reader knew at least the broad outlines of Bernhardi's views. The diaries of several Americans of the time also suggest a familiarity with his work.[37]

American readers did not like what they read. Bernhardi argued that Germans had a biological obligation and a patriotic duty to fight an offensive war in order to impose their will on Europe; the relative weakness of Germany's neighbors, he argued, made the time right to begin a war of conquest as soon as possible. "If people and Government stand together, resolved to guard the honour of Germany and make every sacrifice of blood and treasure to insure the future of our country and our State," he wrote, "we can face approaching events with confidence in our rights and in our strength; then we need not fear to fight for our position in the world." With Britain distracted by the Irish Home Rule crisis, France by domestic discord, and Russia by labor unrest, Germany, he argued, could defeat any combination of enemies, but only if it struck quickly and decisively.[38]

The outbreak of the war suggested that the Germans had in fact been carefully following Bernhardi's script for years. The *Living Age* editorialized that Machiavelli himself would be ashamed of the ideas of a book that had plunged the civilized world into a barbarous war. "To few men," it noted, "has it been given to write a book of which one may say that a swiftly ensuing event of world importance is the fruit." Germany's actions followed Bernhardi's plans "as the report of a gun follows a flash."[39] *Life* compared Bernhardi's ideas to rabies sickening a healthy dog. The disease "will have to be localized and expelled" and the dog killed because "life in a Nietzsche-Bernhardi world would not be worth living."[40]

Bernhardi proved the essential bankruptcy of the German case that it had only acted in self-defense against an aggressive Russia working in a detestable alliance with France and Britain. Harvard historian William Roscoe Thayer said that Bernhardi's popularity in Germany proved that the Prussia of the militarists had finally killed the humanist Germany of Goethe and Beethoven. Whereas German *Kultur* before 1870 had stood for "knowledge, belief, art, morals, law, [and] custom," by 1914 it stood for "whatever strengthens the German Empire under the dynasty of Hohenzollern." Bernhardi had become in Thayer's mind the chief architect of this new German way of thinking.[41] *Life* drew a direct line from German unification under Prussian domination in 1871 to Lieutenant von Forstner's behavior in Zabern to Bernhardi, writing that "Bernhardi and the lame cobbler of Zabern [whom Forstner had struck with his saber] . . . cannot be explained away" by Germany's apologists.[42] They revealed instead the true desires and intentions of the rabid new Germany. Villard wrote that Bernhardi's popularity in Germany augured "a return to the stone age" if his ideas triumphed through Germany's militaristic system.[43]

Historians and journalists soon began to pore over other books coming from Germany. They found echoes of Bernhardi's arguments everywhere. The *New Republic* reviewed Herman Frobenius's *Des Deutschen Reiches Schicksalsitunde* (*Germany's Hour of Destiny*), published in 1913. The editors found in it the blueprint for Germany's argument that, no matter what excuse the regime used to start the war, its propagandists would justify its actions as necessary for its own self-defense. Thus did the government convince the German people that although it told them that they had to go to war to protect their homes from Russia, they had first to "lay waste to Belgium," a small and inoffensive nation that could not possibly threaten German interests.[44]

Frobenius, Bernhardi, and others like them had written the script, and the German military had prepared every detail in secret with the famous organizational efficiency of the Prussians. As Andrew McLaughlin of the University of Chicago noted, "We saw that the whole thing was premeditated; we realized that methods of mobilization, not to speak of strategic railroads, are not mapped out in a moment." Germany's attempts to excuse or defend its actions "affronted our intelligence and added to our distrust" because of the speed and efficiency with which

German forces moved once the war began. To McLaughlin's mind, no state could have done what Germany did in August 1914 had it not been on a hair trigger to fight the very war Bernhardi had envisioned. Still, even McLaughlin placed the blame for the war squarely on the "Teutonic" military authorities in Berlin. Most Germans, he believed, would welcome the defeat of a regime that had started a war that would, sooner or later, lead to their ruin.[45]

These responses help to explain why Germany took more of the blame for the outbreak of the war than did Austria-Hungary or Russia. Whereas the Austro-Hungarians and Russians were certainly guilty of bumbling a diplomatic crisis and turning it into a localized war over the Balkans, the Germans had used that same crisis to justify a global war that it now appeared they had been plotting for years. This viewpoint had wide support across the United States. The African-American Philadelphia *Tribune*, for example, described the outbreak of the war by contending that "Germany has been the aggressor on nearly every occasion since 1870. . . . It is to be hoped that Germany will get such a trouncing that she will never forget it or recover from it for the next hundred years" both for its crimes in Europe and its brutality in Africa.[46] Similarly, the Chicago *Defender* noted that although some Americans might disparage the African-American community for indifference on the subject of war, the opinions of black Americans matched that "taken by every loyal citizen" regardless of race. All Americans, the *Defender* argued, understood that the blame for this terrible war lay in Germany.[47]

Because of the militarist actions of the German regime, Europe and civilization more generally seemed destined for a catastrophe, the likes of which had not struck the continent since the Germanic hordes had destroyed Rome. Now, however, those hordes had modern industrial organization behind them. Barbarian symbolism came easily to cartoonists, and the word *Hun* began to appear in print as early as August as a synonym for all things German. The notion of a return to barbarism gained widespread traction. Booker T. Washington, for example, found himself bewildered by "what [had] gotten into the people of Europe," and half-jokingly offered to send "a group of black missionaries" to see if "something can be done for the White Heathen."[48]

Political cartoonists routinely depicted Germany as a latter-day Cain, slaying his brother, civilized Europe. One cartoon from *Life* on August

27 showed the kaiser pulling a horrified female form wearing a crown reading "Europe" away from a light-infused world adorned with a shining cross and labeled "civilization." Carrying a spiked club, the kaiser drags her into a darkness filled with shadowy images of Huns at war. The cartoon's title reads "Return to Barbarism."[49] Richard Harding Davis described Germany's leaders as "six hundred years behind the times. . . . These men are military mad." Even Davis, however, carefully divided the essentially good "Germans as we know Germans in America" from "the military autocracy of Germany" that he held responsible for the calamity of the war.[50]

Commentators took a condescending tone to the return to barbarism that they saw happening before their very eyes in Europe. They believed that the democratic culture of which they were a part neutralized the worst effects of America's own potential Bernhardis, thus proving the inherent superiority of the American system (and by extension the democratic British and French systems as well). The war revealed how much the New World now had to teach the Old before it slipped back into a new Dark Age. *Life* noted in late August that "the European mind must learn the lesson that the American mind is born to—the lesson of a continental family made up of diverse individuals, actively competitive, but submissive to such limitations of individual action as the integrity and prosperity of the family require. Autocracies, not people, have got Europe into this awful mess."[51] An editorial cartoon in the following week's issue connected autocracy with the war, depicting Kaiser Wilhelm and Austrian Emperor Franz Joseph waving their swords at a woman crucified on a cross. Beneath the cross lies a pile of bodies, while in the background smoke smolders from a burning city. The cross reads "Civilization" and the caption reads "By Divine Right."[52] Henry Watterson, the editor of the Louisville *Courier-Journal*, put his case more directly: "To hell with the Hohenzollerns and the Hapsburgs."[53]

Most Americans saw the distinctions between themselves and the Europeans in positive terms. The United States, a young democratic nation free of the evils of the Old World, could serve as a shining example to Europe. Conveniently ignoring the bloody years of their own Civil War, notable figures across the political spectrum argued that the war should result in the formation of a kind of United States of Europe, a federated continent where states could resolve their disputes peacefully.

Charles Eliot advanced just such an idea in a New York *Times* editorial wherein he wrote that a federation of European states on the American model offered the only chance for avoiding "the vast killing and crippling of men, the destruction of all sorts of man's structures . . . and the physical ruin of countless women and children" that the present war had caused across the most advanced continent in the world.[54] Thus might war between European states someday become as unthinkable as a war between, say, Illinois and Indiana.

America, and the democracy that served as its foundation, could therefore help to set the Europeans right once the war had ended. Europeans would learn from the suffering of war that democracy offered civilization its greatest hope for the future. Ambassador Walter Hines Page wrote from London that the outbreak of so terrible a war proved that the autocracies of Europe had yet to evolve "beyond the stage of tooth and claw."[55] Similarly, a political cartoon in the Little Rock (Arkansas) *Gazette* depicted the warring European powers as "two hairy apelike men attack[ing] each other with hammers."[56] In such an environment, the American child would have to teach the European father how to regain his lost humanity. Andrew C. McLaughlin wrote in a widely distributed pamphlet that Americans could not understand the outbreak of the war because the United States had evolved so far beyond the primitive and atavistic nature that still ruled in Europe. Americans, he claimed, "had no deep-laid scheme for exploitation of inferior races, no colonial ambitions, no determination to force our products on other nations."[57] People from Tuskegee to Vera Cruz to Manila to Beijing might have taken issue with that self-image, but it nevertheless remained powerful.

The war had proved to Americans the inherent superiority of their system and, given that superiority, the need to transplant it to Europe for the greater good of humanity. The war could thus transform the Old World in positive and permanent ways, redeeming its cost in blood and treasure. The Evangelical newspaper *The Independent* noted that an Allied victory would mark the triumph of the Enlightenment ideals of democracy and freedom over the Middle Ages ideals for which Germany fought. "The monarchs must go, and they will." Similarly, the Baltimore *Afro-American* argued that the war might be worth the sacrifices if at the end "kings and czars will be done with for good and all."[58]

From the outset, a large number of Americans saw the war in stark terms and believed that the future of the world would rest on its outcome. *Outlook* called it a contest between the German "reign of the sword" and the democratic "reign of conscience." The Chicago *Tribune* saw a similar duality, and editorialized that the two sides represented the struggle of "the divine right of people" against the "divine right of kings."[59] Once the war ended, the United States would have a chance to help shape Europe's future for good by promoting democracy and greater connections between European states.

Some were predicting that the war might pose a direct threat to America's own future. Writing in the *New Republic* in November 1914, the influential progressive journalist Herbert Croly called the war "the end of American isolation." Because the United States sat so badly unprepared to confront the political, international, and economic dislocations that the war had already created, it could lead to the end of the country's very independence no matter who won. The cover of an early issue of *National Defence*, a New York–based newsletter that argued for higher defense spending, showed Uncle Sam looking at a Europe on fire across the ocean while holding a copy of the Declaration of Independence. The caption reads, "Resolved—To Keep It."[60] If they hoped to do so, Americans had, in Croly's view, to surrender the cherished but "evil spirit of their traditional national delusion—the delusion of isolated newer worldliness." A new American spirit "better able to redeem its obligations both to its own citizens and to a regenerate European system" needed to take its place.[61]

Although hardly any Americans expressed a desire to see their nation get directly involved in the war, they knew that the future of Europe, and perhaps their own future as well, might hang on the outcome. The *North American Review* noted in September that "Europe stands today at Armageddon" in a "frightening holocaust" that had the "giants grappling to the death in a modern Twilight of the Gods" with the fate of the Old World hanging in the balance.[62] The war thereby represented nothing less than what *Outlook* called in mid-August God's desire to end the power of military autocracy.[63] Russia, an autocratic state fighting on the Allied side, might even throw off its reactionary tsarist regime, as it nearly did during the 1904–5 Russo-Japanese War, and join the family of modern, democratic nations. Only if it did so, and Germany followed suit after its own inevitable defeat, could Europe justify the war's price. The only other option, *Life* noted, seemed to be the general suicide of Europe and modern civilization, with the existence of the United States itself in peril.[64] As Woodrow Wilson stated in a public address in the middle of August, "When all this half of the world [Europe] will suffer the unspeakable brutalization of war, we shall preserve our moral strength, our political power, and our ideals." By 1914 he envisioned those ideals as creating the foundation on which the world would begin anew.[65]

From these ideas, it followed that Americans from Pennsylvania Avenue to Main Street saw France and Britain as the defenders (flawed though they may themselves have been) of a democratic order, and Belgium as the irreproachable victim of German aggression. *Life* magazine noted in late August 1914 that "the English, French, and Russians are fighting in this war in [*sic*] behalf of the liberties of the world," while "Germany and Austria are seeking to impose on the world a despotic authority to which it would be ruinous to yield."[66] As Newton Baker, the mayor of Cleveland and future American secretary of war, wrote about the spirit of his country in 1914, Americans had "a very definite conception of the German theory of life and generally disapproved of it."[67]

There were plenty of opportunities to follow the war in as much detail as any American wanted, particularly in the columns of prominent journalists, among them Richard Harding Davis, a veteran correspondent of seven wars who had become famous in the United States after reporting from both the Spanish-American War and the Russo-Japanese War. His name appeared in bold letters in American newspapers nationwide. Others included the *Saturday Evening Post*'s Irvin Cobb, then the highest-paid reporter in the world; Frederick Palmer, who left Monterrey, Mexico, when he heard of the war's outbreak in Europe and hopped the first ship across the Atlantic with an available cabin, the Cunard liner *Lusitania*; and Nellie Bly, self-styled as "America's Greatest Newspaper Woman," who gave accounts of trench warfare on the Eastern front.[68]

Perhaps the most famous of them all was mystery writer Mary Roberts Rinehart, later known as "the American Agatha Christie," who went to both the royal palaces and battlefields of Europe. She was the first female reporter allowed into the trenches of the Western Front. Her departure for Europe made national news both because of the rare circumstance of a female war correspondent at the front and the rumors (true, as they turned out) that her husband had publicly forbidden her from making the trip. She had responded defiantly that "I do not intend to let the biggest thing in my life go by without having been a part of it." He eventually yielded after she agreed to demand that her editors take out a sizable life insurance policy on her. Roberts's reports from Europe led to a remarkable leap of fifty thousand readers in weekly circulation for the *Saturday Evening Post*, which paid her the princely sum of $1,000 per dispatch. She came back to her home in Pittsburgh in March 1915 to even greater fame and increased sales of her mysteries.[69]

All of these reporters developed pro-Allied sympathies soon upon arrival in Europe. Rinehart did so despite being a self-proclaimed pacifist who initially had wanted to cover the war in order to denounce the wickedness of all sides. Once in Europe, however, she recoiled at what she called "the campaign of terrorization" that the Germans were executing across Europe.[70] Cobb spent the first few days of the war traveling with the Germans and saw firsthand both the efficiency and what he called the "pure vandalism" of the German way of war. Although he understood that much of the destruction he witnessed came from the nature of war itself (he titled one column "Sherman Said It"), he placed the blame for the outbreak of the war itself squarely on Germany for encouraging the Austro-Hungarian regime to risk setting the world on fire. Although he, too, had left the United States impartial, within a few weeks he had stopped socializing with German officials and he expressed open relief when he left German-occupied Belgium for France after the fall of Antwerp in October.[71]

The lurid tales about German atrocities in Belgium coming to America through London news services shaped some, but by no means all, of the American response. Most Americans expressed a healthy cynicism about the atrocity stories they heard. The strongly pro-Allied *Life* magazine simply did not report them. Cobb, who reported a number of German violations of the rules of war, nevertheless told his readers that "a dozen seasoned journalists, both English and American," agreed with him that no proof existed to sustain the most sensational charges leveled against the Germans, such as the murder of priests, the killing of children, and the systematic rape of Belgian women. "We need not look for individual atrocities," he told his readers. "Belgium herself is the cap-sheaf [crowning] atrocity of this war."[72] Similarly, Rinehart reported in great detail about the horrors of war in Belgium, but she, too, told her readers not to believe the atrocity tales then swirling in the British media. The Germans, she wrote, in a reflection of the Two Germanys concept, were "not butchers or fiends, but victims of a system against which some day they would rise and rebel."[73]

This view of Germany conditioned a depiction of Britain and France as its antithesis. A writer in the *Review of Reviews* noted that England had evolved from a "Two Englands" concept in centuries past to form one of the world's great democracies. Similarly, France had long since turned its back on monarchs and developed into a republic. Neither nation had therefore sought a war that would kill tens of thousands of its own citizens. This war, the magazine noted, was "made in Germany," where autocrats still made the key decisions, overriding the wishes of their own people, who had had no voice in the decision for war.[74] The Allies, by contrast, were democracies fighting for their very survival in a justifiable war of defense against an aggressor.

Far more than words, Germany's behavior in the war's opening months led the majority of American observers to sympathize with Britain, France, and Belgium, states they saw as standing up to the horrid beast of German militarism.[75] Cobb, Rinehart, Palmer, and other war correspondents warned against a reliance on propaganda in part to keep the focus on the German atrocities that reporters could confirm. Enough evidence existed of real crimes committed by the Germans in Belgium to lead even the staunchly neutral American secretary of state William Jennings Bryan to call German behavior "an outrage against humanity." From London, Ambassador Page wrote to President Wilson on September 11, 1914, that "the horror of the thing outruns all imagination." He had at first disbelieved the terrible reports of German behavior coming out of Belgium but the overwhelming evidence had changed his mind: "Accounts of atrocities are so inevitably a part of every war that for some time I did not believe the unbelievable reports that were sent from Europe, and there are many that I find incredible even now. But American and other neutral observers who have seen things in France and especially in Belgium now convince me that the Germans have per-petuated some of the most barbarous deeds in history."[76]

Belgium evoked some of the deepest sympathy. Cobb, Rinehart, and Davis were among those who depicted Belgium as a David in the path of a Goliath. Davis described Belgium as "smiling and beautiful" before the Germans came, and after as a "graveyard" far worse than anything Sherman had dared to do to the American South. "It looked as though a cyclone had uprooted its houses, gardens, and orchards and a prairie fire had followed."[77] The Belgians, according to Frederick Palmer, were "an unwarlike people, living by intensive thrift and caution—a most domesticated civilization in the most thickly populated workshop in Europe. . . with the door about to be opened to the withering blast of war."[78] J. N. Darling's October 1914 political cartoon for the Des Moines *Register* (and syndicated nationally) depicted the Belgians as a duck surrounded by hunters all taking aim at it. He also drew numerous cartoons showing the plight of Belgian civilians in the face of the German invasion.[79]

The Belgians themselves had earned these journalists' respect and admiration by resisting the Germans instead of rolling over and allowing them to pass through to France. Military strategists (amateur and professional alike) understood that Belgian resistance had likely saved France and Britain from defeat. Thus did Rinehart depict the Belgians as "brave" and "heroic."[80] On August 27, *Life* published an acrostic that read:

Bravery
Energy
Love of Home
Glory
Inheritance
Union
Mettle.[81]

News of the German burning of the "clean, sleepy, and pretty" university town of Louvain in late August generated even more sympathy for Belgium. Richard Harding Davis had been in Louvain when the German Army came through. Furious at the stiff resistance that Belgian partisans had put in their way, the Germans determined to make an example of the town.[82] Davis began to take notes on what he saw unfolding before his eyes. The Germans promptly locked him in a railroad car and threatened him with arrest. Upon his release, German officers responsible for the destruction of Louvain boasted to him of their work in burning the town and expressed no remorse. Davis could see the terror they had imposed on Louvain "in the faces of women and children being led to concentration camps and of citizens on their way to be shot." He reported that "at Louvain it was war upon the defenseless, war upon churches, colleges, shops of milliners and lace makers; war brought to the bedside and the fireside; against women harvesting in the fields, against children in wooden shoes at play in the streets." German soldiers at Louvain, Davis wrote, "were like men after an orgy."[83]

Even the African-American press praised Belgium, despite its past scathing criticism of Belgium's villainous treatment of its colonies in the Congo. One Philadelphia newspaper reported in November on an aid ship going to Belgium that contained supplies paid for with money raised by the city's African-American community. Two African-American children turned over their piggy banks with $1.56 inside. One of the children told a reporter, "I hope these few pennies will help those good white people in Belgium." A sign at the docks read, "This is not our war, but a starving child is any man's problem."[84]

American reporters also wrote damningly of German behavior in France. Davis flatly refuted the German allegation that French soldiers had turned the great cathedral at Rheims into an observation platform and that the Germans therefore had no choice but to fire upon it with heavy artillery. He and others accused the Germans of attacking the cathedral not because of any military necessity but out of a desire to stamp out French culture. The results were horrifying: "Two days before, when I walked through the cathedral, the scene was the same as when kings were crowned. You stood where Joan of Arc received the homage of France. When I returned, I walked upon broken stone and shattered glass. Where once the light was dim and holy, now through great breeches in the walls rain splashed. The spirit of the place was gone." The people of Rheims, he wrote, had become refugees, "trembling, weeping, incoherent with terror, carrying nothing with them." The Germans had, however, managed to shell the city repeatedly without damaging any property owned by neutral nations, evidence, Davis concluded, of German intent.[85] Although Americans could not have known it, the American military attaché in France, Col. Spencer Cosby, agreed, telling the War Department that "there can be little doubt that the shelling of the cathedral was intentional . . . and there was absolutely no excuse for firing on it."[86]

Unlike many of the atrocity stories circulating about Belgium that came from the British press, American journalists saw Louvain and Rheims with their own eyes. The tragedies they saw seemed to show beyond a shadow of a doubt the kind of threat Germany posed to the rest of the civilized world. As *Life* editorialized on November 19, "One sees in Germany immense efficiency, courage, aggressiveness, [and] capacity to suffer, but where, so far, has she been noble? In Belgium? At Louvain? At Rheims?"[87] *Life* answered its own question the following week with a two-page full-color cartoon map for the postwar world titled "A Map of Europe for Permanent Peace." Germany disappears entirely, as an enlarged Belgium expands to the Oder River, taking Berlin with it. The new France recovers Alsace-Lorraine, and annexes Munich, Vienna, and Prague as well.[88] The Philadelphia *Tribune* similarly hoped that the war would result in the kaiser's "ambition crushed and his country, once one of the ruling powers of Europe, dismembered and partitioned by his rivals."[89]

Americans reacted especially strongly against the totality of German warfare and the death and destruction that the Germans wrought, especially on civilians. Reports of a German aerial bombardment of Paris on August 31 led the Charlotte *Daily Observer* to call Germany "a renaissance of barbarism in a new garb."[90] *Life* argued that the war could only have value to humanity if at the end the German people could say "it delivered us from militarism and Pan-Germanism and left us free to live and work and trade in a world no longer unfriendly." Unfortunately, the war seemed only to increase German appetites. *Life* published a satirical proclamation from the kaiser to his "happy people" that read "I have bestowed on Gen. von Havoc the Iron Cross for his noble work at Rheims. God is with us, and I still hope to blow up the Cathedral of Notre Dame at Paris. Rest assured the contents of the Louvre shall not escape us." Then, to mock the stated goals of the German regime, it ended, "We continue to fight in the defense of the Fatherland."[91]

Most Americans saw Britain and France as defending Belgium and holding the line against German militarism. The *New Republic* dismissed

German arguments that France had started the war to recover Alsace and Lorraine. "This is not France's war," the editors of the magazine wrote, despite attempts to appear neutral in tone. "She has necessarily been involved in it, but she did not want it."[92] Davis and Rinehart both wholeheartedly agreed, asking Americans to support the French, although they did not advocate America's entry into the war. Davis argued that the cause of France, America's "sister republic," was also "the hope and prayer of every American." The United States, he said, could not sit back and watch German despotism wipe out one of the birthplaces of democracy. "When we fought for our liberty France was not neutral," Davis reminded his readers, "but sent us Lafayette and Rochambeau, ships and soldiers." He, like Rinehart, urged Americans to help the French in any way they could. "This is no war for neutrals."[93] As we will see, thousands of Americans took up his call.

Americans living and working in Europe shared their own pro-Allied views from the war's opening months. Edith Wharton, who published *Fighting France: From Dunkerque to Belfort* in early 1915, had been in France when the war began. Within weeks she had formed charities to help refugees from France and Belgium and had raised more than $100,000 to provide shelter for hundreds of Belgian children in France. She and the president of the American Chamber of Commerce in Paris visited the front lines. Her book was largely a compilation of her observances of those trips as published in *Scribner's* and other magazines in 1914. It quickly became a bestseller.[94]

A pro-Allied bias from the start of the war was evident among those with college educations and those from old-stock Protestant families, but sympathy for the Allies did not depend only on education and ethnicity. From Washington, British Ambassador Sir Cecil Spring-Rice wrote a friend in November 1914 that "the larger part of the American people are with us or rather against our enemies, not from our merits but owing to the demerits of the antagonist. Their deeds are mightier than their words." In another letter written at the same time, Spring-Rice estimated that 90 percent of America's English-speakers, including 50 percent of its Irish population, were strongly pro-Allied and that German propaganda had backfired in America because of the outrage Americans felt toward German actions in the war to date.[95]

One survey of 350 American newspapers in November 1914 showed that 46 percent expressed pro-Allied sentiments, while just 5 percent (most of them German-language) sympathized with the Germans. The rest claimed impartiality, although they normally expressed their concern for the victims of war in France and Belgium.[96] Even one of Germany's most eloquent defenders, the Danzig-born Harvard professor Hugo Münsterberg, a pioneer in psychology, bemoaned "the almost universal hope in America that Germany will be thoroughly chastised for her ruler's monstrous crimes against the peace of the world."[97] His fear was supported by popular anti-German books published in 1914 like Emil Reich's *Germany's Madness* (also published under the title *Germany's Swelled Head*), George Saunders's *Builder and Blunderer*, and a critical biography called *The Real Kaiser*, published anonymously.[98]

Americans could not easily demonstrate their opposition in ways that would impair Germany's war effort. The effectiveness of the British blockade made a boycott of German goods largely unnecessary and the widely shared view that American firms had a right to trade with anyone they wished would have made a boycott unpopular, even if the majority of Americans would have sympathized with its goals. Instead, those opposed to German behavior looked for ways to solve the problem of Germany and, by extension, Europe more generally once the war ended.

While Americans showed a deep desire to help the Allies, they displayed no desire at all to enter the war. Partly, they saw the war as still being essentially a European problem, but the enormous casualty figures reported in American newspapers undoubtedly contributed to this attitude. American newspapers reprinted sanitized but still shocking photographs of the battlefields, reported on casualties numbering into the hundreds of thousands, and told their readers that the battles of Europe in 1914 were, as the Washington *Evening Star* reported on the first two days of Battle of the Marne, "the greatest on record." That battlefield, the newspaper noted in a typical dispatch, "is now a picture of devastation, abomination, and death almost too awful to describe."[99]

The devastation increased a sense of moral responsibility to help the victims, but this responsibility came with political implications. From the war's first few weeks Americans saw their role as helping to ameliorate the suffering caused by what one writer described as "the wounds inflicted on the world by German *Kultur*," a word the Germans used to describe the best features of their system, but which Americans used pejoratively after 1914.[100] *Life* began a charity fund that raised tens of thousands of dollars for relief in Belgium and France. The magazine published the names (or pseudonyms) of all the contributors. They included contributions from people calling themselves "The Anti-Hun," "The Anti-Kaiser," and one reader who offered to buy Wilhelm a one-way ticket to St. Helena, the exile site of Napoleon a century earlier.[101] Mary Roberts Rinehart also began a relief fund, with all of the money going to Belgium, as did Hampton Institute in Virginia, whose president boasted that every single student had contributed money or goods.[102] Their actions reflected those of tens of thousands of their fellow Americans, as chapter 2 will discuss.

Germany had its defenders, foremost among them Münsterberg. Although he had lived in America for decades, Münsterberg never called himself a German-American, but a German living in America. In the years before the war, he had urged the German government to focus more on what we would today call soft power or public diplomacy instead of military might. In place of militarist blustering, he wanted the German government to open cultural affairs offices in the United States to stress German achievements in literature, art, music, and especially the new medium of cinema, which fascinated him. In his conceptualization, German *Kultur* need not carry the connotation of Prussian militarism that so antagonized Americans and gave Germany a bad name in the United States.[103] When the war began Münsterberg made Germany's case to the American public. In newspaper columns, open letters to Woodrow Wilson, and a book he hurriedly published, Münsterberg blamed the war's outbreak on Russia and the "uncultured hordes of the East" who "begrudged the prosperity of the Fatherland." England and France had made unholy alliances with the Slavic and backward Russians, he argued, in order to gain for themselves a share of German wealth. The American people, Münsterberg claimed, had fallen victim to British propaganda and the anti-German sentiments of media barons. "It is," he contended, "a sin against the spirit of history to denounce Germany as the aggressor."[104] He urged Americans to remain neutral and to keep an open mind.

Münsterberg struggled to gain a following, in large part because Germany had directed the bulk of its armies not against the Slavic peril

Münsterberg demonized, but against Belgium and France. *Life* called him "Iago Münsterberg," a reference to the Shakespearean villain whose enemies eventually exile then murder him.[105] To cite a typical example of the response to his ideas, one of Münsterberg's former students, Boston lawyer Frederick Coburn, wrote to him that "not one [of his fellow Americans] has appeared to be unfriendly to the German people as a whole, but that everyone has expressed the fervent hope that the present German government will get the full measure of drubbing that it deserves for years of arrogance culminating in the present dubious frame-up." Münsterberg's defense of what Coburn called the "paranoiac" and "medieval" German regime put the professor out of step with American views. Such a system as the Prussian, wrote Coburn, "does not deserve the support even of those who happen to be born under it."[106]

Neither did Münsterberg have the support of his Harvard colleagues, although most of them, at least in 1914, defended his right of free speech. Münsterberg pushed that right further than his colleagues believed prudent, however, when he wrote an open letter to President Wilson warning the president that the Democratic Party would lose the German-American vote in the 1914 midterm elections if Wilson did not change his policies toward the war in Europe. Münsterberg found himself ostracized from the social life of Harvard and Boston more generally. Students began boycotting his classes and one wealthy alumnus offered Harvard a generous donation if it fired Münsterberg. Harvard president A. Lawrence Lowell turned the offer down, but he advised Münsterberg against delivering public lectures on politics or bringing his pro-German ideas into Harvard classrooms.[107]

Some German-American newspapers defended German actions against what they described as a corrupt and avaricious alliance of Russia, England, and France. Like Münsterberg, they blamed British propaganda for negative attitudes toward Germany and they depicted Germany as the last bulwark of civilization against a Slavic dominion over Europe. They argued that the British and French served not as the defenders of democracy, but as the unwitting dupes of the reactionary and insidious Russians. These ideas failed to take hold in the minds of most Americans.[108] Gilbert Seldes, a popular writer and theater critic, wrote that the German-American press's "plea failed because before the attorney came to court his client's hands were stained with blood."[109]

Nor were all German-Americans supportive of Germany's war. Nine of ten Americans Palmer met in Europe, "including some with German names," were, he noted, "leaning over backwards to be neutral" on the outside while harboring strong pro-Allied feelings on the inside.[110] A Washington *Post* editorial on August 13, 1914, observed that the German-American press sought less to defend the kaiser's foreign policy than to "protect the good name of everything German" from being smeared with the same brush. German-Americans pointed out that if France had sent Lafayette to help America gain its freedom, Germany had sent von Steuben; and if Germany had produced the hated Hessian mercenaries, they came to America in the pay of the British. German-American newspapers also noted that Germans had fought in all of the nation's wars, producing heroes like Union Army general and future senator and cabinet member Carl Schurz. Congressman Richard Bartholdt (R-Missouri, born in Schliez and an immigrant to Brooklyn in 1872) spoke of the deep links between the United States and Germany and told audiences that "German bankers were the only ones to aid the United States financially during the Civil War," subtly reminding at least his northern audiences of the initial support France and Britain had shown to the Confederacy.[111]

German-Americans, especially those born in the United States, reacted coolly to the open apologia for the kaiser that appeared in George Viereck's *Fatherland*, which began to publish in August 1914. Although he claimed that it had a circulation of more than one hundred thousand issues a week, Viereck had to give most of the copies away for free because of a lack of buyers. He also published under the shadow of widespread accusations (true, as was soon revealed) that the German government was paying Viereck for his efforts. The German government also paid Dr. Bernhard Dernburg, a banker and Red Cross doctor sent to America to head up an office of propaganda in New York City. The Germans recalled him in 1915 when they realized that his efforts were causing more harm than good, even among those who might be sympathetic to the German cause. Allegations that Dernburg had paid American politicians to give pro-German speeches angered the administration and Americans more generally. Bartholdt chose not to run for reelection to the House of Representatives in 1914 in large part due to revelations of his acceptance of Dernburg's money.

German-Americans were one of the most highly acculturated groups in the nation and as such many had ceased to identify primarily as German. Münsterberg and newspaper publisher Edward Rumely both noted that ethnic Germans born in America felt no special connection with their homeland; few had ever bothered to return even as tourists or students. They had instead adopted the individualistic culture of the United States. Rumely noted in a letter to a colleague that German thought "does not coalesce with, nor reach, the great mass of Americans, with the result that although there are some twenty millions of German descendants in this country they have not been able to interpret modern Germany adequately." He wrote that "our democratic instincts and belief in the freedom of the individual tend to emphasize" a distance between Germans born in the United States and those born in Germany.[112]

Major German institutions in the United States either stayed quiet or openly criticized the German government. Protestant church officials mostly remained silent on the issues connected to the war. Socialists and Catholics often blamed the kaiser as much as they blamed the Russians or the British for the war. Socialists, in fact, were often more critical of the German government than any other Americans. German-Americans therefore by no means represented a solid block of opinion.[113]

A few notable mainstream American journalists bucked the general trend of support for the Allies, although they did not necessarily espouse pro-German views as a result. Joseph Medill Patterson, the Irish-American founder of the Chicago *Tribune*, went to Belgium three times to report on the war. He saw hypocrisy in British arguments over Germany's treatment of Belgium given how blithely Britain herself had often ignored the rights of small nations, including, especially, Ireland. The United States, he noted, had also ignored treaties, agreements, and the rights of small nations when it believed that its national interests required it to do so. Patterson argued that no one had any right to complain about Germany's behavior in this regard. In his formulation, all of Europe bore a shared responsibility for the outbreak of a war it should have avoided through arbitration. Even Patterson called Germany the "aggressor," however, and believed that the extension of German control over Europe "is not at all to our American interests." Like Rumely and many other prominent German-Americans, Patterson argued that the

United States should act not out of sympathy for Great Britain and France, but strictly as its own interests dictated. He most certainly did not see a German victory as consistent with those interests.[114]

Americans in 1914 and early 1915 did not view entering the war as even a remote possibility. Most hoped that the war would end soon, and they knew enough about the slaughter of the war's early months to make them wary of sending their own sons and brothers into it. As the Chicago *Defender* put it, "We should be thankful we are not subjects of Europe. We are not at war in this country—let us hope that we never shall be."[115] Still, the American people became neutral neither in action nor in thought, in spite of President Wilson's August 19 address to Congress that ended with an injunction that "we must be impartial in thought, as well as action, must put a curb upon our sentiments, as well as upon every transaction that might be construed as a preference of one party to the struggle before another."[116]

Wilson had misread the mood of his country regarding the war. Americans did not follow his call for strict impartiality. Some close political allies like Henry Watterson, the Louisville editor quoted above, broke with him. Watterson and Frederick Palmer were among those who made no effort to hide their sentiments; as Palmer wrote, "Between right and wrong one cannot be a neutral." Or, as one popular saying went, "Sure, I'm neutral. I don't care who licks the Kaiser!"[117] Despite his public proclamations in favor of neutrality, Wilson privately saw England as possessing a superior system to that of the autocratic Germans. Like his ambassador in Great Britain, Wilson expected his government to act as a neutral in accordance with international law and custom. Unlike Page, however, he thought the American people could translate that legal neutrality into moral impartiality. Page knew better. He wrote to his brother in North Carolina to tell him that he would be neutral in his official behavior, but not in his personal capacity. The American people, he assumed, would do the same because they knew that the war was about "the effort of the Berlin absolute monarch and his group to impose their will on as large a part of the world as they can overrun." Page declared himself willing to resign if Wilson tried to force him into too strict a definition of neutrality.[118] Edward House, the president's closest confidant, seemed closer to Page's worldview than Wilson's. In November, House told the British ambassador that the

American government would have to make protests against some aspects of British maritime policy in order to keep up the image of Wilson's desired neutrality, but that the British should not worry because "general sentiment inside [and] outside the administration was sympathetic" to the Allied cause.[119]

A few Americans did argue for the country to take sides openly. From the battlefields of France and Belgium, Richard Harding Davis wrote in September that while he had read Wilson's August 19 speech, he had also seen the war, and were Americans "nearer to it, near enough to see the women and children fleeing from the shells and to smell the dead on the battlefields, there would be no talk of neutrality" because neutrality placed the United States on the side of wrong. "When a mad dog runs amuck in a village it is the duty of every farmer to get his gun and destroy it, not to lock himself indoors and toward the dog and the men who face him preserve a neutral mind."[120]

The vast majority of Americans, however, did not want to follow Davis into the fight in 1914. They thought that their role in the great conflict should center on the traditional functions of neutrals, such as ameliorating suffering and trying to bring the warring parties to peace. Nationally syndicated political cartoonist J. N. Darling captured American ambiguity in two cartoons published in the war's first week. The first, titled "His Job," featured a female character labeled "Humanity" begging at the feet of Uncle Sam who looks at a burning Europe out his window. Written over the smoke is "The Greatest Conflict in History" and at Uncle Sam's feet sits a sheaf of paper reading "Mediation for Peace," underscoring America's moral responsibilities to try to end the war. But that same week, Darling drew another cartoon that underscored the sense of distance Americans still felt from the war. It showed Uncle Sam staring across the ocean at a Europe at war. The text reads "Moral: See America First." As much as they wanted to help, Americans still saw the war as fundamentally a European problem.[121]

2

A Cause Most Think Is Right

UNTIL SPRING 1915, AMERICANS CONTINUED to count on distance, the Atlantic Ocean, and America's lack of alliances with the European belligerents to protect them from the direct effects of the war. In August 1914, Ambassador Walter Hines Page had written to President Wilson from London, "Again and ever, I thank Heaven for the Atlantic Ocean."[1] Similarly, Cleveland mayor Newton Baker recalled that the "spectacle of all the great nations of Europe in the conflict only heightened our appreciation of our isolation behind the moats of the Atlantic and Pacific oceans."[2] The New York *Sun* had even editorialized that the "quarrels of others" should not cause a neutral state like the United States to "be subjected...to additional care and expense."[3]

As summer turned to fall then to winter, however, even staunch isolationists had begun to face the cold reality that Herbert Croly had articulated in the magazine he had just founded, the *New Republic*: the Atlantic Ocean no longer provided them with the security that it had in the past. The notion of America's physical and ideological separation from Europe sufficing to provide it the security it needed was, Croly argued, an idea that "must be thrown into the accumulating scrapheap of history." The war, he warned in sharp and ominous language, "is a challenge to the United States to justify its independence." No matter what the result of the "madman's dream" then occurring in Europe, the United States would inevitably feel the effects as the old order imploded. If the United States wanted to help shape the new order, Croly wrote, it had to awaken from its slumber and take on the obligations of a great nation.[4] Prominent businessmen and civic leaders nationwide were among the first to sense that the growing interconnectedness of the global trade system made separation from Europe much harder than it had been in decades past. Europe's war, they recognized, could well become America's after all one day. It would at least require considerable care and expense to protect the country from the worst aspects of it.

Responses to the war began with expressions of charity and compassion. A majority of Americans felt connections to Europe on a myriad of levels. They looked with concern at the place from which most of their families had come, and they felt a responsibility to reach out a helping hand. Americans saw Europe as the birthplace of modern civilization: art, architecture, music, science, literature, and fashion all had their foundations there. Now some of its prominent symbols, like the magnificent cathedral at Reims and the fifteenth-century university at Louvain, were literally up in flames. Millions of Americans had been born in places now directly in the line of fire, especially in central and eastern Europe, where Austria-Hungary, Russia, and Germany were engaged in fierce fighting. From the first days of the war, therefore, what they saw happening evoked sympathy and pity.

The war had turned Europe into a slaughterhouse beyond almost anyone's imagination. The Washington *Times* reported with banner headlines that even before the official declarations of war had reached the European capitals, armies numbering in the hundreds of thousands were clashing and thousands of men had died in a single day in a battle on the Franco-German border.[5] Irvin Cobb wrote in the *Saturday Evening Post* of endless streams of Belgian and French refugees "all afoot, all bearing pitiably small bundles. . . . Their heavy peasant faces expressed dumb bewilderment—nothing less" as they fled from homes that no longer existed for an uncertain future somewhere to the west.[6] European armies generally refused to give out exact casualty figures for fear of giving their enemies too much information, but Americans were soon reading about battles in which 60 percent of the soldiers engaged had died from the ferocity of the fighting and men "fell in droves" before the deadly power of artillery and machine gun fire.[7]

Even in the first few weeks, Europe seemed to be imploding with no recovery in sight for years or decades. In November 1914, Page wrote to his son, then living in Pinehurst, North Carolina, that Europe, "the place where man rose from barbarism to civilization is now bankrupt, its best young men dead, its system of politics and of government a failure.... The whole future of the [human] race is in the new countries—our country chiefly." Page ended by telling his son, "Human life there [Europe] isn't worth what a yellow dog's life is worth in Moore County. Don't bother yourself with the continent of Europe any more."[8] The values that had built Europe were being washed away in torrents of blood. The Chicago *Defender* saw the same problem, noting sharply that "if this be the boasted civilization, let us hark back to the so-called dark ages. Conditions were scarcely worse."[9]

With this attitude came an assertiveness of the country's moral superiority. At the same time that Page was writing to his son, Secretary of State William Jennings Bryan gave the ambassadors of the warring parties paperweights in the form of plowshares beaten from swords. One side featured the relevant biblical quotation from Isaiah 2:4 ("They will beat their swords into plowshares and their spears into pruning hooks / Nation will not take up sword against nation, nor will they train for war anymore") and the other side featured a quotation from Bryan himself, his insipid and often-used "Nothing is final between friends."[10] British ambassador Sir Cecil Spring-Rice, who certainly saw no friendship in the Germans of 1914, could hardly contain his exasperation at both America's inability to understand the vital issues at stake and the arrogant moralism of its senior leaders. He could only conclude that Bryan "sighs for the Nobel Peace Prize."[11]

While Bryan wanted the country to provide only a moral example to the world, Page thought that the United States would soon have to back up its words with actions. On August 4 he wrote that the war would likely lead to the "impending ruin of half the world" if the United States did not take action to prevent it. He became one of the first Americans to foresee that America would eventually, if regrettably, have to take a direct role in the fighting and in the formation of a new postwar world order. A German victory would not only erase the progress Europe had made, it would also threaten the values America held most dear. "If sheer brute force is to rule the world," he wrote to Edward House on September 22, "it will not be worth living in." More than shared values were at stake because Germany "would try to conquer the United States; and we should all go back . . . to the domination of kings by divine right." He warned House that the United States should not push for a compromise peace between the warring parties because "the Hohenzollern idea must perish—be utterly strangled in the making of peace." Any other kind of peace would only embolden Germany and endanger the security of Europe and America for years to come.[12]

Few members of the Wilson administration then wanted to hear what Page had to say. Bryan's commitment to neutrality was more appealing, for it allowed the government to avoid the horrors of the war while reaping its not insignificant economic benefits. At the same time, the country could still convince itself that it occupied the moral high ground. Neutrality was also the wisest political course as most Americans hoped to keep their homeland protected from the horrors of war for as long as possible.

If not suffering, some Americans at least had their lives disrupted by the war. Tens of thousands found themselves trapped overseas with no access to money because the war had closed European banks. Six thousand Americans were in Paris alone when the hostilities began. They included sons and daughters of wealthy families who could no longer cash checks or find transportation home. The mayor of Pittsburgh, the president of Columbia University, the celebrated artist Henry Tanner, and other notable figures found themselves among the large groups of tourists whose trips turned overnight from sightseeing to an increasingly desperate attempt to get home from a war-ravaged Europe.

The danger to these individuals seemed real enough. German police warned Americans not to speak English on the street, and one North Carolina woman traveling through Munich recalled a frantic search for American flags that she and her friends could carry in public to show that they were not Canadian or British.[13] One American woman traveling in Germany, perhaps terrified by the atrocity tales and stories of rapes committed by soldiers, slit her throat in panic when she found herself trapped behind the front lines.[14]

Newspapers reported on the whereabouts of famous Americans stranded in Europe and also noted the places in the United States where others had decided to spend the summer in lieu of Europe; the American travel industry received a sudden unexpected boost that summer, as the crisis struck just as the August vacation season was ready to begin.[15] More than 120,000 Americans came from across Europe to the relative safety of London desperate for help, creating what Walter Hines Page called "bedlam" for his small staff.[16] Nicholas Murray Butler, the Columbia University president mentioned above, reached London with just 27 cents in his pocket and no bank that would accept his American lines of credit in wartime. Daniel Guggenheim showed up in London penniless but in an ecstatic mood because he recognized how much money his family's mining empire would soon make from the war.[17]

Rich Americans could depend on connections and friends. Still, they and thousands of less-wealthy Americans needed help to get home. The United States government, unprepared for such an unexpected eventuality, loaded a battleship, the USS *Tennessee*, with $8 million in gold to provide Americans credit in London banks. J. P. Morgan coordinated an effort by ten banks to loan the government another $6 million in gold for the same purpose.[18] Assistant Secretary of War Henry Breckenridge accompanied the gold to London and oversaw its distribution to British banks for use as collateral for Americans in need of British pounds to pay for food, lodging, and tickets home. Government officials also reached out to neutral nations like the Netherlands, Spain, and Denmark to help Americans stranded there. Meanwhile, in London, one of those trapped Americans, engineer Herbert Hoover, had already sprung into action. Along with some British and American friends, he set up offices in the Savoy Hotel to help organize and distribute money from both the *Tennessee* and from private sources to ease the anxiety that the war had placed on Americans abroad.

Being stranded did not automatically equate to sympathy with the Allied cause. The daughter of a former Texas governor who had traveled extensively in Europe before the war resolutely refused to take sides in the war that had kept her from returning home. She praised those who saw the conflict as "a war imposed by a few men upon peace loving nations." Although she saw that the case against Germany was "convincing" in the matter of atrocities in Belgium, she also argued that Great Britain had an imperial and commercial interest in seeing Germany humbled. Thus she remained skeptical of British media reports about some of the most outrageous atrocities in Belgium and argued that American and British interests did not necessarily coincide. When at intermission of a theater performance in London an orchestra played "God Save the King," she and her friends instead sang "My Country 'Tis of Thee," which uses the same tune. She saw her nation's role as that of a strict neutral, helping to ease suffering where it could.[19] She represented an important strand of American thought in the winter of 1914–15.

American officials overseas accepted some of the traditional responsibilities that came with neutrality. Diplomats serving in Europe assumed the care of the citizens and property of belligerent governments in enemy countries. Diplomatic staffers hung American flags outside the embassies and consulates of states at war, hoping to protect them from looting and vandalism. Walter Hines Page assumed the care of more than seventy thousand Germans living in London and jokingly began to refer to himself as the "German ambassador in Britain," despite his own anti-German sentiments. In Berlin, American ambassador James Gerard took on the same responsibility for the British and French embassies, driving around the city in a big car festooned with American flags so that no one would mistake his English-speaking staff for Britons or Canadians.[20]

By early September, once the last of the stranded Americans had gone home, Hoover and Page turned their organizational skills to providing relief to Belgians. In October, Hoover formed the Committee for Relief in Belgium, eventually raising hundreds of millions of dollars and providing five million tons of food. His efforts caught the attention of President Wilson with whom he began a regular correspondence.[21] Other Americans came to Europe as doctors, nurses, and aid workers of all kinds. That same month the first American Red Cross ship arrived in France, bringing 170 doctors and nurses. They were the vanguard of thousands of Americans who risked their lives and futures to help France and Belgium in the face of a global emergency.[22]

Virtually all American volunteers came to Europe to aid the Allies, a clear indication of where Americans placed their sympathies. J. P. Morgan's energetic and talented daughter, Anne Morgan, became one of the leaders of this movement. She had been traveling in France when the war began and had decided to stay after a visit to the front lines convinced her of the need for Americans to help. She dedicated herself to raising money for the relief of civilians and the improvement of the French ambulance service, beginning a lifelong commitment to helping France recover from the devastation of the war. Mary Borden, a wealthy Chicagoan living in England in 1914, funded a field hospital for the Allies and served in it herself from 1915 to 1918.[23]

These movements usually began with the wealthy, but Americans from all walks of life saw themselves as the only hope for Europe amid global disarray. "We ought to get into this European war harder," wrote the editors of *Life*. "Since it is not proposed that we shall fight in it, we ought to get into the rescue work with more power," especially when it came to helping the Belgian and French civilians hit most directly by the war. The editors proposed a number of ways for Americans to help, including the suggestion that all college football ticket sales from the 1914 season go to Belgian relief efforts. While the universities showed little interest in that idea, students did pass around buckets at football games for fans to contribute to various charities involved in helping civilians, especially those in Belgium and France.[24]

In the war's early months, Americans of all classes reached deep into their pockets to provide money. Virtually all of that aid went to Belgium, France, and another suffering member of the anti-German alliance, Serbia.[25] By October, New York City's contribution to relief in the Allied nations since the outbreak of war amounted to $636,853. Columbia University led a drive to rebuild the library at Louvain and restock it with either donated books or books to be printed and published expressly for the purpose. The school had pledged to raise $35,000 of the estimated $1,000,000 the project would cost.[26] Philadelphia's millionaire merchant and civic leader John Wanamaker called for a public campaign to raise the astronomical sum of $100,000,000 in relief for France and Belgium.[27]

No equivalent to this movement existed for the Central Powers; although German and Austrian subjects living in the United States sometimes returned to Europe to fight, there are no records of American citizens serving in either the German or Austro-Hungarian Army. By contrast, and despite threats from government officials to revoke their citizenship if they did so, tens of thousands of young men went to Canada to enlist in the British Army or joined the French Foreign Legion at the French consulate in New Orleans.[28] By the end of August, a few dozen Americans had joined the French Army in France itself, training in the courtyard of Les Invalides under the watchful eye of a former United States Army officer who had relocated to Paris before the war. These young men provided ready-made heroic stories for journalists eager for news that Americans wanted to read, and the French news service proved more than willing to help publicize this link between the United States and France. The volunteers included poet Alan Seeger, who joined the French Foreign Legion on August 24, 1914, and Billy Thaw, a son of one of the wealthiest families in America, who told reporters that he was willing to give his life in the "fight of civilization against barbarism."[29] When one American volunteer, Edward M. Stone, a Harvard graduate, died on the Western Front in March 1915, he received flattering obituaries from newspapers across the nation. The Harvard *Crimson* depicted him as a hero, noting that "we do much talking around the Yard about the war, taking sides (usually the same side) with earnest eloquence; but here is a fellow, happy, rich, strong, with a promising life before him, who did not hesitate to volunteer under a foreign banner and sacrifice his life for the cause he thought (and most of us think) right."[30]

The blood, money, and sacrifice of these Americans formed a transatlantic bond between the American people and the Allied cause that had grown intense since the outbreak of the war. One such volunteer, the poet, suffragette, and nurse Caroline King Duer, visited the Marne battlefield in September 1914 en route to her post at a field hospital. She noted that the stark battlefield stood as a monument to the freedom that England and France had defended during the battle and she expressed her hope that all Americans who came to France "will be able to give thanks for that freedom" by helping the Allies as she was then doing.[31]

Support for those Allies came from every corner of the United States. The African-American press took great pride in the departure of a group of highly trained black nurses to France; the Chicago *Defender* noted that such volunteerism should come naturally to African-Americans because "of all the countries, France is the fairest to every man regardless of his nationality, creed, or color."[32] Heavyweight boxing champion Jack Johnson had successfully defended his title in Paris the night before the assassination of Archduke Franz Ferdinand. When the war began a few weeks later, Johnson, the first African-American champion and a hero to people on both sides of the Atlantic, was in Russia. He announced that he would return to Paris by motorcade and that when he arrived he would donate his vehicles to the French Army. News of his offer preceded his arrival in Paris, where an ecstatic crowd came out to meet him on the Place de la Concorde. The French Army made him an honorary colonel of a regiment and Johnson spoke to reporters of his interest in joining the French Army in more than an honorary role. Back in the United States, the African-American press celebrated the French Army's respect for the "bravery and strategy of the Afro-American" as symbolized by the 150,000 Africans fighting for France.[33]

American volunteers thus created tangible links between the United States and the Allies. So, too, did the economic aspects of the war, as the vast majority of American trade went to the Allies. The start of the war occurred as the American economy had fallen into recession. The sudden collapse of the global economic system destroyed the bases of the American export and financial markets and created a genuine crisis in an already fragile economy. In a matter of just a few hours the price of cotton fell from thirteen cents a pound to six cents a pound, leading to calls from Southern politicians for the United States government to fix prices or to subsidize farmers at the rate of five cents per pound. Even at deflated prices, American cotton sales plummeted, owing to the disruption of overseas markets, finance, shipping, and insurance. In October 1913 the United States had exported 257,172 bales of cotton; in October 1914 it exported just 21,219, devastating a vital American industry on which both the Northern and Southern economies depended.[34] The value of the US dollar fell from $4.86 to the British pound to $7 to the pound overnight. American traders soon found themselves with no access to European markets, insurance, or credit. British ambassador Spring-Rice warned his government of the possibility of the complete failure of the American economy.[35]

This unprecedented crisis, every bit as shocking and disorienting as the subsequent crashes of 1929 and 2008, forced the New York, Chicago, and Philadelphia stock exchanges to close their doors on July 31 in order to prevent European governments from selling their American securities and converting the proceeds from the dividends into gold. On July 28 alone, Europeans had removed more than $14,750,000 in gold from New York, more than five times the amount European traders normally withdrew in an average month. At that rate, American banks would not long survive, and the country would risk losing the gold that backed its paper currency. By a 231 to 6 margin, the House of Representatives passed an emergency bill that transferred millions of dollars of government-held gold to private banks in order to restore consumer confidence. Secretary of the Treasury William Gibbs McAdoo ordered the gold sent to banks in trucks arriving on pre-announced routes as part of a publicity stunt to show Americans the steps their government was taking to ease the crisis. Banks in thirty-nine states borrowed more than $368,000,000 in gold and paper currency, helping to mitigate the effects of the global economic crisis, but the doors of the New York Stock Exchange remained closed for a remarkable four long months, not reopening until November 28. Chicago's did not reopen until December 11.[36]

The ripple effects of this titanic economic disruption directly hurt Americans nationwide. Customs revenues fell sharply, leading to a genuine crisis in the federal budget and reenergizing the highly controversial idea of introducing a national income tax to make up the difference. A political cartoon titled "First Fruits of Europe's War" by the nationally syndicated Clifford Barryman from early August showed Uncle Sam looking over papers called "Income Reduced," "US Customs Revenue Greatly Reduced," and "Increased Income Tax Plan."[37] The administration's inability to react to the crisis with sufficient dexterity badly hurt the Democrats in the 1914 midterm elections. They lost more than fifty seats in the House of Representatives. Even in the solidly Democratic South the president's party came under heavy criticism, which the Virginian Woodrow Wilson took personally.

Relief began to come in the late fall (just a few weeks too late for Democrats at the polls) as the belligerents turned to America to fill orders for weapons, raw materials, finished goods, timber, food, animals, and, eventually, cotton. Daniel Guggenheim's vision of high profits for American companies had begun to come true. Because Britain controlled the high seas, owned the vast majority of the world's merchant vessels, ran the international credit markets, and dominated the maritime insurance industry, American recovery depended on trade with the Allies. American attempts to fix the problem of its own small merchant marine fleet had come to naught in the years before the war, largely because of congressional unwillingness to devote sufficient funds and the concomitant debate over the creation of a Federal Reserve Bank. As a result, America's financial recovery in 1914 depended heavily on British benevolence.

That benevolence fit in with a certain definition of American neutrality. As Wilson understood, economic recovery meant far more to most Americans than maintaining a strict legal neutrality on matters connected to the war. Americans would therefore seek to trade with whomever they could whenever they could. As one newspaper in the American heartland noted, international law protected America's "perfect right to carry on a world trade with whatever countries it can reach with its products."[38] Circumstance dictated that those products could most easily reach Canada and Britain; that the vast majority of trade went to the Allies was thus a happy coincidence of the circumstances of the war, national sentiment, and economic self-interest. The British helped the United States by not listing cotton (critical to the packing of artillery shells) as a contraband of war, thus helping to rehabilitate not just the economy of the South, but of the North, even though the world cotton markets in particular took a long time to recover from the shock of 1914.

Industry, agriculture, and labor all benefited from the new boom in trade. The African-American newspaper Chicago *Defender* saw opportunity for its readership as thousands of recent European immigrants who "strove to elbow the Afro-American from labor and occupations at which he formerly labored" returned across the Atlantic to fight for their native countries. The war would shrink the American labor pool while the economy grew, thus removing competition from European immigrants, increasing wages, and giving the African-American worker renewed access to jobs "in which he was formerly engaged before Europe began sending her hundreds of thousands here annually."[39]

That economic recovery depended on old connections and the building of new ones as well. The senior vice president of Philadelphia's Baldwin Locomotive Works made two trips to Russia in the war's opening months, securing contracts for more than $127,000,000 to provide railroad cars, munitions, and other war supplies. A Baldwin subsidiary, Eddystone Ammunition, soon held contracts for the manufacture of millions of shells and rifle cartridges for the British and French armies. By the end of 1915 they were providing ammunition for the Pennsylvania

National Guard and the United States Army as well. With these contracts, of course, came jobs and infrastructure investment in the Philadelphia area and beyond. Baldwin and Eddystone had to rely on British ships to transport all of their overseas commerce given that less than 10 percent of Pennsylvania's trade to Europe traveled in American ships. Without British shipping, American firms like Baldwin simply could not fill the millions of dollars of orders coming in to their firms every month.[40]

Economic interest, political preference, and cultural affinity thus coincided nicely. Such circumstances, however, put the United States in an awkward international position given how manifestly they ran counter to Wilson's desire to put a strictly impartial face on American thought and behavior. As Secretary of the Interior Franklin Lane, a man with his own strong pro-Allied sympathies, wrote to an American businessman in Rome, "The position of a neutral is a hard one. We are being generously damned by the Germans and the aggressive Irish for being pro-British, and the English press people and sympathizers in this country are generously damning us as the grossest of commercialists who are willing to sell them into the eternal slavery of Germany for the sake of selling a few bushels of wheat."[41] Or, as the Chicago *Tribune* noted, "The truth is that abroad the United States is the object of an almost universal dislike" because no matter what it did, its actions benefited one side over the other.[42] To cite one example, the United States protested Britain putting copper on the contraband list despite its evident military utility in the construction of shells and other armaments. Britain's *Punch* magazine criticized the contradiction between American principles and materialism by publishing an "American" poem that read: "So while we pray for Prussia's fall / And look to your stout arm to whop her, We mean to answer every call / She makes on us for copper."[43]

Even Americans making money from the war agreed with the sentiment in *Punch*, both for political and moral reasons. The nation's eagerness to profit handsomely from the tragedy in Europe sat uneasily with those, like Secretary of State Bryan, who sought a purer definition of neutrality, as well as with socialists who blamed the war's outbreak on the arms trade. The United States, they alleged, fueled the fires that killed men by the tens of thousands in Europe's new hecatombs while reaping a blood-stained profit in the process. Pro-Allied Mary Roberts

Rinehart felt uneasy about her native Pittsburgh "fattening on catastrophe" even though she knew that orders for steel and finished goods (like a British order through Westinghouse for five million artillery shells) would benefit the city tremendously.[44] A cartoon by J. N. Darling in the Des Moines *Register* from December 1914 showed the contradictions and hypocrisy in American neutrality. In the first panel, an American says to his wife, "This war is a terrible thing! The country ought to stop the slaughter some way." In the second panel a lawyer arrives to tell him, "Sir, your Uncle Ezra is dead, leaving to you his New Jersey ammunition factory." In the final panel the man is in Europe selling a weapon labeled "guaranteed to kill everything within 8 miles" and holding an order form for "300000000 rounds of ammunition."[45]

Moral qualms notwithstanding, Americans vigorously defended their right to trade freely, even if their particular definition of neutrality brought with it the anger of the European belligerents, especially Germany. Public statements from Germany's ambassador to the United States criticizing America for its effectively pro-British trade policies evoked ire from one Iowa newspaper. Germany's criticisms, its editors argued, were "unfair to the people of this country, who as innocent bystanders have had to suffer a good many hardships from this war and have endured patiently a good many unpleasant things." The economic recovery that accompanied the new wartime trade thus served as America's just compensation for the economic dislocations of the war's first few months. "We did not stir up this war," the editors continued. "Let those who are responsible for it bear the blame."[46] Americans, as was their right under international law, would reap the benefits of Europe's self-immolation.

As the American economy began first to slowly recover, then to grow, some Americans saw an opportunity for the United States to supplant Europe as the world's leading financial and industrial powerhouse. On August 20, 1914, at the very nadir of the Stock Exchange crisis, millionaire Boston investment banker Henry Lee Higginson wrote to Woodrow Wilson to tell him that "England has been the exchange place of the world, because of [its] living up to every engagement, and because the power grew with the business. Today we can take this place if we choose." The war, Higginson told the president, "is our chance to take first place."[47] Manufacturers saw the same chance. "The demand for

American-made goods abroad is increasing," said one Midwestern newspaper publisher in January 1915. "But, better still, the demand for American-made goods is increasing at home. You and I have bought all too many 'Made in Germany' products heretofore. There is a 'Made in America' movement on foot now, to which we should all lend our aid." Although, or perhaps because, Europe seemed likely to undergo yet another bloody year of war, the newspaper argued that Americans could make 1915 "the best year of our lives."[48] Notably, although the editorial focused on economics, not politics, it singled out Germany and did not mention Great Britain or France. One Pittsburgh newspaper took a wider view, but also hoped openly that America would profit from Europe's misfortune. "The United States," it editorialized, "cannot but be the gainer if Great Britain, France, Russia, and Germany engage in hostilities" because of the increased European demand for American goods and the resultant destruction and militarization of European industry.[49]

The war thus opened a seemingly endless series of opportunities for Americans to make money. Businessmen in Pensacola, Florida, reacted by forming a Gulf Coast Development League to draw investment money from the newfound "overwhelming prosperity" of the nation to the Gulf Coast's railroad, lumber, and tourism industries. The league sought to take maximum advantage of the "unusual situation" that the war presented.[50] Similarly, a January 1915 editorial that ran in several small Midwestern newspapers (probably supported financially by the railroad industry) predicted vast profits for American farmers from the war. Despite the "miserable shipping facilities" of the United States merchant fleet, and despite the need for federal funds to modernize the nation's railway network, the war offered American farmers an opportunity "to reap a larger profit from the chaotic conditions which exist in Europe than any other class of tradesmen in our country." European trade with the United States in food had already grown 25 percent in a year, with nearly limitless growth possible in flour, pork, beef, and mutton. The editorial highlighted two important points: first, that Americans could base their economic recovery on war trade and, second, that the American merchant fleet's small size meant that the United States did not entirely control its own economic destiny.[51] The opening of the Federal Reserve Bank of New York in November 1914 (long planned by Progressives but held up due to strong congressional opposition) helped to stabilize the American economy, support the dollar as an international trade currency, control the flow of gold, and allow the stock exchanges to reopen with confidence.[52]

As Americans saw it, the growth of American trade need not benefit only the United States. *Life* saw the growth of American trade as helping everyone, even the Germans, whom the magazine's editors clearly held responsible for the war. "No doubt our great part in this vast disturbance is to mind our own business and keep our general apparatus of production and distribution going for the benefit not only of ourselves, but all of Europe" because the United States would have to play the dominant role in European reconstruction after the war ended. American prosperity and European recovery thereby became one and the same.[53]

The war presented an opportunity for the United States to supplant Europe beyond the economic sphere as well. The president of the American Medical Association and dean of the University of Michigan medical school argued that Germany's "petty" bid to extend its power over Europe would cause it to forfeit its role as a leader in education, medicine, and science. "Some other country must take her proud place, must dominate the scientific world. This country should be America." In a similar vein, the New York *Times* reported that the war would have the unintended benefit of keeping America's best students at home and enticing more foreign students to come to American universities instead of German ones.[54]

Although most Americans aimed their venom at the Germans, they had disagreements as well with the British who used their commercial and maritime supremacy to interfere with American trade. Lloyds of London so dominated the overseas insurance markets that it alone could influence American commerce or even stop some overseas shipments altogether. The British were most concerned with shipments to Germany disguised as trade with neutral states that bordered Germany like Holland and Denmark. The Royal Navy could not always interfere with trade between two neutrals, but Lloyds could make such trade exorbitantly expensive by refusing to insure it if the British thought the Germans were using neutral ports to gain access to American goods.[55]

By stopping and searching American shipping headed to Germany or nearby neutrals, the British stirred up memories of the infringement of

American rights during the War of 1812. The British government drew up a series of contraband lists, detailing which goods it would capture and which it would let pass. "England is making a fool of herself by antagonizing American opinion, insisting on rights of search which she has never acknowledged as to herself," wrote Secretary of the Interior Franklin Lane to a friend in January 1915. "If she persists she will be successful in driving from her the opinion of this country, which is ninety percent in her favor."[56] British economic policies created a tension with Americans that the latter saw as unnecessary. Theodore Roosevelt's shrewd daughter Alice Roosevelt Longworth thought that virtually all of the anti-British sentiment in the United States came not from those who opposed the Allies on political or moral grounds, but from people economically disadvantaged by Britain's shortsighted contraband policy.[57] British ambassador Spring-Rice and foreign secretary Sir Edward Grey saw the same problem. Together they convinced the British government to keep many items off the contraband list in the interests of maintaining good relations with the United States. They thereby prevented American attitudes from turning even more anti-British.

Nor did anger about Louvain, Rheims, and other German atrocities cool as the weeks passed. To the contrary, Germany's attempts to justify its actions kept that anger alive. In October, ninety-three prominent Germans signed the so-called Appeal to the Civilized World defending German actions "in a struggle which has been forced on her." The signatories represented the elite of German intellectuals and included several Nobel laureates.[58] Americans saw the appeal as further proof of how deeply the war had corroded the morals of the German people. In December, the *New Republic* called the appeal "pitifully feeble" and said that it represented the "sign and seal of success of *Kultur* in making all her subjects accept the Kaiser without question.... Just when monarchs by the grace of God are disappearing from the earth, the Germans would have us listen devoutly to the archaic utterances of their king and emperor."[59] Harvard historian William Roscoe Thayer, who knew some of the signatories personally, said that the manifesto proved "the complete subservience of the German university professors to the Kaiser and his Ring. Not in our generation," he concluded, "will German scholarship recover its prestige after such an exhibition."[60] The New York *Tribune* called the document "the wildest, most arrogant and fantastic document of its kind that the war has yet produced."[61]

In December, the *New Republic* further noted that as a result of the appeal and statements by the German people in favor of the war, Germany's "best friends are disappointed in them, and forced to face the problem of how obtuseness is to be reconciled with all the admirable intellectual traits which we have come to associate with Germany." Revealing how far American attitudes had come since August, it concluded: "The Germans would have us accord them a position of racial supremacy; just when the world is becoming unified economically and scientifically, the Germans clamor for an exceptional position in the brotherhood of nations."[62] The *New Republic*'s evolving position on Germany reflected both the increasing sense of American charges of guilt at the German people more generally, and the developing vision of a postwar world of greater interconnectedness and the imposition of democratic values.

Other American publications followed a similar path. *Life* ran a cartoon in December showing a boy running away from a wild pack of pursuing men, children, and dogs while women yelled at him from windows. The text read "Moral: If you are in favor of the Kaiser, keep it to yourself."[63] At the same time, former Harvard president Charles Eliot wrote an editorial in the New York *American* openly questioning whether the United States and Germany could coexist in the same world.[64] Chicago *Daily News* war correspondent John Bass grew so angry at what he saw in Europe that he tried to join the French Army before another reporter talked him out of it.[65]

Prominent Americans publicly lent their voices both to the growing mistrust of Germany and frustration with Wilson's policy of neutrality. Civil War veteran and railroad executive Charles Francis Adams wrote in a March 1915 editorial that the war had proven the basic incompatibility of the American and German worlds. German thinking, he wrote, represented "the absolute negation of everything which in the past tended to the elevation of mankind, and the installation in place thereof of a system of thorough dishonesty, emphasized by brutal stupidity. There is a low cunning about it, too, which is to me in the last degree repulsive." If the world were to come to think like Germany, he wrote, "I would rather cease thinking at all."[66] Similarly, the progressive educator and philosopher John Dewey argued that the United States, Britain, and France shared a system of national values that was "basically opposed to the German character" and that those values "offered the most striking contrast to German absolutism."[67]

Notable German-Americans knew that Germany had lost the sympathy of their countrymen. Minister, theologian, and Social Gospel proponent Walter Rauschenbusch compared sympathy for Germany in an "overwhelmingly hostile" America to being a supporter of Protestantism in Bourbon Spain. Being a sympathizer of the German cause, he noted, marked one as a member of a "disreputable family."[68] Hugo Münsterberg wrote with sadness that few German-Americans born in the United States saw the righteousness in Germany's position. He lamented the fact that German-Americans only agreed on one issue, their opposition to prohibition. Younger German-Americans failed to understand that the war "is fundamentally a war of Russian brutality against German civilization." As a result, they followed the general trend of American popular opinion, which Münsterberg thought showed a "lack of insight into the European mind" as German-Americans had become less German and more American.[69]

Münsterberg's desires notwithstanding, a strict adherence to neutrality became the main reaction of German-Americans to the war. H. C. Bloedel, the head of the Pittsburgh chapter of the National German-American Alliance, argued that the war represented for Germany a "most momentous struggle for 'to be or not to be,' fighting for its very existence in a war wrought upon them by hate." He called on German-Americans to aid Germany in its time of trial, but carefully noted that German-Americans must stand with America first and foremost.[70] To Bloedel and many other German-American leaders that meant arguing for strict American neutrality, not pleading the merits of Germany's case to one's fellow Americans as Münsterberg was doing.

Americans, especially Protestant Americans, worried, too, about the passions of Europe causing violence on American streets. Newton Baker, then-mayor of Cleveland, called in his police chief on the outbreak of the war to share his fears about ethnic violence on his city's streets. Cleveland then had 750,000 residents, three-fourths of whom were either first- or second-generation immigrants. "The racial antagonism and bitterness of this war in Europe," Baker warned his chief, "will inevitably affect our people and we are likely to have a war in miniature in our streets." The chief promised the mayor that he would take reasonable precautions, but he told Baker not to worry. The citizens of Cleveland may have come from every corner of Europe, but they had now become Americans. "Most of these people," he told Baker, "came from Europe to escape the very thing now going on there and their chief emotion will be thankfulness that they have escaped it and are not involved." The chief predicted that there would be no war-related violence on the streets of Cleveland.[71]

The chief had read the pulse of his community well. Cleveland police made no arrests related to the war in 1914 or 1915. In the Pittsburgh area, the only war-related arrest occurred in the steel community of Homestead, where a drunken man of Slavic descent roamed the streets shouting insults about Austro-Hungarian emperor Franz Joseph.[72] The cities remained calm, although native-born Americans sometimes continued to express worries that events in Europe would eventually cause trouble on American streets. They would not have been reassured had they known of a conversation Ambassador James Gerard had had with German foreign minister Gottlieb von Jagow in Berlin at the start of the war. Jagow tried to frighten Gerard by warning him that America risked "civil war" if it did not behave in a strictly neutral way because Germany had 500,000 army and navy reservists living in the United States. Gerard, whose own mistrust of Germany had grown quickly since the outbreak of the war, chillingly replied, "I do not know whether there are 500,000 German reservists in the United States, but I do know there are 500,000 lampposts in my country and that every German residing in the United States who undertakes to take up arms against America will swing from one of those 500,000 lampposts."[73]

Some American officials knew that the German government had taken steps to, if not start a civil war, at least foment trouble on American soil. Germany's ambassador to the United States had returned to Berlin on the outbreak of the war and came back to Washington with millions of dollars in cash for propaganda and related activities. American law enforcement agents soon got wind of a German scheme to buy passports of American longshoreman and give them to German reservists so that they could travel back to Germany without fear of being arrested by British officials or captured on the high seas. Because American passports did not then carry photographs, the British would have no way to identify German reservists and would have no choice but to let them travel to Germany or a neutral state like Holland, even if they transited through Britain en route.

A German national living in the United States ran the passport scheme out of offices in lower Manhattan. In January 1915 federal agents arrested another German national who had in his possession a typewriter that matched the one that had typed a list of the German officers given purchased passports. He was convicted and given three years in a federal penitentiary in Atlanta. His arrest in turn led to the arrest of yet another German national who produced forged American birth certificates with which agents hoped to obtain genuine American passports. Seeking to avoid an international incident, the State Department decided not to raise a formal objection to the German government, but it did begin to insist on photographs being pasted into passports to prevent the practice continuing in the future.

Americans also knew that the German government wanted to plant pro-German stories in American newspapers or to buy American newspapers outright. German agents approached H. L. Mencken early in 1915 with an offer to buy his magazine *Smart Set*; Mencken refused. The Germans then turned, as we've seen, to subsidizing George Sylvester Viereck's *Fatherland*, which he began publishing on the outbreak of the war. Viereck, born in Munich, had lived in the United States since age eleven and had developed a reputation as a talented poet and a much less talented political commentator. His pro-German sentiments were well known to people on both sides of the Atlantic. Viereck himself promoted the rumor (likely false) that his father had been the illegitimate son of Prussian king Wilhelm I. His 1908 book *Confessions of a Barbarian* both established him as one of America's great Germanophiles and got him kicked out of several prominent social clubs, including the New York Athletic Club, for his views. To get away from the heat, he took a job as a professor of poetry in Berlin in 1911, but he returned to America in 1912. Viereck's newspaper had some limited appeal among first-generation Germans, but only aroused the ire of non-German Americans. In early 1915 most Americans simply ignored it or dismissed it as a propaganda tool of a foreign government.

Of much greater concern to American policemen and the American people more generally, a suspicious trail of fires and potential sabotage of facilities providing supplies to the Allies began. In January 1915, the SS *Orton*, taking munitions from Brooklyn to Great Britain, caught fire. The same month a mysterious fire began in a steel mill in Trenton, New Jersey. In February, sailors found bombs on two ships headed to Great Britain, and explosions rocked a DuPont munitions factory and a gunpowder plant in Illinois.[74]

Three other German-based plots made national headlines at this time. The first involved a failed attempt to dynamite the Welland Canal in Ontario, which Canadian authorities traced to a professional spy named Horst von der Goltz, who had lived in Mexico before the war then moved to New York City. A frightened von der Goltz found his way to England after the plot failed, promising the British secret information about zeppelin raids over London in exchange for amnesty on the Welland Canal charge.[75] The British refused and sent him to the United States, where he also went to jail in Atlanta. Next came the arrest of a German national named Werner Horn on similar charges. Horn, who had been living in Guatemala before the war, devised a scheme to blow up the railroad bridge between Vanceboro, Maine, and St. Croix, New Brunswick. Canadian officials asked for his extradition, but, he, too went to the federal jail in Atlanta. Then in early April 1915 came word of a plot to dynamite the railroad bridge connecting Vancouver, British Columbia, to the United States. British agents based in the consulate in San Francisco uncovered the plot. They also arrested two of the Germans traveling on purchased passports when they transited through England. The Americans asked for extradition, but the British sent them instead to the Tower of London, where one committed suicide and the other died at the hands of a British firing squad.[76]

The United States government reluctantly accepted the German embassy's explanation that German nationals were acting on their own initiative and without any connection to the German government.[77] That distinction was critical, as it cleared the German government of charges of interfering with American rights and also absolved Wilson of having to take action. Wilson remained anxious to preserve the appearance of neutrality and sought to downplay the incidents as much as he could. Federal agents did not, therefore, investigate further, despite growing circumstantial evidence that a network of German government officials based in New York City had links in one way or another to all of these plots. Wilson's timid response to these events helped to convince his rival Theodore Roosevelt to begin a more open criticism of administration policy. Roosevelt soon began writing regular columns in a number of outlets, most importantly nationally syndicated articles for the Kansas City *Star*.

While Wilson refused to do anything at the federal level, local authorities decided to take action on their own. In early 1915, the New York City Police Department, which Roosevelt had once headed, formed the wonderfully named "Bomb and Neutrality Squad" in response to the suspicious trend of damage to the property of companies doing business with the Allies. Led by Thomas J. Tunney, a twenty-five-year Irish-American veteran of the NYPD and brother of boxer Gene Tunney, the squad had thirty-five members, all of them veteran detectives from Manhattan or Brooklyn. They had previously worked together on a "Black Hand" squad formed to track anarchists. Now they set their sights on the German spy network they believed to be operating in New York City.

The squad's suspicions quickly fell on the crews of German merchant ships stranded in New York and Hoboken harbors by the outbreak of the war. Unable to take to the open seas for fear of capture by the Royal Navy, the ships and their men became a beehive of pro-German activity. Police could not monitor activity on the ships themselves, but they could trail the sailors when they went ashore in New York and New Jersey. Tunney particularly focused on Paul Koenig, the chief detective for the Hamburg-Amerika shipping company. Trailing Koenig led Tunney and his men to the German Club near Central Park and the Hamburg-Amerika building in the financial district, where Koenig attended meetings with two German diplomatic envoys, naval attaché Karl Boy-Ed and commercial attaché Franz von Papen. Tunney suspected all three men of plotting sabotage, and while he could not yet arrest them, he did succeed in getting one of New York City's first telephone taps in order to listen in on conversations at the Hamburg-Amerika offices.[78]

These events created an atmosphere of suspicion that made the German position on the war that much more unpopular inside the

United States. Those German-Americans who continued to plead Germany's case therefore changed tack. Knowing how much Americans objected to the argument that Germany was fighting a war of survival against a Slavic peril, they developed a new strategy. By early 1915 they had turned to denouncing the influence of a pro-British media for poisoning American minds. They also argued for an arms embargo, whereby the United States would agree not to sell weapons to either side, as the European neutrals had agreed to do during the Franco-Prussian War. An arms embargo would obviously benefit Germany, as it would stanch the flow of weapons coming from American factories to the United Kingdom and France.

In January 1915, fifty prominent German-Americans, including Hugo Münsterberg and former Missouri congressman Richard Bartholdt, met in New York City to discuss ways to promote an American arms embargo. The idea dovetailed nicely with the arguments of socialists who opposed the armaments trade on the grounds that it allowed wealthy Americans to profit from the war. It also fit in with the newly formed American League to Limit Armaments, a Quaker-led movement backed in large part by Andrew Carnegie's money. Prominent clergymen like John Mott, a close friend of John D. Rockefeller and Woodrow Wilson, also argued for an arms embargo.[79]

They did not, however, represent the views of the American people, as demonstrated by the response to the meeting and its call for an arms embargo. The New York *Times* called the gathering "completely subservient to a foreign power" and the fifty men gathered in the city "agents of German propaganda." The *Nation* similarly said that the group had acted "plainly in the interest of a foreign power."[80] At the same time, *Life* announced that while it was "not yet after Germans" in the United States, their actions, too, had begun to raise questions. "Are our neighbors here of German derivation potential spies of the Kaiser and potential allies of the Kaiserland against this Republic that has sheltered them?" If so, the magazine knew how high the stakes could get, for a German victory would mean that "the world would be delivered to a succession of barren struggles, ending in such suspicion and despair as creation has never witnessed" and the United States under the domain of "Kaiserism, Prussianism, the rule of might, blood and iron, *Deutschland Über Alles*, force [as] the higher law, and all that."[81]

Protestant and native-born Americans led this charge, but Catholic and Jewish Americans had begun to change their views as well. At the start of the war, the Irish-American community found itself divided. The largest group supported Irish politician John Redmond, who wanted Catholics in Ireland to fight alongside Britain as a way to prove that the concept of Home Rule could work. A minority of Irish-Americans instead supported the *Clan na Gael* movement, which argued for complete Irish independence and noncompliance with Britain's war. The *Irish World*, one of the two most important Irish Republican newspapers publishing in the United States, called Redmond "the recruiting sergeant of the British Army," and one woman wrote to the newspaper from Brooklyn to say, "I hope and pray England will suffer as Ireland did under British rule." The Republicans hoped that the war might produce not Home Rule but complete independence for Ireland.[82]

Still, Irish-Americans had to proceed with caution. Most understood that the community could not risk losing the benefits of assimilation that the previous generations had gained. Despite their mistrust of England, they knew that any open expression of support for Germany or Austria-Hungary could produce a backlash. Most wanted America to remain neutral and at least grudgingly accepted Redmond's position. The Irish-American press also took careful note of the meaning of the words of President Wilson's dedication of a monument to Irish-American naval hero John Barry in May 1914. Wilson said that Barry's "heart crossed the Atlantic with him" unlike those who "need hyphens in their name because only part of them has come over."[83]

Outside pressure may have played a role in setting initial Irish attitudes, but internal dynamics within the Irish-American community mattered much more. In 1914, Redmond's position of cooperation with Britain had the greater pull on Irish-Americans, especially its leadership.[84] Only the most radical Republicans openly expressed sympathy for the Central Powers. As the war went on, German treatment of Catholic Belgium and Catholic Poland made the German model seem much less appealing than the Home Rule model Britain had grudgingly proposed just before the war. Thousands of Irishmen were, moreover, fighting and dying in the British Army, making support for Germany seem treasonous to many Irish-Americans. Most Irish-American newspapers thus advocated neutrality for the United States; such a position both fit in with general sentiment of neutrality in the country and offered a middle ground between an avaricious Germany and a British government that most Irish-Americans still suspected of false motives toward their homeland.[85] Most charitable contributions from the United States to Ireland, therefore, went to help families who had men in the British Army fighting the Germans.[86]

A similar process of internal and external pressures existed inside the Jewish community as well in 1914 and 1915. The intense hatred for the notoriously anti-Semitic Russian regime led many Jews to support the Central Powers at first. "The Jews support Germany because Russia bathes in Jewish blood," reported the *Yiddish Times*. "Who will dare say that it is a crime for Jews to hate their torturers, their oppressors and murderers?"[87] Nor had Jews forgotten the nasty anti-Semitism that the Dreyfus Affair had shown just under a surface of public tolerance for Jews in France. By contrast, Germany and Austria-Hungary had become relatively tolerant places for Jews, as shown by the prominence of Jews like Sigmund Freud, Albert Einstein, and German industrialist Walther Rathenau.

Still, hatred for Russia did not necessarily mean support for the Central Powers, and enthusiasm for Germany especially began to fade quickly. German society in 1914 did not have the vituperative anti-Semitism that plagued Russia, but the kaiser and his regime had their own well-known anti-Jewish sentiments. As one Yiddish newspaper noted in October, the Germans did not necessarily provide much of an alternative to reactionary Russia. Echoing the Two Germanys idea, it argued that "German victory shall not mean the triumph of German culture, of German philosophical thought, of the German labor movement and socialism... it shall be a triumph of German reaction and the monarchy, of the Hohenzollerns and Junkers; it shall retard democratic development in Germany for decades and wipe out Belgium and Luxembourg... it means the coming of a new, great, inevitable World War, wherein Russia shall play an even more prominent role as the 'defender of civilization.'"[88]

Germany's behavior in the parts of Poland it conquered, moreover, suggested that life for Polish Jews under German dominion might not be much better than under Russian. Rather than liberating Jews, German armies stole food and committed acts of random violence, as

Forverts, a New York City–based Yiddish-language newspaper reported in September 1914: "Three elderly frightened folk, in their bed clothes, were tied up and shot in front of everyone. German soldiers looted and plundered. The city [Kalisz, west of Warsaw] is now a ruins, partly bombed and partly burned. Corpses are strewn about as if after an earthquake."[89] The American Jewish community also contained a large number of socialists, who saw the war as proof of the faults in capitalism.

Like the Irish community in the United States, Jews understood full well that they had only recently begun to climb the social ladder and that standing out too much from American opinion more generally could lead to their taking a step back. Many assimilationist Jews read the situation in Europe exactly as the police chief in Cleveland had predicted. When one mother wrote to the Jewish daily *Forward* advice columnist to ask how she should respond to the desire of her son and his friends to return to their native Austria and fight the hated Russians, the paper replied, "Let them give thanks that they are in America and not forced to kill or die needlessly."[90]

A desire for self-interested neutrality notwithstanding, by the spring of 1915, a growing number of Americans had begun to awaken to the dangers that the war posed to America and to the distasteful aspects of their own neutrality. Some turned on Wilson, with William Roscoe Thayer calling the president's policy "tantamount to acquiescing in the German doctrine that might is right, that matter and not spirit rules the universe."[91] Such men and women found their champion in Theodore Roosevelt, who began an intense and virulent campaign against Wilson's lack of response both out of principle and in the hopes of finding a wedge issue for the 1916 presidential campaign. As his daughter Alice recalled, Roosevelt (and she herself) had had enough of the "vacillating policy" coming from the White House. "No atrocity could stir him," Alice Roosevelt Longworth wrote of Wilson. "He just wrote notes—and then more notes."[92]

Notwithstanding their instinctive sympathy with the Allies and the deepening economic ties to Britain and France, the war still seemed to be a European problem. Mary Roberts Rinehart noted upon her return to Pittsburgh in March 1915 her relief that the United States remained neutral. "As a family, we were still safe," she happily noted in her diary.

"The boys were young, and long before they were of fighting age the war would be over."[93] Most people, however, could sense the war creeping closer and closer to America every day. On May 2, 1915, American ambassador to Great Britain Walter Hines Page wrote to his son in North Carolina with an astonishing premonition. "If a British liner full of American passengers be blown up, what will Uncle Sam do? That what's going to happen."[94] Page would not have to wait long to find out.

3

The Impossible Middle

WALTER HINES PAGE DID NOT have long to wait to see his premonition come true. Nor had he been particularly clairvoyant in making it. In February 1915 the German government had announced its intention to sink ships headed into active war zones. On March 28, one American died when a German ship sank the liner *Falaba* off the coast of Sierra Leone.[1] On May 1, a U-boat had struck the American oil tanker *Gulflight* off the coast of Cornwall, killing three more Americans. The German government apologized and blamed the latter incident on a case of mistaken identification. Wilson pledged to hold the Germans to "strict accountability," but the incidents soon faded from public view.

Just a few days later, however, the issue of submarine warfare catapulted back onto center stage when a U-boat sank the *Lusitania*, the world's foremost luxury liner, a ship that had transported statesmen, journalists, businessmen, and tourists between the United States and Europe in war and peace alike since its celebrated launch in 1906. Edward House had sailed on it earlier in the war, as had war correspondents Frederick Palmer and Irvin Cobb when they left for Europe to cover the German invasion of Belgium. The *Lusitania* was therefore more than just any ship. It represented to many people, on both sides of the Atlantic, a pinnacle of Western civilization; the Cunard Liner company advertised its magnificent ship as "a perfect epitome of all that man knows or has discovered or invented up to this moment in time."[2]

American and British leaders saw the sinking of the unarmed and vulnerable *Lusitania* as a symbol of the threat that Germany posed to the vital links between them and to civilization itself. Page had not mentioned any specific ship by name in the letter to his son, but just days before the sinking King George V had specifically asked House, "Suppose they should sink the *Lusitania* with American passengers aboard?"[3]

Germany had announced its intention to sink passenger liners; German officials had even taken out advertisements in New York newspapers, warning Americans that they traveled into the North Atlantic war zone at their own risk. Several people with bookings on the ship's ill-fated voyage, including playwright Justus Miles Forman, had received mysterious phone calls in the days before the ship's departure from men with German accents urging them not to travel on the ship. They had all ignored the warnings, presuming them to be a hoax or some kind of sick joke. No one in the United States seemed to believe that the Germans would actually target a famous and luxurious ocean liner carrying innocent civilians.[4] The *Lusitania*, a massive ship with four distinctive funnels, was not the *Falaba* or the *Gulflight*; in this case, there could be no claim of mistaken identification. Most believed that the famous ship was safe from harm; in any case it was supposed to be fast enough to outrun submarines.

Nonetheless, a German U-boat did sink the ship off the coast of Ireland on May 7, 1915. Almost 1,200 people died in the frigid waters of the North Atlantic, including 128 Americans. The tales of horror told by the 764 survivors, as well as the photographs of their hollowed, traumatized faces, first shocked and then outraged Americans. Although there were no anti-German riots in the United States—as there were in Canada—anti-German sentiment ran hot.[5] Newspapers brought out what they called their "Second Coming Type" for once-in-a-generation size headlines.[6] The German embassy's statement that the ship had been carrying war contraband failed to convince contemporaries of the justice of sinking it and the German government's celebration of the event, including the casting of commemorative medals, only added to American fury. *Life* responded with a cover image showing a submarine's periscope (sliding menacingly westward) across an ocean with a caption reading "The Assassin."[7]

The *Lusitania* sinking proved that the European war had finally become America's. American lives had now been lost, including those of innocent women and children. Fifty children under one year of age had died on the *Lusitania*, and several newspapers reprinted a photograph of a Philadelphia couple and their six children with the caption "all lost with the *Lusitania*."[8] The ensuing diplomatic crisis created a need to come together and face an unprecedented international crisis with one voice. Virtually all Americans felt an impulse to demonstrate that, whatever their views on the war, they now stood shoulder to shoulder with their countrymen in a time of need. From Richmond, Virginia, came a pledge from the Jewish community to prove that "Good, red American blood had not disappeared from the face of the earth." Patriotism, they noted, "asserted itself," both inside the Jewish community and out.[9] One newspaper pledged that American Jews "will take their stand with the body of patriotic Americans who are intent on preserving the honor of the Republic and on safeguarding the welfare of its people."[10] The *American Hebrew and Jewish Messenger* urged calm but noted that the nation faced a moment of truth as grave as anything since the sectional crisis that had produced the Civil War. The sinking was, in the eyes of the editors, "a demonstration of the terrors that war can bring to noncombatants innocent of any thought of human destruction." If America had believed itself immune from the nightmare of that terror, the sinking of the *Lusitania* definitively proved otherwise.[11]

The African-American press agreed. The New York *News* argued that despite past injustices, African-American men had a duty to stand with their white countrymen should the *Lusitania* incident lead to war. The Philadelphia *Tribune* praised the stance of the *News* and added that African-Americans should support "the United States against Germany as long as a man of them is needed to properly man the warships and fill the ranks of the Army."[12] The Baltimore *Afro-American* urged its readers to prove wrong the recent statement of a federal judge overheard predicting that African-Americans would not support the United States in its hour of crisis.[13]

The leaders of the Hispanic community in New Mexico responded to the sinking by declaring their allegiance to the United States. In the 1898 war against Spain, New Mexican identities came under intense scrutiny; in 1915 there would be no such cause for concern, and in the months after the sinking Hispanic-Americans came to constitute half of the New Mexico National Guard. Neuvomexicanos saw a moral imperative to join the outrage at German behavior, as well as a benefit to their own community, which had only just attained the full rights of citizenship when New Mexico became a state in 1912.[14]

For Italian-Americans, the sinking of the *Lusitania* coincided with Italy's entry into the war on the Allied side. While the German-American press railed at the Italian government's perfidy (Italy had had an alliance with Germany in 1914, but did not join the war on the German side), the Italian-American community mobilized itself to help its country of birth. By 1917 more than ninety thousand Italian men living in the United States but not yet naturalized returned to Italy to serve in its armed forces. Immigrant aid societies in New York, Philadelphia, Boston, and elsewhere stopped using their resources to help new immigrants settle in the United States; instead they helped Italian reservists return home to fight.[15] The events of spring 1915 tied those who stayed more closely both to the Allied cause and the general shift of anti-German sentiment. Many Italian-Americans had family actively fighting in Europe and therefore the closest connections to the war of any recent immigrant group. They tended to follow news closely and, with the exception of some socialists, increasingly saw the goals of Italy and the United States as overlapping. Some joined the American armed forces in anticipation of the day that the United States would enter the fight alongside Italy.[16] In New Haven, one group responded by creating an all-Italian machine gun company in the Connecticut National Guard.[17]

The *Lusitania* sinking had the further effect of suggesting that perceptions of the Two Germanys might be inaccurate. Rather than respond with anger and fury at their government's "horrible" and "shameful" massacre on the high seas, the German people seemed elated. The *American Israelite* was speaking for more than its Jewish readership when it concluded that it could no longer draw such a fine distinction between the German government and the German people. "Many Americans have been startled by the change that seems to have been brought about in the German nation. A kindly people whom we habitually liked and respected seem to have been somehow transformed by wrath and fear."[18] An editorial in the mainstream *Saturday Evening Post* agreed, noting that "the war has turned the German people into barbarians—the *Lusitania* [is] evidence."[19]

Similarly, the Nashville-based *South Atlantic Quarterly* argued that the German reaction to the sinking of the *Lusitania* showed "the perfect accord between the German people and their government." Both had proven beyond a shadow of a doubt that they "were in no mood to urge the maintenance of friendship with the United States." Sadly, the American people had to conclude that "the Germans were not so innately pacific as we had wished to consider them." At the start of the war the journal had subscribed to the Two Germanys thesis and attributed Germany's crimes, not to the nature of the German people, but to the "Prussianization" of German state and society. After the *Lusitania* incident, the magazine called its former views "absurd."[20] Writer Arthur Gleason, a man with clear nativist sympathies, wrote that the good German spirit had been "misdirected by the handful of imperialistic militarists in control. There has been no instance of a noble force so diverted since the days of the Inquisition." The United States could no longer satisfy itself with hoping that the German people would demand changes from their own government. There could be no peace in Europe as long as the Germans, with their barbaric customs, "invade that soil, burn those homes, and impose their alien ideas."[21] Rabbi Samuel Price shared those sentiments, noting in his diary that people in his community in Springfield, Massachusetts, were "enraged against Germany."[22] The notion of the German people as innocent in war crimes faded, although the idea of them as victims of their government did not.

The *Lusitania* incident revealed how woefully inadequate early American responses like giving aid to French children or pledging to reconstruct the library at Louvain had been. While Americans had been focusing on reconstruction and aid, the German war machine had been taking steps to move the bloodshed closer to America's own shores. An ever-growing number of Americans saw the *Lusitania* as a symbol of a newer and more immediate threat from Germany to their own security, liberty, and prosperity. One rural newspaper in Iowa wrote that the *Lusitania* had revealed some stark truths, most notably that "Germany intends to draw this country into the war." Although it stopped short of urging that the administration declare war, it clearly stated that any further hostile actions "will mean war with Germany and, serious as such [a] conclusion may be, ought to mean war."[23] In the American heartland and in the South, no less than on the East Coast, the *Lusitania* sinking led to much harsher feelings toward Germany and a greater willingness to see the Wilson administration take a firmer stand.

Exactly what Americans wanted to see their government do in terms of concrete action, however, still ran the gamut. Ideas varied from going to war or severing diplomatic relations with Germany, still a minority view, to the even more unrepresentative view at the other end of the spectrum, embodied by Secretary of State William Jennings Bryan, who believed that the United States should enforce its neutrality more strictly, even if that meant banning Americans from traveling overseas and curtailing trade with the European belligerents. In the immediate aftermath of the *Lusitania*, tensions had clearly risen, and although the nation avoided going to war in the end, the possibility of war seemed to hang in the air for several weeks. Edward House, for one, thought war might result within a month, although he thought it would be a function of American weakness much more than strength. "If war comes with Germany," he wrote shortly after May had come and gone, "it will be because of our unpreparedness and [Germany's] belief that we are more or less impotent to do her harm."[24]

Nevertheless, the impulse to stay out of the war remained prevalent, with some sharing Bryan's desire for isolation from a Europe grown sick and murderous. W. E. B. Du Bois's argument about what the war really stood for did not represent a majority opinion, but it expressed the common feeling that something at the core of European civilization had rotted out. "European civilization has failed. Its failure did not come with this war but with this war it has been made manifest," Du Bois wrote. "Whatever of brutality and inhumanity, of murder, lust and theft has happened since last summer is but counterpart of the same sort of happenings hidden in the wilderness and done against dark and helpless people by white harbingers of human culture." Thus did he express another facet of the general American disenchantment with Europe and America's traditional deference to it. Wilson may not have shared Du Bois's diagnosis, but he recognized some of the same symptoms. Something had gone terribly wrong in the heart of civilized Europe and, Wilson believed, the United States would have to play a role in righting it. More immediately, however, Wilson could not see a way to force the Germans to resolve the *Lusitania* crisis to America's satisfaction. The president opted for an exchange of diplomatic notes with the German government that lasted into July.[25] He hoped to convince the German government of the error of its ways, force some kind of a change in German behavior, and pull America back from the risk of a war that few people wanted, however deep their anger.

Although they did not want war, Wilson's actions struck Americans across the political spectrum as insufficient. He made no public statements at all for several days and kept to his regular routine, including playing golf and courting the wealthy widow Edith Galt, who had recently rebuffed one of his marriage proposals. Most controversially, Wilson gave a speech in Philadelphia on May 10, three days after the sinking of the Lusitania, in which he declared the nation "too proud to fight," a phrase that aroused ire nationwide, and cost him the public support of many prominent Republican politicians who had recently rallied around him.[26]

A furious Theodore Roosevelt was among them. Already disapproving of the Wilson administration on foreign and domestic matters, he accused the president and his advisors of giving in to Germany's murderous behavior. In a letter to a Chicago *Tribune* reporter, Roosevelt said that "Wilson and Bryan have quarreled over what seems to me an entirely insignificant point, that is, as to the percentage of water they shall put into a policy of milk and water." The administration's stress on an increasingly tenuous legal neutrality made the nation less safe, not more. In a democracy leaders must set the tone or the people will be tempted to follow the path of least resistance. "If Lincoln had acted after the firing on Sumter in the way that Wilson did about the sinking of the *Lusitania*, in one month the North would have been saying they were glad he kept them out of war and that they were too proud to fight."[27] Roosevelt had not yet ruled out challenging Wilson in the 1916 election.

Roosevelt became the champion of those who wanted to see a more forceful American response and at least a sharper rhetoric from the Wilson administration. The editors of the *North American Review* warned Wilson to stop negotiating with an "incorrigible" Germany, which was "a self-confessed murderer of helpless American men, women, and children." While deploring Roosevelt's verbal attacks on Wilson as "too severe," they noted that "a great majority of the American people accord with his [Roosevelt's] conclusion that the limit of patience has been reached." The editorial concluded, "We remembered the *Maine*, God forbid that we should forget the *Lusitania!*"[28]

Wilson had attempted since the outbreak of the war to find a middle ground, but in doing so he had only inflamed critics on both sides. He also isolated his own secretary of state in the process. William Jennings Bryan resigned in early June because he felt that the diplomatic notes Wilson had sent did not do enough to ensure American neutrality. He had urged Wilson not to insist on the rights of American citizens to travel in a war zone, but Wilson did not heed his counsel. Bryan therefore concluded that his own views on the war did not fit the president's. Bryan's colleagues in the administration, frustrated with his pacifism and his endless moralizing, reacted with a mixture of anger and relief at his resignation. Interior Secretary Franklin Lane called him a traitor, and Assistant Secretary of the Navy Franklin D. Roosevelt said that he was "disgusted clear through" with Bryan for walking away at a time of national emergency.[29] They also saw how out of step Bryan's views were with those of the American people more generally. In a widely circulated pamphlet, Packard Motor Car Company president and social activist Henry Bourne Joy even compared Bryan to Benedict Arnold for sowing discord at a time of national crisis. "Mr. Bryan saw fit to desert his post of duty, the most important office next to that of the Presidency itself, in a time of serious international negotiations, being carried on in an effort to secure peace and respect to Americans. He saw fit to compel us to show a divided front to a possible enemy."[30]

Bryan had criticized Wilson for acting too forcefully. Far more Americans sided with Theodore Roosevelt and criticized the president for being too weak. Hundreds of telegrams arrived at the White House from people furious with the "too proud to fight" phrase, words Wilson himself soon regretted. From Fort Bliss, Texas, the future American Expeditionary Forces commander, General John Pershing, asked his wife, "Isn't that the damndest rot you ever heard a person get off?" He continued, "What do you suppose a weak, chicken-hearted, white-livered lot as we have in Washington are going to do?"[31] The soldier in Pershing, however, knew enough to keep his thoughts private, but not everyone felt so constrained. Arthur Gleason contrasted Wilson's shameful words with the brave actions of American volunteers in France. Those volunteers better expressed the nation's true sentiments than did the president. Praising the service of men and women at the American hospital established in the Parisian suburb of Neuilly not long after the Battle of the Marne, Gleason wrote, "'The quarrel none of ours?' The suffering is very much ours. 'Too proud to fight?' Not too proud to carry bed-pans and wash mud-caked, blood-marked men." The *Lusitania* sinking led to a marked increase in both money and volunteers going to France to help the Allied cause. More than two thousand local relief committees across the United States contributed $45 million in cash and $60 million in supplies to French hospitals in the ensuing weeks. By the summer of 1915, at least forty-five thousand Americans were serving as volunteers in Allied hospitals or in the Allied armies themselves, including three hundred of the first four hundred American Rhodes Scholarship winners.[32]

The columns of war correspondent Richard Harding Davis, who was still reporting from Europe as he had been since the war's start, underscored the sense of dishonor that many Americans felt from the president's lukewarm response to the *Lusitania*. Davis wrote that the French remained grateful for American generosity but that they saw America's response to the *Lusitania* as the reaction of a "cowardly nation, but [one] assuming superiority over the man who not only would fight, but who was fighting." In England, Davis reported on seeing a recruiting station with a poster showing fat, lazy Americans that read, "These are too proud to fight! Are you?"[33]

The most publicized rage against Wilson's tepid response came from Roosevelt, who in November publicly called Wilson the worst president since James Buchanan.[34] The words "too proud to fight," he said, had only "aroused the heartiest contempt for us in foreign countries."[35] James Gerard, the American ambassador to Germany, also grew critical of Wilson, telling him, "The Germans fear only *war* with us—but state frankly that they do not believe we dare to declare it, call us cowardly bluffers, and say our notes are worse than waste paper."[36] The Boston *Post*, echoing Kaiser Wilhelm's blithe dismissal of the treaty guaranteeing Belgian neutrality a year earlier, ran a cartoon showing the kaiser holding one of Wilson's speeches above the caption "Another Scrap of Paper."[37]

To no one's surprise, Roosevelt became one of the leaders of the movement to force Wilson to take more aggressive action against

Germany. Popular opinion in smaller neutral states—such as Spain, Sweden, and Norway—was also horrified by German atrocities. Unlike those states, however, Roosevelt argued, the United States had sufficient power to force changes in German behavior if only the president would take forceful action. The *Lusitania* crisis was thus a test of America's capacity for global leadership, a test Wilson was obviously failing. Roosevelt's increasingly shrill criticism of the president provided for excellent newspaper copy; journalists across the country soon waited on his every word. On learning that Wilson had exchanged another diplomatic note with the Germans, Roosevelt asked sarcastically, "Did you notice what number it was? I fear I have lost track myself; but I am inclined to think it is number 11,765, Series B." Wilson, Roosevelt claimed, belonged to a group of "professional pacifists... flubdubs and mollycoddles... every soft creature, every coward and weakling, every man who can't look more than six inches ahead, every man whose god is money or pleasure or ease."[38] Roosevelt undoubtedly meant the last part to strike right at the heart of the deeply religious Wilson.

Roosevelt wasn't the only one to question Wilson's morality. Sharp criticism of Wilson also came from American church leaders. Lyman Abbott, an influential Congregationalist theologian who preached from Henry Ward Beecher's pulpit in Brooklyn, also compared Wilson to Buchanan and argued that Wilson's timid policy only brought America closer to war on the terms of an "insane" and "barbaric" Germany. *Outlook* magazine, a progressive Christian journal with ties to Roosevelt, argued that the time had come for "national action," although the magazine did not specify what kind of action it thought best. Another leading Presbyterian publication called the sinking of the *Lusitania* "the worst crime of responsible government since the crucifixion of Christ." It, too, failed to offer any concrete policy options.[39] Like Abbott, American Christians had begun to accept the view that war might in some circumstances be preferable to an unjust or unsustainable peace. Notable Washington, D.C., theologian (and Confederate Army veteran) Reverend Randolph McKim began the war a pacifist and a firm supporter of Wilson, but the sinking of the *Lusitania* led him to break with Wilson and support ending diplomatic relations with Germany. He called for placing "the immense weight of our influence [onto] the side of humanity and law and liberty."[40]

Moral outrage was the order of the day, but in the early summer of 1915 it was inchoate and unfocused. Still, the rhetoric of these leaders symbolized a growing discomfort with neutrality. Anti-Wilson sentiment was echoed widely in the press, too. Influential journalist Irvin Cobb blasted the idea of the nation being "too proud to fight" by saying that the shameful words "should be nailed in letters of flame across the national firmament and kept burning there" as a reminder of national cowardice.[41] In the Des Moines *Register*, editorial cartoonist J. N. Darling—one of the most influential cartoonists of the age—depicted a club-wielding ape labeled "Barbarism" dragging away a fair maiden wearing a sash labeled "Peace." Wilson is pictured sitting dazed in the wreckage of the room, with Uncle Sam knocked out in one corner. Next to Wilson sits a box of chocolates labeled "Sweet Nothings" and a crushed bouquet labeled "Flowers of Rhetoric." The caption reads "Faint Heart Never Won Fair Lady—At Least Not with That Kind of Rival."[42] Darling did not specifically identify the Germans as the rival, but he did not have to.

The phrase "too proud to fight" and the fate of the *Lusitania* had given journalists and cartoonists plenty of material to work with. In the absence of a desire to go to war, commentators could at least critique what they saw as Wilson's ineffectual and dishonorable response. Influential political cartoonists, including Nelson Harding, Rollin Kirby, and Robert Carter (all future Pulitzer Prize winners) espoused increasingly pro-Allied positions after the sinking.[43] The once-neutral New York *Times* argued that the sentiments behind "too proud to fight" would lead to the end of America's aspirations to global power status. "From our State Department," the newspaper implored, "must go to the Imperial German government at Berlin a demand that the Germans shall no longer make war like savages drunk with blood."[44] Belittling the supposed higher-ground morality of "too proud to fight," it argued that a great nation "cannot act on this theory if it desires to retain or regain the position won for it by the men who fought under Washington and by the men who, in the days of Abraham Lincoln, wore the blue under Grant and the gray under Lee." A dishonorable peace might come at too high a cost.[45]

The sinking of the *Lusitania* put the remaining defenders of Germany and its wartime policies on the defensive. The *North American Review* accused Germany outright of "manifold murder." Although the journal did not see American goals as overlapping with those of the British and French, it nevertheless concluded that the Allies were fighting for the cause of "liberty, of humanity, of Christianity." The greedy England that had fought the Boers in South Africa and oppressed millions in its empire had, the journal argued, been replaced by the England that had once been the liberty-loving "hope of the human race." In its war against "the Satanic powers of Germany," it had become that freedom-loving nation once again.[46]

The change in the national mood had immediate consequences. It was a clear turning point, not so much in pushing America toward war, but in making Americans realize the growing danger that they faced from Germany. Even those Americans with only indirect links to the Germans suffered by association. In Chicago, Democratic mayoral candidate Robert Sweitzer unexpectedly lost by 150,000 votes to Republican William "Big Bill" Thompson, whose only political experience had been as an alderman thirteen years earlier. A good deal of old-fashioned Chicago trickery played a role in Thompson's surprising victory, but Sweitzer's pre-*Lusitania* appeals to German-American voters and a Democratic Party flyer distributed just before the sinking defending the foreign policy of the Central Powers badly backfired and helped to produce a stunning upset at the polls.[47] H. L. Mencken withdrew from a contract to write a flattering piece for a German-American publication about the philosophy of Nietzsche because, although he had expressed admiration for Germany before the war, the sinking of the *Lusitania* had changed his mind. "I do not want to appear a spokesman for Germany," he said, "for I am an American by birth and the son of native-born Americans."[48] His German and American identities suddenly seemed in conflict to him in a way that they had not just a few weeks earlier. Similarly, the German-American Walter Lippmann noted in *The New Republic* that his readers should not confuse his unwillingness to contribute to the growing hatred toward Germany with taking a pro-German stance on the war. His need to note that silence did not imply support for Germany's behavior speaks volumes.[49]

The sinking also increased the scrutiny Americans applied to German espionage and sabotage activity inside the United States. Around the time of the *Lusitania* sinking, an Irish-American stevedore working on the docks of New Jersey told the New York *World* that he had grown suspicious when a man with a German accent approached him and his colleagues with an offer to pay them to go on strike. He decided to go to the newspapers as soon as he had deduced that the money was likely coming from German agents based in New York City. The plot resembled another one run at the same time by Austro-Hungarian agents to foment strikes in American munitions plants in Pennsylvania and the Midwest.

Suspicions and fears of German plots had grown to the point that federal agents began to track the movements of suspect Germans. On July 24, American Secret Service agents trailed *Fatherland* publisher George Sylvester Viereck after a meeting with Dr. Heinrich Albert, a German commercial attaché, at the Hamburg-Amerika offices in lower Manhattan. Several versions of the story exist, but they all agree on the basic outlines. Viereck and Albert left their meeting together and boarded an uptown Sixth Street elevated train on a sweltering New York City day. Viereck left the train at the 33rd Street station. One agent followed him while another stayed on the train with Albert, who soon fell asleep in the hot and stuffy car. At 50th Street he suddenly awoke, leaping off the train at the station in such haste that he left his briefcase behind. The American agent trailing him quickly grabbed the case and left the car by another door, running away as fast as he could from a screaming Albert. In some (likely exaggerated) versions of the story, the American agent pulled out his gun and badge, ordering a passing driver to pick him up and not stop until they were safely away.

The agent with the briefcase then went to a Secret Service safe house, where he met with his boss. They took one look at the documents inside Albert's briefcase, realized the magnitude of what they revealed, and decided to call Treasury Secretary William Gibbs McAdoo, then on vacation in Maine. When McAdoo heard what they had to say, he ordered them to bring the case to New Hampshire where they would brief a vacationing President Wilson.[50] The papers outlined German and Austro-Hungarian plans to buy American newspapers, publish incendiary propaganda, start strikes, bribe politicians, and commit acts of industrial sabotage. Wilson wrote to House that the documents proved that "the country is honeycombed with German intrigue and infested with German spies," but he chose not to make an official protest because he did not want to put his careful diplomacy at risk in the wake of the *Lusitania* notes.[51] Albert officially worked for the Hamburg-Amerika line, a private company. Wilson thus believed that the American government might have trouble proving a direct link between the plots and the German government.[52] Wilson did, however, leak the documents to his friend and political ally Frank Cobb, publisher of the New York *World.* The paper printed the documents in full in a series of articles in the *World* that ran from August 15 to 23 and were syndicated in newspapers nationwide in the ensuing weeks. No doubt with an eye toward sales, the *World* called the papers evidence of a plot to "annihilate American rights for the advancement of German arms."[53]

The leaked documents were part of a growing pile of evidence of German intrigue on American soil. In August, British agents seized and published papers found on a journalist named James F. J. Archibald, who was traveling through Britain to neutral Holland en route to the Eastern front. The papers included communications from Austrian and German agents active in the United States to their masters in Vienna and Berlin calling for the organization of strikes and sabotage in American factories in Bethlehem, Pittsburgh, and Cincinnati, all cities with large populations of people born in Germany. One letter in particular from German commercial attaché Franz von Papen caught the attention of American newspapermen. It called Americans "idiotic Yankees" and warned that, instead of challenging Germany, Americans should "shut their mouths and better still be full of admiration" for German power. American journalists then hounded von Papen, tracking him down at Yellowstone National Park where, as it later turned out, he was en route to San Francisco to plot further incidents of sabotage. Von Papen refused to give them any more headline fodder, but the papers did publish photographs of him sneering, the reporters said, in contempt at American displeasure with his comments.[54]

Meanwhile, the mysterious fires and explosions discussed in chapter 2 continued. In the post-*Lusitania* age, they seemed even more sinister than they had the year before. Thirteen American ships carrying munitions destined for Britain caught fire at sea in the second half of 1915. In late May, a DuPont munitions ship exploded outside Seattle. Agents arrested a German national who had in his possession dynamite and fuses. Nonetheless, with no surviving physical evidence from the sunken ship, they could not directly tie him to the explosion and a judge released him.[55] Explosions also rocked factories in New Jersey, Delaware, and Pennsylvania. Although no hard evidence existed to tie German government officials to these incidents, they all targeted American trade with the Allies and they seemed to prove the perfidy behind the Albert and Archibald documents.

Investigators based in New York City got the break they needed when French officials in Marseilles found three metal objects roughly the size of cigars inside sacks of sugar on board a ship that had arrived from the United States. The French soon discovered that the "cigars" contained two chambers separated by a thin copper disk. The chemicals in the two chambers (potassium chlorate and sulphuric acid) slowly ate away at the disk until they came in contact with each other, resulting in what police called "instant fire."[56] In the Marseilles case, the copper disks had been cut too thick to erode completely; thus the chemicals never combined. French police then deduced that the suspicious fires at sea always occurred on ships carrying both munitions and sugar. The latter provided fuel for the fires and came in sacks that were both easy to open and easy to sew shut again, thus leaving virtually no trace of tampering. The New York City police bomb squad had enough clues to lead them to Robert Fay, a chemist and reservist in the German Army. Because Fay lived in Weehawken, New Jersey, across the river from Manhattan, New York City police had no jurisdiction. They therefore called in federal agents, who raided Fay's garage. There they found 450 pounds of chemicals, 200 empty cigar bombs, a German Army–issue pistol, and charts of New York harbor. Fay's arrest led to the arrests of two other German nationals; all three said that they had received help from Germany's military and naval attachés in New York. They received prison sentences of between four and eight years on the only charge prosecutors could make stick with the laws on the books in 1915: insurance fraud.

These arrests, however, did not solve the problem. The mysterious fires continued. An undercover agent who spoke fluent German infiltrated another network that led him to a chemist named Charles von Kleist in Hoboken. Von Kleist had devised a method of tying the cigar bombs to the rudders of ships, whose motion would increase the chemical dissolution of the copper disks. The disks could therefore be thicker, which made handling the dangerous chemicals in the cigars safer. Police soon discovered two important facts. First, they concluded that von Kleist's cigar bombs, not Fay's, had caused the mysterious fires, and second, that von Kleist had been receiving money from German agents based in New York City for months. Much to the police's surprise, von Kleist proved more than willing to cooperate with them. His German handler had refused to reimburse him $117 for supplies he had purchased to make the cigar bombs. The two had argued and now von Kleist wanted revenge. He took American agents to his lab in Hoboken and showed them how he assembled the cigars. He also told them that the Hamburg-Amerika ship *Friedrich der Grosse*, interned at Hoboken harbor since the start of the war, had its own bomb lab and had served for a time as a base of operations for Franz von Rintelen, a German naval officer who masterminded many of the German sabotage and intelligence efforts in the United States.

American officials had already begun to link von Rintelen to Victoriano Huerta, who had been a thorn in the American government's side during the Mexican Civil War and had been living in exile in Spain since 1913. American agents suspected that von Rintelen had made huge cash deposits into Huerta's bank accounts in Cuba and had sent German agents to Texas to work on plans to reinstall Huerta as Mexican president. Federal agents detained Huerta in El Paso where he had gone to meet with German agents before trying to sneak back into Mexico. They then took him to Fort Bliss, where he died shortly afterward of yellow jaundice. Working with British agents, the Americans also discovered that von Rintelen had decided to return to Berlin via England and Rotterdam on a false Swiss passport. British agents arrested him when the ship docked on the English coast.[57]

Only after von Kleist's arrest and von Rintelen's departure from the United States did the ship fires finally stop. Still, tensions, especially in the New York area, remained high. German agents helped Fay to escape from a federal penitentiary in Atlanta to Mexico, leading to fears of a wide international plot. The investigations also revealed the problems in law enforcement, which had multiple, overlapping jurisdictions and no laws that forbade the manufacture of explosives, even those designed to destroy shipping.[58]

By the end of 1915, notwithstanding his desires to keep the issue quiet, even Wilson had finally had enough. Matters had gone beyond dime-store novel material to suggest a genuine threat to national security. The final straw came when American agents discovered check stubs directly linking von Papen and Karl Boy-Ed to agents involved in sabotage plots. Wilson directed the State Department to inform the German government that he now considered both men *personae non gratae*; Germany soon recalled them.[59] An unusually contrite Wilson then addressed Congress, apologizing for allowing men "born under other flags" to pour "the poison of disloyalty into the very arteries of our national life" and "debase our politics to the uses of foreign intrigue." He offered the excuse that "a little while ago such a thing would have seemed incredible. Because it was incredible, we made no preparations for it."[60] Clearly, events would now force the administration to take firm action, though what action and when was still unclear.

While the *Lusitania* sinking was clearly a pivotal event, there were contributing factors to the hardening of America's attitudes toward Germany. The same week as the sinking saw the publication of the *Bryce Report into German Atrocities in Belgium*.[61] Although defenders of Germany dismissed it as the work of British propaganda, most Americans put great faith in James Bryce, a well-respected and well-liked former British ambassador to the United States. A scholar, author, and diplomat, Bryce brought with him the authority of a wise and fair arbiter who had studied the atrocity reports in Belgium since September 1914 in great detail. The *Bryce Report* seemed to confirm many of the tales of outrageous German behavior coming out of Belgium. Though many later proved to be false or exaggerated, at the time the report that contained them highlighted to Americans the worst aspects of the German war machine, and the timing of its release coincided with a sharp rise in anti-German sentiment more generally. The New York *Evening Post* concluded that the report showed that Germany "now stands branded with a mark of infamy such as in our times has not been stamped upon the face of any people." Senior American leaders, such as Agriculture Secretary David F. Houston and Nobel laureate Elihu Root, accepted the report at face value, with Root calling German behavior in Belgium "barbarity unequaled since the conquests of Genghis Khan."[62] American artists George Bellows and Man Ray both read the *Bryce Report* and became firm advocates of American intervention into the war; Bellows took up the cause in his art, conceiving paintings about the death of

Edith Cavell, a British nurse shot by the Germans in October 1915 for assisting the enemy, and a horrific piece that became "The Germans Arrive" showing German soldiers cutting the hands off of Belgian civilians and terrorizing Belgian women.[63] *Life* responded to the *Bryce Report* by noting, "For us the great clear issue of this war is Belgium." The report showed the editors that "Belgium is a martyr to civilization, sister to all who love liberty or law."[64]

Events in Washington and New York added to the sense of fear. In early July, a man first identified as Frank Holt tried to assassinate financier J. P. Morgan Jr. at Morgan's Long Island home. He succeeded in shooting Morgan in the thigh and stomach, although Morgan survived. Sir Cecil Spring-Rice, the British ambassador to the United States and Morgan's weekend guest, escaped unharmed. Police soon discovered that Holt was in fact Erich Muenter, a former graduate student of German at Harvard and a devoted admirer of Hugo Münsterberg. Muenter had in his possession a list of the names and ages of Morgan's children. Muenter soon admitted that he had planned to kidnap Morgan's wife and children in order to force him to stop financing Allied industrial purchases in the United States. A search of Muenter's apartment revealed 134 sticks of dynamite that his wife said Muenter intended to stow on ships bound for Britain. Police then matched the dynamite's chemical composition to the dynamite that destroyed a telephone exchange near the vice president's office in the Capitol building in Washington the day before the attempt on Morgan's life. The explosion had not resulted in any serious injuries, but it had rattled the nation's capital and put the city on high alert. Boston police then linked Muenter to the mysterious death of his first wife in 1906, after which Muenter had moved west and changed his name to Frank Holt.

Later investigations showed that Muenter suffered from mental disorders and had no link to the German government nor had he had any association with Münsterberg since his time as a student at Harvard. At the time of his arrest, however, newspapers speculated widely that he must have had the support of foreign agents to pull off not one but two audacious crimes in as many days. Muenter hanged himself in his jail cell, thus, reporters speculated, taking whatever secrets about the German government he possessed to the grave with him. Some newspapers even reported that he had died not from hanging but from a gunshot fired by a German sniper into his cell in order to keep him quiet.[65]

These incidents destroyed much of the momentum that pacifists like the legendary social activist and founder of the first Hull House, Jane Addams, had built for their position. Addams had, in fact, led a peace meeting at The Hague just weeks before the sinking of the *Lusitania*. Her calls for peace and arbitration quickly seemed anachronistic in the wake of the *Lusitania* sinking and the spate of domestic terrorism incidents.[66] Roosevelt unleashed a series of vicious attacks on her upon her return to the United States, and the New York *Times* called her a "silly, vain, impertinent old maid... who is now meddling with matters far beyond her capacity."[67] Addams and her fellow pacifists had to address the charge that their pacifism sat at cross purposes to the interests—and the very well-being—of the United States. Other groups once pro-German or advocating neutrality moved to separate themselves from the Germans, including Samuel Gompers's American Federation of Labor, most American socialists, and most Irish-American leaders. They did not abandon their own beliefs in the peace process, but they ceased to see Germany as a fellow traveler or worthy of their sympathy.[68]

The events of 1915 increased American fears that their security was being compromised. A series of popular fiction books depicting invasions of the United States appeared. Some of the books, like William Skaggs's *German Conspiracies in America*, Frederic Wile's *The German Plot*, and a four-volume series by H. Irving Hancock, specifically named the Germans as the aggressors.[69] Others, like Hudson Maxim's *Defenseless America*, avoided the word *German*, but left little to the imagination. Maxim's 1915 book became a popular 1916 movie, *The Battle Cry of Peace*. Henry Ford criticized the movie as propaganda for its author, a manufacturer of machine guns. The studio sued Ford for $1 million, and the resulting publicity helped to sell tickets and spread the message that the nation stood defenseless against external enemies. Memoirs and firsthand accounts of American volunteers in France also sold well. Leslie Buswell's bestselling *Ambulance No. 10: Personal Letters from the Front* drew praise from literary critics and from admirers like Theodore Roosevelt. Buswell returned to the United States in 1915 a hero, having won the French Croix de Guerre for his service.

German-Americans, too, began to distance themselves from Germany's cause, sometimes for fear of attracting attention to themselves, though often because of a sincere revulsion toward the actions of the German government. The Germanistic Society of Chicago had hosted an annual lecture series on topics of interest to new immigrants. In the 1914–15 season (from November 1914 to April 1915) the society had dedicated five lectures of the thirteen from the series to the war. Germany's head of propaganda in the United States, Dr. Bernhard Dernburg, had delivered one on German economics in wartime. In the 1915–16 season, the society hosted no lectures at all on the war and saw a one-third decline in season-ticket sales. A year later, for the first time in its history, it offered no series at all.[70] The papers in the Archibald documents also proved the point, as Austrian officials noted that the American people had developed such pronounced anti-German and anti-Austrian sentiment that schemes for bribing newspaper editors offered little hope of success.[71] A few German-American newspapers were still willing to plead Germany's case. They argued that Germany had warned Americans not to travel on the *Lusitania*, an argument that, although technically correct, insulted the honor of Americans who believed they had the right to travel overseas even in wartime. To many Americans, moreover, the warnings against travel seemed less like fair notice than evidence of willful premeditation.[72]

These newspapers also argued that Britain bore the responsibility for the sinking because it had used the *Lusitania* to transport munitions. Britain, not Germany, lay at fault for the deaths even if a U-boat had directly caused them. This argument reflected at best a minority of American opinion in the first few days after the sinking, but it quickly faded as outrage overcame narrow legalism.[73] Americans generally did not accept the argument that people, including women and children, traveling on ships carrying munitions deserved to die as a result because they could not have known what lay in the cargo holds.[74] Seeing that neither of these core arguments stood much of a chance of changing public opinion, most of the German-American press resorted to arguing for continuing the American policy of neutrality.[75]

Another strategy was to frame the debate in familial terms. German-Americans talked about the dispute between the two countries as an argument between a man's mother, who had raised and nurtured him, and his wife, with whom he now lived and had made a solemn vow of fidelity. The Milwaukee *Germania-Herald* used that comparison after the *Lusitania*; it also made it clear what choice it would make in the event of conflict. "If war ever came between this country and Germany or any other country, we would be American citizens, just as we were in the Civil War."[76] Cardinal George Mundelein in Chicago made the same analogy. What happens, he asked his congregants, when a wife and mother feud? "My experience has been that almost invariably the wife won out, and I suppose yours is the same. That is the answer."[77]

Few Americans questioned the loyalty of German-Americans, especially those born in the United States. They mostly reacted as Claude Wheeler, Willa Cather's protagonist in *One of Ours*, did. Wheeler does not even consider breaking off the close friendships he has with his Bohemian and German friends, nor does anyone else in his community before American entry into the war. Mrs. Wheeler praises local German immigrants, noting that the Wheeler family "never [knew] one that wasn't kind and helpful." Their housekeeper, reacting to anti-German political cartoons in the local newspaper, asks, "How comes it all them Germans is such ugly lookin' people? The Yoeders and the German folks around here ain't ugly lookin'." Claude replies by telling her that the ugly ones are those doing the killing while the Germans on the home front are "nice, like our neighbors."[78]

Clearly, however, German-Americans began to feel the pressure of association with a foreign government that most blamed for atrocities abroad and sabotage at home. In the weeks after the *Lusitania* sinking, applications for American citizenship from German nationals increased fourfold, an indication of how German-Americans wanted to identify themselves. Hugo Münsterberg adopted a far less public profile after the *Lusitania*, although the few speeches he did give were increasingly controversial. He died suddenly in 1916 in the middle of delivering a lecture at Radcliff College at age fifty-three; those close to him blamed the stress of reconciling his position on the war with that of the United States more generally.[79]

Münsterberg was not the only one feeling the strain. Most observers thought that Wilson might have been able to get a declaration of war at several points in 1915 had he wanted one, although he himself doubted it. Upon hearing Wilson's doubts, Roosevelt characteristically responded,

"That depends on the leading."[80] Still, both Wilson and Roosevelt knew that the majority of Americans, outraged though they were by the *Lusitania* and the acts of espionage on American soil, still did not want war. They did not want to see thousands die to avenge the deaths of the 128 who had died on the *Lusitania*. Some middle ground had to exist that would both uphold American interests and avoid war. Americans in 1915 needed something between the moral sterility of "too proud to fight" and the bloody-mindedness that later characterized "Over There."

Wilson also understood that the nation was in no position to fight a modern war, as did members of Congress, only a small handful of whom supported going to war in 1915. They knew, moreover, that this war was many orders of magnitude more complex and murderous than the "splendid little war" against Spain in 1898. Just a few weeks before the sinking, Germany's introduction of asphyxiating gas (what one eyewitness described to an American reporter as "a dense cloud of suffocating vapors") at the Second Battle of Ypres made headline news in the United States, indicating that the war had crossed yet another terrible threshold.[81] Wilson found himself trapped between those, like Roosevelt, who called for swift and, if necessary, violent responses, and Bryan, who called for a more isolationist understanding of American neutrality. Wilson's middle course—reflective though it was of the national mood—only exacerbated the problem. To many Americans, it highlighted the nation's essential weakness. Herbert Hoover, then in Belgium, wrote a letter to Wilson that revealed the ambivalence in American views. He told the president that the words "too proud to fight" filled Americans in Europe "with humiliation." He recoiled at the idea that "we are prepared to submit to the continued cold-blooded murder of our women and children."

At the same time, however, Hoover did not want to see the president push the country to the brink of war. Rather, he wanted Wilson to find some firm middle ground that could force the Germans to accept the American position without war. "Our one desire," as he expressed the views of Americans in Europe, "is to help to find some solution which would prevent our own country from being joined in this holocaust, but the belief on our part is that only a strong line of constructive character could prevent this catastrophe." America's primary responsibility, Hoover noted, lay in finding a path "towards the ultimate redemption of Europe from the barbarism in which it is slowly but surely drifting from all sides." Like most of his fellow Americans, Hoover urged Wilson to follow "a policy which will not necessarily lead to war but which in its vigor might bring an end to at least some phases of these violations of international law and humanity."[82] It was, as Wilson knew, a dangerous tightrope walk.

American attitudes remained conflicted at the end of 1915. The extreme pacifism of William Jennings Bryan no longer held purchase with most Americans, who, although not eager for war, wanted the government to defend American rights and American honor with greater force. Iowa senator Albert Cummins noted, in a swipe at Bryan (who had once represented Nebraska in the House of Representatives), that "between the armed camp of William of Germany and the open dove coat of William of Nebraska there must be an honorable abiding place for a great nation which is prepared to lead the world toward peace, but will not submit to injustice or indignity."[83] In short, Americans wanted it both ways, as their increasingly bellicose rhetoric suggested.

Never one to mince words, Alice Roosevelt Longworth excoriated Wilson in terms far less diplomatic than Cummins's. Living in heavily German Cincinnati when she heard about the "too proud to fight" speech, she and her husband, Nicholas Longworth (a member of the House of Representatives and future Speaker of the House), were convinced that the time for action had arrived. "There was no doubt in our minds either that our fellow citizens of German-American descent would be with us without a murmur. Then came 'too proud to fight,' that psychological moment was over, and the battle to keep some shred of self-respect was on again."[84] Like her father and countless other Americans, Longworth concluded that Wilson had lost the support of the nation.

Charting a course through such choppy seas presented Wilson with a formidable challenge. The new secretary of state, Robert Lansing, recognized the dilemma in a letter to Wilson on July 14, eight weeks after the sinking of the *Lusitania*. "As I read the state of mind of the majority of the people," Lansing told the president, "it is that they do not want war, that no war spirit exists, but at the same time they want the government not to recede a step from its position but to compel Germany to submit to our demands." Achieving that aim without war, Lansing noted, was "well-nigh impossible," in large part because he knew that the United States lacked the kind of army and navy that might compel Germany to accept American terms.[85]

In short, the United States found itself in the position of having to uphold the nation's honor without engaging in military action for which it was utterly unprepared. Most of the Wilson cabinet had initially urged the president to, in Lansing's words, "bring things to a head regardless of the consequences." Cooler heads, however, soon prevailed, particularly as the *Lusitania* furor receded somewhat. Even Lansing knew that "to speak bluntly would have been a personal satisfaction though it would have accomplished no more than polite phrases [would have]" because the United States stood in no position to back up any of its tough talk with meaningful action.[86] Lansing struggled to find the right diplomatic and legal wording to convey America's difficult position. Had the *Lusitania* been an American ship, he could have written more forceful defenses of American interests. Bryan had not helped Lansing's hand when he told the Austro-Hungarian ambassador just before he resigned on June 9 that the sinking did not rise to the level of an act of war.

Lansing brought a new approach to the State Department, even if he could not change the weakness of the American position. Soon after taking office, he noted that America's friendship with Germany "is a matter of the past."[87] German-American relations threatened to worsen in late August when a German submarine sank the *SS Arabic*, a British passenger ship heading toward the United States. Three of the forty-four dead were Americans. The Chicago *Herald* saw in the sinking a replay of the *Lusitania* and argued that the United States should break diplomatic relations rather than exchange more ineffective notes with the murderous German government. "The floor of the ocean bed," the newspaper wrote, "is being paved with the good intentions of the German government."[88] Still, the far smaller loss of American life, combined with initial reports that the *Arabic* had tried to ram the German submarine, moderated the public outcry. The Germans, too, seemed to have learned their public relations lessons from earlier in the year and took a remorseful tone. Wilson, learning his own lesson from his "too proud to fight" speech, adopted a firmer line with the Germans. They, in turn, promised to stop the sinking of ocean liners without warning and even offered financial compensation, a tacit admission of their guilt.

Although the German position had more to do with the pressures inside the German government not to risk any expansion of the conflict, Wilson drew praise nationwide for resolving the *Arabic* crisis peacefully, and on terms favorable to the United States. The New York *Evening Post*, although critical of Wilson during the *Lusitania* affair, wrote that in the *Arabic* incident, "without rattling a sword, without mobilizing a corporal's guard of soldiers, or lifting the anchor of a warship, [Wilson] won the greatest diplomatic victory of generations."[89] Unlike the *Lusitania* sinking, in this case the Germans had admitted wrongdoing and pledged to act with more discretion in the future. Those pledges seemed good enough for the vast majority of Americans, who still hoped beyond hope for peace. Herbert Hoover wrote in praise of Wilson's firmness without resort to belligerence that war "is a condition which no good American could for one moment consider except as the last alternative to continued transgression."[90] That point seemed not to have arrived, at least not yet.

Roosevelt, predictably, argued that Wilson had only attained a pledge from the Germans that they temporarily "intend to stop the policy of assassination." Both the Philadelphia *Evening Ledger* and the Providence *Journal* (which gained a national reputation after the *Lusitania* incident for its tough anti-German tone) suspected a German trick, with the *Journal* noting that Germany "looks pleasant because she has to. But wrath and resentment still fill her mind and heart."[91] The Brooklyn *Eagle* noted that Germany had only promised to bark before she bit, but the American people seemed content to take what Germany had offered.[92] Wilson had won a diplomatic victory and removed any need for America to enter the war, but he had not, in the eyes of many Americans, solved the basic problem nor had he done much to keep the war from creeping ever closer to American shores.

Whether they wanted to get ready to meet the growing German menace, develop the strength to defend themselves from any future threat, or be in a position to enforce their own view of peace, most Americans now accepted that they needed to do much more to prepare their country for potential conflict. In the case of the *Arabic* words had worked, but the future remained uncertain. Secretary of the Interior Franklin Lane wrote to a friend that Wilson's notes, though ultimately successful, had amounted to talking "Princetonian English to a waterfront bully." Lane certainly sympathized with Wilson's enormous responsibilities, but he also felt that Wilson had not done enough to guarantee the future security of America.[93]

Lane was far from alone. Social reformer Arthur Gleason likened neutrality to "reveling in fat money vaults" while innocent people in Europe suffered at Germany's hands. He lambasted what he termed the un-American belief that "prosperity is greater than sacrifice" on behalf of liberty. Gleason, however, saw hope in the thousands of Americans of privilege who gave their money or went to France to help the Allies. Enough Harvard graduates had gone to France in the months after the Lusitania incident, he proudly noted, to allow them to open a Parisian chapter of the Harvard Club.[94] Frederick Palmer, covering the war in Europe in spring 1915, observed Canadians at the front, "with perhaps a 'neutral' from Wyoming in his company fighting the Germans in Flanders." The sight impressed him. "If there must be a war . . . , why to my mind the Canadians did a fine thing for civilization's sake. It hurt sometimes to think that we could not be in the fight for the good cause, too, particularly after the Lusitania was sunk, when my own feelings had lost all semblance to neutrality."[95] The Brooklyn Eagle, too, called for a firmer American response, blaming the lack of action from "the weak-kneed and phrase-loving" Wilson for all of the affronts to American honor since the "Lusitania murders."[96]

The Lusitania and the events that occurred around it did not lead the United States to war, but they did force Americans to begin choosing sides. As the New York Evening Sun journalist and short story writer Nelson Lloyd described it, "blinking eyes began to open."[97] Former president William Howard Taft, former secretary of war Henry Stimson, and Harvard president Charles Eliot all publicly broke with Wilson over his handling of foreign affairs. In June, Taft and one hundred leading American thinkers formed the League to Enforce Peace, which called on the United States to support the ideas of collective security and international arbitration rather than isolation and neutrality. The League posed a direct challenge to Wilson's leadership, even if it shared some of his ideas. Writer Henry James, who had spent most of his life in the United States, renounced his American citizenship in sympathy with the Allies. His "defection" made national headlines, although few Americans supported his decision. One American newspaper said that James's departure proved "that the dividing line between a genius and a plain ass is hard to see."[98] Criticizing America seemed fair as a response to Wilson's diplomacy, but abandoning America most certainly did not.

Problems kept multiplying in what the Chicago *Tribune* called the "Anno Diabolos" of 1915.[99] Rumors of German activity in an increasingly unstable Mexico worried Americans. Historian William Roscoe Thayer saw plots to Germanize America and Mexico as a direct product of Wilson's waffling. "Such a campaign," he wrote, "would not have been tolerated by an Administration which had possessed either courage or regard for American honor." Although Thayer did not doubt the loyalty of German-Americans, he did fear "the almost limitless extension of the German spy system" sent to North America "for an explosion against this country."[100] In July Secretary of the Interior Franklin Lane, once strictly neutral, looked forward to the next cabinet meeting so he could give the president his views on the "damned goose-stepping Army officers" in Germany who would "spit on the American flag." He planned to use "short and somewhat ugly Anglo-Saxon words, utterly undiplomatic" that he hoped Wilson would use in his meetings with German officials in order to impress upon them the danger of stirring up trouble for the United States in Mexico.[101]

Lansing saw the dangers as well. On July 15, 1915, he wrote the following memorandum for the record: "I have come to the conclusion that the German Government is utterly hostile to all nations with democratic institutions because those who compose it see in democracy a menace to absolutism and the defeat of the German ambition for world domination." He predicted that if the Germans defeated the Allies in Europe, they would then attempt to form alliances with Latin American states in order to threaten the last remaining great democracy on earth, the United States. "A triumph for German imperialism," he had therefore concluded, "*must not be....* We must in fact risk everything rather than leave the way open to a new combination of powers, stronger and more dangerous to liberty than the Central Allies [*sic*] are today." Lansing began to advocate a series of concrete steps to reduce German influence and power in Latin America, including supporting the head of the Mexican "Preconstitutional Government" Venustiano Carranza in his struggle for power against Pancho Villa and Emiliano Zapata. Lansing also wanted the United States to open negotiations with Denmark about purchasing the Danish West Indies in order to keep them out of German hands. He worried that Germany might invade Denmark, take the West Indies as war booty, then build a naval base that could threaten the Panama Canal. The Danes proved anxious to remove a potential source of friction with Germany and opened negotiations that resulted in the sale in August 1916.[102]

German intrigue in Mexico wasn't the only danger seeming to face the nation. In July war correspondent Floyd Gibbons of the Chicago *Tribune* chartered a fishing boat to sail from Los Angeles to Cedros Island off the coast of Baja California. Gibbons had heard rumors that Mexico, possibly with German encouragement, had invited Japan to build a naval base on the island. Disguised as fishermen, he and another correspondent sailed around the island for ten days. They reported seeing no signs of Japanese personnel, but plenty of physical evidence that the Japanese had begun to explore the construction of a base there.[103] With concerns about Japanese naval activity in Mexico and acquisitive German eyes on the Danish West Indies, the war in Europe increasingly seemed to be not merely approaching the United States, but surrounding it.

To Americans on the eastern seaboard especially, the war seemed ready to arrive at any moment. The rash of sabotage and explosions made officials anxious for the very security of the American homeland, a fact so recently taken for granted. In late August, House warned Wilson that he feared that "attempts will be made to blow up waterworks, electric lights and gas plants, subways, and bridges in cities like New York."[104] Shortly after the Robert Fay arrest, the New York *Tribune* warned that "Germany is now waging war within the United States" and told its readers that the "suitcase next to you in a street-car or a quiet house on your street may hide enough explosives to wreck a block." The Brooklyn *Eagle* agreed, claiming that the Fay scandal proved "that the German government, through its representatives, is responsible for a conspiracy worse than any other feature of the pro-German campaign in this country." Both newspapers urged the administration to do more than write notes and counsel patience. "Even Job got sick of it," concluded the Chicago *Tribune*.

Officially, the United States government claimed that it could not determine if the ship fires, bomb plots, and attempted assassinations were the work of a German government plot or the actions of individual Germans. The former could constitute an act of war; the latter would not. Increasingly, the media, especially on the East Coast where the danger seemed the greatest, did not care. The New York *Evening Sun* referred to "guerrilla warfare being...systematically waged by outsiders against the legitimate business of our citizens." It featured a cartoon showing a German sowing seeds from a spike helmet over an American city. The seeds were labeled Arson, Hate, Incendiarism, and Treason.[105]

In such an environment, Americans saw that the war in Europe was fast becoming, whether they liked it or not, their war too. Writer Samuel Taylor Moore noted in November that before the *Lusitania* Americans had seen the war as "a fantastic panorama of varying interest to America. But always in the layman's mind it was distant, as far away as though Europe were on another planet." Neutrality in those days struck Americans as both profitable and "a patriotic duty." But the events of 1915 showed the Germans to be, in Moore's words, "monsters, fiends, beasts, creatures lacking every concept of decency and humanity."[106] Even if Americans were unwilling to go to war, they had awakened to the danger and wanted their government to take steps to protect their property and their lives.

Perhaps most important, the events of the spring and summer of 1915 opened a debate about Preparedness, the specific actions that the United States should take to defend itself. Roosevelt had come to the conclusion that if the president and his administration would not take the steps needed to prepare the nation for future troubles, the American people would have to do it themselves, in the spirit of his Rough Riders from 1898. By the fall of 1915, more and more Americans had come to agree with him, though the devil remained in the details.

4

1916 and the Wages of Guilt

AT THE END OF 1915, reliable accounts about the massacre of tens of thousands of Armenians had begun to reach the United States. A Christian population living inside a predominantly Muslim empire, their plight elicited deep sympathy from Americans, a small handful of whom saw the tragedy firsthand. Clarence D. Ussher, an Episcopal missionary with the American Board of Foreign Missions and a physician practicing in a hospital near the ethnically diverse town of Van in the Caucasus Mountains, had been among the first to learn of the massacres. He knew the local Ottoman Army commander, Jedvet Bey, personally. Ussher had been the family's physician for a time and he had been a frequent guest at the Jedvet home for tea. The growing anger toward Armenians that Ussher sensed from Ottoman officials after the war began had deeply alarmed him. Ottoman attitudes had turned harsher and more violent early in 1915 as Ottoman officials became convinced that the Armenians were acting as a fifth column in support of advancing Russian forces.

In April, Ussher received a report that the Ottomans had torched every house in the Armenian village of Aikesdan. He also heard Jedvet Bey pledge to kill all of the Armenians in the region and shell the American hospital if any American tried to come to their defense. He intervened anyway on behalf of the Armenian community, and for his efforts Ottoman troops surrounded and besieged his hospital for four weeks. A temporary change in battlefield fortunes allowed the Russians to reach the hospital, giving Ussher, his wife, and their American staff time to get safely away, although his wife died of typhus en route to St. Petersburg. By the fall of 1915 the surviving American staff members of the Van hospital were in the United States being interviewed for newspaper articles, speaking constantly on behalf of Armenian charities, and urging the United States government to do everything in its power to protect the orphaned children of Armenia. Ussher believed that those children represented the best hope for the future of the Caucasus region if, under postwar American tutelage, they learned democracy and industry. Those Armenian children had first to survive a series of massacres in a place that one newspaper remembrance of Mrs. Ussher called "ravished, martyred Armenia," a land run by the sultan's "bloodthirsty" Turkish troops and the site of "wholesale massacre and the seizure of thousands of young women."[1]

In speeches and interviews in the first half of 1916, Ussher connected the tragedy in Armenia to America's lack of Preparedness. He spoke about the country's weakness and how that weakness helped to enable the massacres themselves and to create the dangerous situation that Americans overseas faced. While besieged in his hospital in Van, Ussher was convinced that had the American staff surrendered, Jedvet would have killed them all because the Ottoman commander knew that "there would be little danger of his ever being called to account by our Government." Ussher also spoke of an earlier incident when Turkish officers had stolen medicine from the hospital; when he threatened to protest their actions to the US ambassador in Istanbul, one Turkish officer replied, "We are not afraid of America. America has no army."[2] The hospital, which had been in operation since the 1840s, became the latest victim of America's inability to defend its interests or project its values; once battlefield fortunes changed in its favor, the Ottoman Army burned it to the ground.

Even allowing for a degree of exaggeration, Ussher's accounts underscored the national sense of global weakness in an era of total war, as evidenced by the events in Belgium, Armenia, Serbia, France, and elsewhere. As report after report documented the scale of the Armenian tragedy, Americans grew increasingly frustrated at either the inability or the unwillingness of the government to act. Theodore Roosevelt added his voice to the calls of criticism when he alleged that the American neutrality that had "kept Americans from doing their duty in Mexico, in the Belgian outrages and in the *Lusitania* case has made the murder of women and children by the Turks possible."[3] Not all Americans shared his views about what the duty of Americans was, but they tended to share his outrage.

Unable to help either Belgium or Armenia in their hours of need, the United States risked watching helplessly as the war in Europe rendered it insignificant on the world stage. If the nation could not help Armenia, which one South Carolina newspaper called the original "land of martyrs," the kingdom of the first large-scale converts to Christianity, and (some Christians believed) the site of Noah's landing after the flood, then of what use were American power and values to the world?[4] To stand neutral in the face of such a tragedy, Ussher, Roosevelt, and many others argued, was effectively to side with the evil that sank the *Lusitania* and massacred innocent civilians. Such a condition, they believed, was inappropriate for a nation with the kind of growing global role that America seemed destined to play.

Dismay at American global ineffectiveness spread exponentially after the reports from Armenia. The city of Philadelphia covered the entrance to all public buildings in black crepe for a day of mourning in recognition of the people "so murderously treated by the Turks." Above the crepe sat an American flag and the word ARMENIA stretched underneath.[5] Similar ceremonies occurred across the country as people tried to find some way to acknowledge the victims. Around this time, the Lebanese-born Maronite Catholic poet Khalil Gibran, then living in Boston, wrote a eulogy for his homeland, "Dead Are My People," a poem about the destruction the war had wreaked on Lebanon and Syria.[6] Awareness and the desire to help alone, however, would not suffice to help the suffering. The logistical difficulty of getting money, food, and supplies to Armenia only added to the sense of frustration and ineffectiveness.

Americans blamed not just the Ottoman Empire but Germany for the tragic plight of the Middle East more generally, and Armenia specifically. They assumed that the German government must either have approved the massacres or done nothing to stop its Ottoman ally from committing them. The New York *Tribune* ran a haunting cartoon of an Iron Cross–wielding Kaiser Wilhelm wearing a fez and holding a scimitar dripping with blood. The caption reads "Allah Mit Uns," a sardonic satire of the German slogan "Gott Mit Uns" (God Is with Us).[7] An editorial in that same newspaper noted that Armenia's tragic fate "should open our eyes to what would threaten us should *Germany* win and to our supreme interest in preventing her winning."[8] Armenia sat alongside Belgium and the *Lusitania* as specifically German crimes. The growing list of such crimes was itself proof that the Allies sat on the side of the right.[9]

But believing themselves to be on the side of the right only led Americans to the vexing question of what they should do about it. They increasingly came to believe that neutrality did not conform to their vision of the country's proper global role. The noted Episcopal bishop William Manning, rector of Trinity Parish in lower Manhattan, argued that America's safe and profitable peace was "not a peace Christ would have.... We have been neutral, but not great." He urged a stronger pro-Allied stance. From her place in France running aid programs, Anne Morgan argued in American newspapers that American prosperity combined with neutrality in the face of German aggression "is jeopardizing our soul." She urged her countrymen to "cast aside the veil which appears to obscure our divine obligation and give generously to the stricken of France."[10]

In the first half of 1916, American anger at Germany rose, largely as a result of the events in Armenia and the torpedoing of the passenger ferry *Sussex* in the English Channel carrying dozens of American citizens. Anger continued to rise throughout the year as events both at home and abroad showed the threat that Germany posed to American values and interests worldwide. Still, few believed that entering the war was the right response, as they retained sufficient faith in diplomacy, and awareness of the practical limits of Preparedness.

The hard truth was that living with this dilemma benefited millions of Americans as neutrality continued to feed the country's growing economy. Awareness of this dilemma came to a head in the national debate over a billion-dollar loan for the Allies that Anne Morgan's father, J. P. Morgan, pledged to help underwrite. Even those who warned that the loan could tie the United States more closely to the Allies diplomatically nevertheless found economic reasons to support it. Thus did the German-American newspaper publisher Edward Rumely note that a close friend of his opposed the loan on political grounds but the friend's heavy investment in overseas wheat sales and the manufacture of agricultural tools outweighed his political objections.[11] Rumely and most of his fellow newspaper editors came out in favor of the loan, though they were aware of the potential risk of tying the American economy more closely to that of Great Britain and France.

The loan, which made millions of dollars available to Britain and France from the end of 1915 and into 1916, had become critical to the wartime American economy and thus to the well-being of millions. Virtually every sector of the economy had grown as a direct result of wartime contracts with the belligerents (mainly Britain and France), increased trade with European neutrals, and higher sales at home. American businessmen saw an unprecedented opportunity to move into European markets as German, British, and French agriculture and manufacturing increasingly went into war production. Between 1914 and 1917 American exports to Europe increased exponentially from $1.4 billion to $4.3 billion. To cite one example, exports to Spain, also a neutral country, more than doubled in the years of American neutrality, going from $30.8 million to $76.9 million. The United States sent its first commercial attachés to that country late in 1915 and the National Chamber of Commerce soon followed by opening its first office in Madrid. The United States, which accounted for just 14 percent of total Spanish imports (most of them agricultural) in 1914, accounted for 45 percent of imports in 1917. Most of the increase came at the expense of Germany, whose ability to trade with Spain came to a crashing halt because of the British blockade and the closure of overland trade routes through France.[12] A similar pattern occurred in Portugal, Norway, and Sweden, as American firms sought to take advantage of the war by opening new markets and building new international commercial links. These firms also moved aggressively into Latin American markets to take over market share from European rivals.

Most Americans understood early on in the war that they stood to gain tremendously from their neutrality. In April 1915, John T. McCutcheon, the Chicago *Tribune*'s political cartoonist, had drawn "Coming Our Way:

The Money Center of the World" in which the docks of New York appear as giant magnets, pulling bulging bags containing the hard currency of Europe across the Atlantic. A gleeful Uncle Sam sits on the docks with his arms stretched wide open to welcome the pounds, francs, and marks moving across the Atlantic to America. Britain's John Bull, a Paris banker, and a spike-helmet-wearing German officer watch in shock and frustration from their coastlines. The spirit continued the following October when McCutcheon drew another cartoon titled "The Prosperity That Depends on the Suffering of Others."[13]

Some were uncomfortable with what one Tennessee minister called "citizens whose only passion has been greed for money and whose chief solicitude has been for dollars and dividends," but as a rule most Americans—across the political spectrum and up and down the socio-economic scale—saw a chance to reorient the world economy to their favor for as far into the future as any of them could dare to dream. One news report from late 1915 predicted that the destruction and reorientation of European industries to war production had already guaranteed American dominance of the world economy for the first two decades after the return of peace because of the European need for American reconstruction money and goods. Everyone seemed to be profiting from the tragedy on the other side of the Atlantic, from pencil manufacturers to steel companies to high-tech optical glass makers.[14] Even American Bible salesmen reported record profits of $2.8 million, a jump of more than 50 percent in two years, as European printers abandoned the trade in favor of war work.[15]

The American dilemma as the war ground through its second year involved the guilt-inducing paradox of a neutrality that was both profitable and morally questionable. This paradox set the context for the continuing debates in early to mid-1916 about the country's ambiguous and fraught relationship to the war as well as the presidential election of 1916, which began to take shape. By the end of the year, Americans had a consensus view of how they viewed the war but were no closer to a consensus view about what they should do about it.

Almost everyone had become more alert to the dangers that the war in Europe presented to the country's security. Unlike two years earlier, the war in Europe was no longer just about "them" but, increasingly, about "us." What happened in France, Armenia, and Poland had now come much closer to the core interests and values of the American people, especially as the economy increasingly depended on the course of events overseas. The sense of a shared threat had become more pronounced and avowed, as the alleviation of the suffering of others seemed less important than ensuring a security that Americans had so recently taken for granted. Whereas in 1914 Americans could respond with pity and charity, by 1916 those same Americans saw clearly that charity would never be enough. In January, for example, journalist Ray Stannard Baker spoke at the Hudson Guild Settlement House on Manhattan's Lower West Side and praised it as a model for Europe to follow in solving many of its own social problems. Theodore Roosevelt, who blanched at Baker's idealism in a time of existential crisis, responded with a searing letter that read: "Do you think in Belgium it makes much difference now whether its people do or do not believe in the Hudson Guild spirit? If we can't defend ourselves, it will be of no more consequence what we think of the Hudson Guild than what the Chinese think." Roosevelt's conclusion was that the United States in 1916 needed soldiers rather than muckraking progressives like Baker. If the United States could not defend itself, then the progressive Hudson Guild spirit might be crushed by the German military or sapped of funds by the near permanence of a large standing military. Baker himself feared that militarism would mark the end of the Progressive reform spirit that he held so dear. Still, he ruefully recognized that Roosevelt was right, writing that as time passed he became more convinced "that the Germans and all they stood for had to be defeated."[16]

Popular journalist Irvin Cobb had come to the same conclusion, declaring evocatively that "I am not a neutral any more. I am an American!" His comment shows the contradictions and the evolving definitions of neutrality. Cobb, back from the battlefields of Europe and publishing his accounts in various newspapers and magazines nationwide, warned Americans that the horrors he had seen in Europe, mainly the killing of civilians and the burning of towns in Belgium, could one day come to pass in the United States. "In all fairness," he warned at the end of 1915, "I can conceive [atrocities on the Belgian model] as being all the more likely to happen should the invading forces come at us under that design of black vulture which is known as the Imperial Prussian Eagle. Given similar conditions and similar opportunities, I can see Holyoke,

Massachusetts or Charleston, South Carolina, razed in smoking ruins, as Louvain or Dinant [were]."[17] Cobb had been particularly frightened by the German Army's killing of civilians in Belgium.

Life captured the fears of Americans with an arresting image on the cover of what it called its "Get Ready Number" on February 10, 1916, which consists of a map of North America in the near future should the United States take no steps to defend it from a host of avaricious enemies. Most of the United States is labeled "New Prussia" with cities like New Berlin (Washington), Kruppsburg (Pittsburgh), and Schlauterhaus (Chicago). Notably, Boise, Idaho is labeled Von Papen and another nearby city is marked Boy-Ed City after the two German conspirators recently expelled from the United States for their roles in planning the sabotage plots of 1915. Florida appears on the map as "Turconia," Baja California as "Austriana," and Mexico as the "German-run Province of Mexico" with "Wilhelmsburg" as its capital. A small area marked "The American Reservation," with "Goosestep" as its capital, appears roughly where New Mexico exists today.[18]

The west coast of the map is labeled "Japonica," with cities like "New Kobe" (Portland, Oregon), "Nagaseattle" (Seattle), and "Yohohanjalee" (Los Angeles), a reflection of abiding anti-Japanese fears and the sense that Japan might well join in any carving up of the United States led by Germany. Japan had shown an unusually aggressive naval posture in the Pacific by sending warships to the waters off Hawaii and Mexico between August and December 1914. As part of that effort, the Japanese, by agreement with the British, seized the former German colony of Tsingtao on mainland China as well as German Pacific island colonies north of the equator. Thus did Japan take control of critical positions astride American maritime communications to the Philippines, Hawaii, and China, notably the Caroline, Marshall, and Marianas Islands. United States Navy leaders began to call for American or international control over parts of those island chains in order to keep them from falling entirely into Japanese hands; some even argued for the islands returning to German hands as a check on Japanese growth. Japan also began a program of construction of modern *Dreadnought*-class battleships and battle cruisers, giving them eight of each by 1918.[19]

The fears that the *Life* map played to were to rise to center stage a year later in the wake of the Zimmermann Telegram crisis, but as the map clearly indicates, as early as February 1916 Americans had begun to envision a dark future brought about by this war. The Atlantic Ocean, labeled the "Von Tirpitz Ocean" on the *Life* map after the commander of the German Navy, no longer represents protection from Europe, as Walter Hines Page had envisioned it in August 1914, but an enemy-controlled waterway threatening and containing America. The threat was everywhere, and close to home. On the *Life* map the Great Lakes are renamed Pilsner Laken, Muenchner Laken, Culmbacher Laken, Hofbrau Laken, and Lager Laken. Canada itself appears on the map as "Barbarians," a reference to the fear that Germany might claim much or all of British-controlled Canada as part of war spoils in the event of its victory on the Western Front.

Thus could the United States face a future of German control of the Atlantic Ocean, Canada, and British possessions in the Caribbean, while German allies Turkey and Austria took possessions in North America. Japan, an abiding concern, especially for Americans on the West Coast, might well use its increasing power to take advantage of the situation for itself. The outcomes of the 1916 battles, particularly on the Somme and at Verdun, which had started in February and would continue for nearly a year, thus now became central to America's own security. Moreover, the British or the French always had the option of giving up parts of their North American possessions (including parts of Canada and Caribbean islands, such as Martinique and Guadeloupe) to the Germans as part of a treaty to end the war. The European war might well devastate the United States even if, or perhaps especially if, America remained neutral. In this environment, Cobb's statement shows an inherent contradiction between being neutral and being American; to be the former might well put at risk everything dear to the latter. These were extreme fears but they were growing in intensity. Even the senior American aid administrator in Europe, the strictly neutral Warwick Greene, warned that the war had made "human life as precarious and of as little value as in the Middle Ages." The United States would need to do more than relieve the suffering of victims; if it did not stop "feathering our nests a bit too ostentatiously while the best manhood of Europe is dying" there might be no civilized world left in a few years.[20]

It appeared for a time in the spring of 1916 that interventionists might get the crisis to jolt Americans out of their complacency. In February, the German government announced that it would return to a policy of sinking even those merchantmen carrying civilian passengers. The announcement led to a public debate about appropriate American responses and a proposal in Congress called the Gore-McLemore Resolution that would have banned Americans from traveling on ships heading into war zones. The resolution had some initial support in Congress, although Wilson opposed it from the beginning as tying the country's hands, as well as his own. Newspaper reports that a German-funded lobby directed by the National German-American Alliance, formed in 1915, was behind the resolution sapped national support.[21] Key senators moved to oppose it and the resolution died, although the debate surrounding it reopened discussions about how the United States should respond to Germany's submarine warfare campaign.[22]

The debates soon moved from the theoretical to the practical. On March 24 came news that the Germans had torpedoed the English Channel ferry *Sussex* with dozens of people killed, including a Persian prince, the famous Spanish composer Enrique Granados, and noted Anglo-Irish tennis star Manliffe Goodbody.[23] The *Sussex* was clearly a civilian ship and even the Germans admitted that they did not suspect it of carrying contraband. The Germans had therefore had no military reason to target the ship, all of whose passengers were either neutrals or noncombatants. Several Americans were injured although fortunately none died (despite early media reports of American deaths). Four other ships carrying American citizens, all of them British, had also been torpedoed by German submarines in March. Government officials responded with fury at the Germans for targeting what one rural newspaper called "unarmed, unwarned steamers" that posed no threat to anybody.[24] They worried that the incident would reawaken all of the anxiety of the year before following the *Lusitania* sinking. Secretary of State Robert Lansing called for breaking off diplomatic relations with Germany, and House urged that the president send the German ambassador back to Berlin in protest.

A crisis certainly seemed inevitable. Germany's initial response to the torpedoing of the *Sussex* was, in the words of Secretary of Agriculture David F. Houston, "singularly unsatisfactory. It was even trivial." The Germans first claimed that the ship sunk had not even been the *Sussex*, a claim that Houston noted showed the American government that the

Germans "failed to appreciate the gravity of the subject" to American eyes.[25] It also revealed how little respect Germany was giving to the United States in this latest crisis. The Germans evidently had no more reason to fear American reprisals than the Ottomans had, especially given German views that by this point America's trade policies made it a member of the British-French alliance in all but name anyway.

Thus began another round of tense diplomacy. As with the *Lusitania* crisis the year before, Wilson and Lansing tried to be firm with the Germans but the president did not want to risk a diplomatic break. Wilson had to be ready to address critics like Roosevelt who would argue that he had done too little to defend American honor as well as those like William Jennings Bryan who would argue that the president's actions had unnecessarily increased the risk of war with Germany. Most Americans wanted their government to be firmer with the Germans this time, given that the *Sussex* had revealed the bankruptcy of German promises of the year before. Too proud to fight wouldn't cut it again. The antiwar Progressive William Borah (R-Idaho) supported breaking diplomatic relations with Germany if it did not reply satisfactorily to the *Sussex* sinking, a step he had not advocated after the *Lusitania*. By March 1916 his views had changed significantly, leading him to say "I am not afraid of war if it is necessary to protect American rights."[26] Still, he also led a bipartisan group of members of Congress who supported Wilson's efforts to find a peaceful solution consistent with American honor. War had, to Borah's mind, become acceptable, but still not desirable. Even the New York *Evening Mail*'s generally pro-neutrality Edward Rumely warned a friend in Freiburg, Germany, that the German government must respect "this country's final and imperative demand that this murder be stopped."[27]

Wilson did indeed take a firmer line in 1916 than he had in 1915, addressing a joint session of Congress and threatening to break diplomatic relations with Germany if it did not alter its submarine warfare policies. Germany then changed its justification for the attack, arguing that the *Sussex* had been acting as a minelayer and that it could only have exploded as it did if it had been carrying munitions. American naval experts (correctly) rejected both points, concluding that the ship must have been hit by a torpedo, a point the Germans did not officially concede until May.[28]

The suggestion of Germany paying an indemnity for the *Sussex* seemed like one way out of the crisis, in part because an indemnity came with the implication that Germany had violated international law. But the idea of taking money from the Germans struck a raw nerve.[29] In what it sardonically called its "Humiliation Number" issue of April 13, *Life* featured a cover image of a poor, bent-over Woodrow Wilson picking up the loose change that a haughty Wilhelm tosses on the ground while an American eagle bows his head in shame in the background. "Here's money for your Americans," the kaiser says. "I may kill some more."[30] Two weeks later, *Life* featured another cover image with a German officer flirtatiously stroking the chin of Columbia over the words "How long will she stand it?"[31] Indemnity claims with the European powers had resolved similar situations in the American Civil War, but almost no one in 1916 seriously considered that model, in part because Americans now saw a new, more powerful, role for their country than they had half a century earlier. What had once been a normal part of the international arbitration system now looked like an insult to the nation's honor and self-image. Older definitions of neutrality, in other words, no longer seemed appropriate to the situation at hand in 1916. The country was now in new and entirely uncharted waters.

Wilson opted for an ultimatum demanding not arbitration or indemnification but "strict accountability" from the German government. His note read, in part: "If the sinking of the *Sussex* had been an isolated case the Government of the United States might find it possible to hope that the officer who was responsible for the act had willfully violated his orders or had been criminally negligent in taking none of the precautions [the German government] prescribed [but]...it unhappily does not stand alone." The torpedoing of an unarmed and totally harmless passenger ferry was, the note concluded, "one of the most terrible examples of the inhumanity of submarine warfare as the commanders of German vessels are conducting it."[32]

Almost everyone feared that war would result from the *Sussex* incident. From Springfield, Massachusetts, Rabbi Samuel Price noted that if Germany rejected the ultimatum a crisis would no doubt follow. "Diplomatic relations will be severed which will probably lead to war," he wrote in his diary. Americans had only to recall what had happened when Serbia had accepted every condition but one in Austria-Hungary's

July 1914 ultimatum to grow fearful for the future. Two days later, on April 22, Price noted that his community was "preparing for war in case the answer of Germany is not satisfactory."[33] Several newspapers were reporting the comments of one official in the German embassy in Washington that while "Germany regrets that Americans have been killed" by submarine warfare, the German government "cannot accept the terms of the United States government" as laid out in Wilson's note. Thus, concluded one Pennsylvania newspaper, "the crisis is not far distant."[34]

As with the *Lusitania* incident, however, few Americans—and fewer public officials—actively pushed for war, which still seemed too drastic a step no matter how high the anger level. The Washington *Post* polled members of Congress, asking them if the *Sussex* incident provided "sufficient provocation" for war. Of the 24 senators who replied to the questionnaire, only 1 said yes; of the 152 members of the House of Representatives who replied, just 3 said yes.[35] Americans were generally united behind the forceful diplomacy of Wilson, which one rural newspaper in Ohio called "the only [course] compatible with the dignity of the nation," and, one presumes, the only course feasible given the manifest weakness of the American military.[36] Walter Lippmann saw in Wilson's *Sussex* ultimatum proof that "if America had to fight" it would. Nevertheless, the country would go to war not for territory or power but for the more noble goal of assuring "the peace and order of the world." By contrast, he concluded, Germany showed itself mostly interested in a "peace of intrigue" as shown by its response to Wilson as well as Germany's sponsorship of "intrigue and conspiracy on American soil."[37]

Their hands already full fighting a major battle at Verdun—one which showed no signs of letting up after three months and in the end would result in one million total casualties—and sensing the intensity of American opposition to their actions, the Germans yielded. On May 4, they issued the Sussex Pledge by which they promised to stop sinking all merchant and passenger ships, adding the meaningless proviso that they expected the British to abide by the pledge as well. Samuel Price read the tone of the German reply as "brisk and insolent," but thought it just good enough to avoid war.[38] Secretary of Agriculture David Houston read the German pledge in a similar way, noting that it resolved the crisis temporarily, but that Germany "as usual promised nothing absolute" and that it was still "up to us to deal with Germany killing Americans," which Houston presumed would happen again, with or without the Sussex Pledge.[39]

The pledge was nevertheless a major victory for Wilsonian diplomacy and the basis for the "He Kept Us Out of War" slogan of Wilson's 1916 election campaign. A survey of more than seventy editorial pages and speeches by national politicians found the American people, as one editorial put it, "overwhelmingly in support of President Wilson."[40] But not everyone was satisfied. Roosevelt predictably called it "a crime against the nation" for knuckling under to the Germans. In his eyes, Wilson had allowed the German attack on the *Sussex* and the victimization of the Americans on board to go unpunished. German diplomacy having proved itself to be dishonest in the past, Roosevelt put no faith whatsoever in its latest pledge. The Germans, he believed, would violate the pledge whenever they decided it was in their best interests to do so.[41]

Nor did the conclusion of the *Sussex* affair lead to a greater sense of security nationwide. Writer and critic Gilbert Seldes believed that Germany's pledge had solved nothing and remarked that it made Americans "at last realize that their isolation is at an end, that the expedients of peace had been exhausted, and war was a possibility."[42] Franklin Martin, one of the doctors who helped to form the Committee of American Physicians for Medical Preparedness, wrote in the summer of 1916 that "we seemed destined to be drawn into the maelstrom" despite the Sussex Pledge. He, like many Americans, continued to hope for peace but felt "impelled by a growing conviction that the forces of evil were on trial and the combined hosts of righteousness would be required to prevent the world's destruction."[43] From her position at the center of American politics, Alice Roosevelt Longworth remarked that "the war seemed to be all that anyone thought or talked of," even after the Germans issued the Sussex Pledge.[44] Mary Roberts Rinehart agreed but added ruefully, "not one [American] in ten thousand knew what it would mean, in blood and cost." She took an extended trip out West in the hopes of getting a break from increasingly depressing war news.[45]

Though it removed the immediate threat of war, the Sussex Pledge had the effect of galvanizing a national reaction. Some communities took active steps in their own defense. More than three thousand Philadelphians formed a Citizens' Army to defend the city in case of

German attack.[46] A few individual Americans grew so frustrated with their country's lack of action that they volunteered to fight for one of the Allied armies. Among the most notable was Algernon Charles Sartoris, a grandson of Ulysses S. Grant, who volunteered for the French Foreign Legion because of his anger with the feebleness of Wilsonian diplomacy. "From the moment the war broke out, it had been my intention to serve the Allied cause," he later wrote. The sinking of the Lusitania and other examples of "Hun 'Kultur'" had persuaded him that war was inevitable but the "*Sussex* affair clinched it, so far as I was concerned, and finally, despairing of my own country doing her duty, like many other Americans I decided to enlist in the French Army and 'do my bit.'"[47] One Washington, D.C., newspaper praised him for joining "that strong corps of heroes where princes and poets battle shoulder to shoulder against the Germans with ditch diggers and peasants."[48]

Sartoris's enlistment came at approximately the same time that poet Alan Seeger died in the service of France on the Somme, symbolically enough on July 4. He died, as one woman who knew him wrote, "as he had often expressed the wish to die, in the service of France, a nation fighting for Right and Justice."[49] The New York *Sun*, which had published much of Seeger's wartime poetry, celebrated the life of the man they called a "Poet Warrior" with a combination of American and French symbols. In a front-page story, the *Sun* praised Seeger's "enthusiasm for the cause of France" as well as his "inherent American sense of humor and his unusual bravery."[50] His death in the service of France drew praise nationwide. The deaths of Harvard football hero Dillwyn Starr, also killed on the Somme while serving in Great Britain's elite Coldstream Guards, and of the grandson of Civil War hero Philip Kearny, killed while fighting for France that summer, similarly provoked national admiration.[51]

Thousands of Americans either took inspiration from these sacrifices or saw the storm clouds coming and decided that they, too, would volunteer for the Allies. More than six thousand Americans were serving in the British Army in 1916 and tens of thousands more were serving in the Canadian Army.[52] By October 1916 the American Field Service had 349 American students serving as volunteer ambulance drivers, including eighteen Rhodes Scholars, eighty-nine Harvard students, and eighty-seven students from other Ivy League schools. Eighty other volunteers had no college experience, indicating that more than simply men from the American elite were volunteering.[53] C. Earl Baker, a young man interested in a career in publishing, reacted to the events surrounding the *Sussex* sinking by joining the Pennsylvania National Guard along with 123 other men from his community and taking a job in a munitions plant. "Germany's aggression," he noted in explaining his decision, "seemed certain to pull America into the war soon" despite Wilson's attempts to keep the United States out of the war.[54] He and his friends concluded that they had little choice but to join the National Guard to get some military experience before the crisis struck.

No group of American volunteers attracted more attention than the men of the Lafayette Escadrille. Americans who had joined the French Foreign Legion in the early months of the war came together in 1916 to form a volunteer squadron in the French Air Service originally named the Escadrille Américaine. When Germany protested the name as a violation of American neutrality, the group changed the name to honor the Marquis de Lafayette, the young French nobleman who fought alongside George Washington in the American Revolution. Most of the members came from wealthy families; cofounder Billy Thaw's father was president of the Pennsylvania Railroad and Thaw was the first man to fly an airplane around the Statue of Liberty and underneath the Brooklyn Bridge.[55] The men of the Lafayette Escadrille openly expressed their love for France and hatred of Germany. University of Virginia student James McConnell, destined to die in the air in March 1917, said in 1916 of his decision to join: "The more I saw the splendor of the fight the French were fighting, the more I began to feel like an *embusqué*—what the British call a shirker. So I made up my mind to go into aviation."[56]

Given their backgrounds and their pro-French stance, they made for perfect newspaper copy. Roosevelt wrote newspaper and magazine articles praising them.[57] W. K. Vanderbilt gave them the princely sum of $10,000 a month to fund a lavish lifestyle that included huge banquets and two lion cubs as mascots named, appropriately, Whiskey and Soda. On top of the flash and the wild tales of parties in Paris, the Lafayette Escadrille compiled an impressive fighting record in the skies over Verdun and the Somme. Although technically they put their American citizenship at risk by fighting for a foreign army, their massive popularity put them above reproach. Colonel Spencer Cosby, the American military attaché in France, who could have pressured them to stop flying for France, instead expressed admiration for them for returning "the courtesy formerly paid to our country by La Fayette and [Yorktown commander the Comte de] Rochambeau" during the American Revolution.[58]

The pilots of the Lafayette Escadrille became media heroes on both sides of the Atlantic. The French instantly recognized the propaganda value of Americans putting their lives on the line for the cause of France, and, like American editors, saw how the Escadrille's heroic deeds could sell newspapers. An article in *Illustrated World* described them as "the daredevil Americans. You know the type. You have seen them often—making headlong tackles on the football field, diving feet first, spikes flashing in a wild slide for third base, galloping madly across a polo field, diving from a platform higher than someone else had dared—they are the youth of America."[59] Thaw especially made headlines when French newspapers reported him killed in combat. He then appeared very much alive in New York at a memorial held in his honor. The whole episode fit in beautifully with the death-defying public persona of the pilots of the Lafayette Escadrille—and readers loved every bit of it.[60]

Not all of the Escadrille pilots were as lucky as Thaw. Tennessee-born and North Carolina–raised Kiffin Rockwell died over the skies of Alsace in September 1916, leading the French ambassador himself to write a letter of condolence to Rockwell's mother. Poet Edgar Lee Masters was inspired to write a poem in his honor.[61] Newspapers across the country praised Rockwell's heroism and his sacrifice while mourning his death in a cause they increasingly came to see as their own.[62] His brother Paul kept his brother's legacy alive by also flying with the Escadrille and amassing an impressive combat record of his own.

Real help—not just expressions of sympathy and compassion—also continued to arrive in France from the United States in the form of volunteer medical personnel. A July 1916 ship brought nurses to France from New England, New York, and the Midwest as well as money from across the country. By midsummer doctors and nurses had come to France from forty-seven of the forty-eight states.[63] In one week in July, American money funded fifty field hospitals that provided 63,095 dressings for wounded men. With furious battles still raging at Verdun and the Somme, Americans reached deep into their pockets to provide enough money to fund care for 107,530 dressings in early August alone. A group in San Francisco paid for cars for a hospital, and a group in Ann Arbor, Michigan, purchased an entire operating room.[64] Another relief fund, dedicated to the care of French soldiers blinded by poison gas, had as its leaders the daughter of former president Grover Cleveland and the granddaughter of former president Ulysses S. Grant, both of whom moved to France for the duration of the war.[65]

The American people saw the volunteers in Europe, from fighter pilots to nurses, as a direct link to the war. Their sacrifices put the United States on the front lines in some capacity, fighting for the side that most Americans thought right. Evangelical leader Frederick Lynch saw Americans volunteering in Europe as "those who are truly Christian [and] anxious to have the United States become the savior of impoverished, distracted, disrupted, groaning Europe after the war is over." To Lynch's mind, the United States had to ensure that the war ended with wicked Germany punished because "ending the war without achieving righteousness would betray the cause of Christ himself." In Lynch's eyes, America's goals did not necessarily overlap with those of Great Britain and France, but they surely contradicted those of Germany, and the volunteers in France were making contributions toward those holy aims.[66] No records exist of any American citizens volunteering to fight for the Central Powers and only a small handful went to Germany or Austria-Hungary as medical personnel.

Americans unable or unwilling to go as far as Frederick Lynch, Billy Thaw, and Anne Morgan still found ways that they could contribute. Journalist Richard Harding Davis offered "Hints for those who want to help" in a January 1916 column. He reminded Americans that "owing to the war, many have suddenly grown rich" at home while "in France, the war has robbed everyone" of their fortunes.[67] A wide variety of charities existed to help those in need, mostly in Belgium, France, Poland, and Serbia, thus continuing the traditional neutral role of alleviating suffering and also ensuring that at least a symbolic share of America's wartime profits served a noble role. Notable charities included the French Women and Children Fund, the Aid to Serbia Fund, the Relief for the Allies Fund, Relief in Armenia Fund, the American Jewish Relief Fund, and the Kits for French Soldiers Fund. Together, they raised more than $1.5 million in contributions from individual Americans in December

1915 alone. The Rocky Mountain Club of New York City gave $500,000 of the $1 million it had raised to build a new Midtown Manhattan headquarters to Belgian relief instead, because its directors had been "moved by stories of woe" in that country.[68]

Notable Americans such as Helen Keller lent their fame to such efforts and helped to organize charity drives like one for Belgium in April 1916 that distributed cards featuring both American and Belgian flags and a paraphrase of Abraham Lincoln's words from the Gettysburg Address, "Let Us Highly Resolve That This People Shall Not Perish from the Earth."[69] A December 1916 event, "The Enslavement of Belgians: A Protest," demanding that the United States do more to help Belgium, sold out New York's Carnegie Hall. Nobel Peace Prize winner, Preparedness advocate, and former secretary of both state and war Elihu Root gave the keynote address.[70] These events show that Americans had political as well as philanthropic goals.

The sinking of the *Sussex*, the massacres in Armenia, and continuing American anxieties over internal security increased suspicions of Germany and its leader. Yale historian Robert J. Menner wrote in April 1916 that Americans saw Kaiser Wilhelm as "scarcely better than the Devil." He represented "a spirit which most Americans have come to consider destructive of our ideals and perhaps dangerous to our safety." Calling the Two Germanys idea of 1914 "absurd" in the light of the events of 1915 and 1916, he concluded that the American people had to accept the unpleasant truth that "public opinion in Germany was at least as bellicose as its rulers."[71] Arkansas governor Charles H. Brough lampooned German *Kultur* with a newspaper editorial in which he wrote "**K** stands for killing; **U** stands for U-boat; **L** stands for lies; **T** stands for Treachery; **U** stands for Unfaithfulness; **R** stands for Rudeness."[72]

Americans returning from Germany made the case as well. Frank Bohn, an Ohio-born son of a German socialist who had immigrated to the United States before the Civil War, spent part of 1916 in Germany. He returned horrified by what he had seen there. "Three years ago," he wrote, "the virtues of the German people and their distinguished services to the world made Germany loved throughout America. Today both are coming to be despised by nearly all but the Germans themselves." Germany and its regime, he argued, had "failed to play her allotted part in this century because she failed to win democracy and political civilization in 1848." In their place had come a reactionary regime that posed a peril to the entire world. In matters of government, he wrote, "Germany remains stolid, medieval, hopeless."[73]

Another German-American, Herbert Bayard Swope, won a 1917 Pulitzer Prize for his highly critical series of essays about modern Germany. Published in book form as *Inside the German Empire*, his writings began to appear in the New York *Sun* after his return from Germany in mid-1916. Swope told his readers that the Germans "dream of a Germanized world" firmly under their thumb and that they would not yield until they had achieved it. The German people, not only their government, Swope warned, hated Americans for their support of the Allies and for their beliefs in individual rights and democracy. Germany, he warned, was preparing to wage war on the United States in both Europe and in North America in order to impose its own set of values.[74]

In such an environment, leading advocates for peace and strict neutrality found themselves more and more on the outside. Andrew Preston estimates that by the end of 1916 the ranks of pacifists "had dwindled down to a small cast of hard-core activists who were willing to serve prison time for their beliefs."[75] Their spiritual leader, William Jennings Bryan, largely faded from public view as his extreme isolationism found fewer and fewer supporters. The pacifist and recently retired president of Stanford University, David Starr Jordan, came to Yale to speak against Preparedness and the war in general. The student body there, as one student recalled it, knew that "anti-German sentiment was growing" at Yale "with more and more talk of the probability of our being in" the war at some point in the near future on the Allied side. Officials at Yale thus worried that Jordan would receive a "rude reception" because his views stood at such sharp odds with those of the community. Only a plea for quiet from Yale's legendary English professor and former football star Billy Phelps calmed the tension and allowed Jordan to make his speech without disruptive protests.[76]

The arguments of the extreme end of the German-American press became more ludicrous and harder to accept, perhaps as a desperate way to gain any media attention at all. George Sylvester Viereck's *Fatherland* (the name itself implied a dual loyalty for German-Americans) claimed that a great secret scheme was built into diamond magnate Cecil

Rhodes's 1877 will to fund a plot by the British to take over the American government. America's pro-Allied foreign policy and calls from prominent Americans to break off relations with Germany were all part of this secret forty-year-old scheme. Viereck claimed that J. P. Morgan, Andrew Carnegie, Roscoe Thayer, Charles Eliot, and Theodore Roosevelt were among those prominent Americans committing "high treason" by receiving money from the clandestine Rhodes fund to destroy American democracy and put the United States back under the heel of the British monarchy.[77]

Even most German-Americans gave Viereck and his schemes little credence. The majority ignored him or assumed (correctly, as it turned out) that he was fully in the pay of German propagandists. Other, more subtle, statements showed the general trend of American antipathy toward Germany. A magazine advertisement for books describing "The War from All Sides" appears impartial by its title, but a closer examination shows a different pattern. The ad included books on Germany like *Pan-Germanism: A Critical Study of the German Scheme for the Conquest of the World, The War Makers of Modern Germany*, and another book showing the "startling contempt" of Germany for the rights of small nations. By contrast, books about the Allies included one that promised readers that they would "like the lively French soldier" who is a "tremendous worker" as well as a book about the brave Belgians who defended their homeland in the face of German invasion. For good measure, there is also a book on Preparedness that claims that "a government is the murderer of its citizens which sends them to the field uninformed and untaught." Perhaps the magazine thought the ad an expression of impartiality, but American biases clearly showed through in what publishers thought Americans wanted to read.[78]

Fears of German intrigues inside the United States continued despite the departures of Karl Boy-Ed and Franz von Papen. In April, soon after the *Sussex* torpedoing, eight more German nationals were arrested in connection with bomb plots. The Indianapolis *News* noted that "almost from the beginning there has been a war carried on against the American people and their government—and a war of a most detestable kind—by German agents, some of them officers of the German government." The article connected the recent arrests to the cigar bomb plots of 1915 and to Erich Muenter's bombing of the Capitol building. The United States, the newspaper noted, has been "the victim of a war waged against it by the agents of a foreign power," and predicted that the worst was yet to come.[79]

Anti-German sentiment after the *Sussex* incident did not always translate into greater pro-Allied sentiment. German-Americans especially remained reluctant to see American foreign policy tied to the goals of the British, French, and Russians. Their presumed desires to annex German and Ottoman territory, gain commercially from the war, and extend their imperial control in Asia and Africa did not curry much favor with Americans. Still, the positive reactions to the heroism of men like those in the Lafayette Escadrille showed the general tenor of American feeling. So, too, did a proclamation signed in April 1916 by five hundred prominent Americans. The signatories included 212 university presidents and professors, 37 bishops, 27 judges, 10 former cabinet members, and a host of well-known authors. The proclamation was a statement of "brotherly sympathy for, and intimate understanding of, the ideal for which the Allies are fighting." It read, in part: "Our judgment supports your cause, and our sympathies and our hopes are with you in this struggle. In saying this, we are confident that we are expressing the convictions and feelings of the overwhelming majority of Americans."[80] By this point, some senior French officials had already begun to refer to the United States as France's "great neutral ally."[81]

A particular outpouring of affection for France appeared throughout 1916, much of it coming from people who had recently gone to France and seen the war firsthand. Anna Murray Vail, a noted botanist and the treasurer of the American Fund for French Wounded, wrote an article for the *Atlantic* that compared wounded French soldiers to "Crusaders resting from their labors. And they *are that* for have not they been fighting for the Cross and all the civilization that that stands for?" In a letter to one of her patrons, she compared the Germans to "devils" and accused them of using airplanes to target the jewels of French, and by extension Western, civilization like the Louvre and Notre Dame.[82]

By the end of 1916, fewer and fewer Americans used the term "neutrality" any longer. They sensed themselves part of a larger global war that already involved them whether they had wanted it to or not. Nevertheless, they resisted taking the final step of entering into war. One British journalist traveling through Ohio told writer Gilbert Seldes that people he spoke to had "an active horror" of the idea of entering the war. Although they were pro-Allied, that viewpoint was "sentimental and detached; passive not active." Ohioans wanted the Allies to win the war but they also wanted to limit their support to indirect measures. Only if "direct attacks were made on American ships" or American interests, the reporter concluded, would enough Americans decide that they must participate in the "bad dream" of the European war.[83] The question during the tense spring and early summer of 1916 was when such an attack would come.

On the night of July 31, 1916, a massive series of explosions rocked the mile-long Lehigh Valley Railroad terminal in Jersey City, New Jersey. The terminal, nicknamed "Black Tom," served as the single largest depot for the transshipment of ammunition and explosives from the United States to Great Britain, accounting for almost three-fourths of all munitions shipments overseas. On the night of the attack it held more than two million pounds of explosives on its docks. At 2:08 A.M. an explosion and a fire began, setting off smaller explosions as the fire engulfed railcars loaded with artillery shells and bullets. A second large explosion occurred at 2:42 A.M. and the resultant infernos made it impossible for firefighters to extinguish it for days.

The explosions were unlike anything America had ever experienced. They blew out windows in Times Square and St. Patrick's Cathedral. Fragments of metal damaged the Statue of Liberty. People as far away as Baltimore and Philadelphia felt the effects of the blast, estimated at the equivalent of 5.5 on the Richter scale. Souvenir seekers picked up entire artillery shells almost two miles from the scene. The explosions produced hundreds of injuries and six deaths, including that of an infant thrown from its crib in New Jersey.

It was, we know now, the costliest act of terrorism in American history prior to the attacks of September 11, 2001. German agents had been watching Black Tom and planning ways to keep the munitions on those docks from killing German soldiers at the Somme and Verdun. To the Germans, any nation that would not only permit, but would profit from, such shipments of weapons was no neutral. It was, by contrast, a belligerent in all but name and therefore a perfectly legitimate target.[84] At the time, however, the docks were far too badly damaged to permit anything like a proper investigation. Fires smoldered for days and the wreckage of six piers, thirteen warehouses, and two hundred rail cars remained on the devastated site. Police initially thought that the blasts might have been caused by smudge pots lit by the night watchmen to keep mosquitoes away on a hot, humid summer night. Other officials suspected that perhaps the president of the Lehigh Valley Railroad had destroyed the piers himself in order to collect the enormous insurance premium. The extensive damage meant that there might never be a way to determine the exact cause of what appeared to most to be a terrible accident.

New York–based investigators, the same men who had broken the 1915 German plots, immediately suspected foul play. The smudge pots, they soon concluded, could not have touched off the blasts. The explosions, moreover, had begun in the perfect places to do maximum damage while protecting a saboteur from the prying eyes of night watchmen. The second major explosion, detectives further deduced, could not have been the result of spreading fires from the first and therefore also had to have been set deliberately. One explosion might be accidental; two explosions definitively proved sabotage. Further investigations showed that the explosions had most likely begun with devices planted in freight cars.

The evidence was enough to raise suspicions and fears of German intrigue, for only Germany benefited from such an attack. The wealthy socialite Eva Stotesbury must have suspected the Germans of involvement in the destruction of Black Tom because she included stories about it in the massive scrapbooks of war clippings that she kept. One of those clippings quoted an investigator as saying, "Fires don't start in freight cars accidentally. . . . We have insidious enemies who want nothing better than to prevent shipments abroad." Another article noted that the evidence of German complicity remained unclear but that the destruction of Black Tom not coincidentally "must prove cheering news to Berlin and Vienna."[85] The Philadelphia *Evening-Ledger* blamed a shadowy "German plot" for the fire, although it noted that the evidence was as yet insufficient to prove the charge beyond a reasonable doubt.[86] A few weeks later, the Washington *Times* reported on an "alien plot" involving Norwegian agents in the pay of the German government.[87] If true, German intrigue to destroy Black Tom would qualify as an act of war. Soon, however, the evidence against the Norwegians fell apart and the police were left with no leads.

Investigators got their first big lead when a landlady in Bayonne, New Jersey, told police that her tenant had come home at 4 A.M. on the night of the explosion pulling at his hair and crying out "What I do? What I do?" He turned out to be a twenty-three-year-old Slovak immigrant named Michael Kristoff. The police found money, maps, and nautical charts of the New York and Jersey City harbors in his room. From here, the details of the case grow murky. Police seem to have doubted Kristoff's sanity and released him from custody so they could trail him in the hopes of finding the masterminds behind the plot. The trail led to a few suspects, but not enough evidence to prove the case of deliberate sabotage. Soon thereafter, several of the men under suspicion disappeared, evidently to Mexico with the help of German agents.

The story continued to have far more than its share of bizarre twists and turns. Kristoff later enlisted in the United States Army under a false name, but soon after was medically discharged. Living under yet another assumed name he was arrested in Albany in 1921. A subsequent investigation into his many identities led to the eventual discovery of the entire German plot to destroy Black Tom. A national inquiry concluded its work in early 1933 and found German agents and the German government responsible. By then the chancellor of Germany was none other than Franz von Papen, the attaché whom Wilson had declared persona non grata and expelled from the United States in 1915. West Germany finally admitted its guilt in 1953 and agreed to pay $50 million in compensatory damages, making the final payment in 1979.[88]

Although no one in 1916 knew for sure who had been responsible for Black Tom, the explosions reminded Americans of the sabotage plots of the year before. Before the year ended, five ships leaving from West Coast ports caught fire in ways all too similar to the cigar bomb fires of 1915. Investigations always seemed to falter on jurisdictional issues or a lack of police authority to investigate. Thus did judges often have no choice but to release suspects they wanted to hold, only to find that the suspects disappeared at the first opportunity.[89]

Black Tom notwithstanding, the enormous profitability of neutrality gave the nation an additional reason to look the other way when it could. There can be no doubt that wealthy Americans made enormous sums of money from the war. The Guggenheim mining empire, for example, reported its single most profitable year in 1916.[90] The profits reached deep into the American economy as virtually all sectors grew as a result of the war. Almost anything the American people could grow, mine, or manufacture could find a market either overseas or as a replacement at home for an import no longer coming from Europe. Trade with Asia and Latin America also increased sharply as European manufacturers largely abandoned those markets in the war years.

Americans still had the luxury of having it both ways. Farmers benefited from both increased demand for American crops and meat and the good harvests of 1915 and 1916. One Southern journal lauded this favorable circumstance, noting with glee that "Virginia farmers are to share in the general prosperity" of the country after several years of relatively hard times.[91] The change in fortunes especially helped the South, which depended on tobacco and cotton, two crops that rebounded from the disastrous year of 1914 less quickly than did wheat. With the demand for wheat rising sharply in Europe, the American Midwest had already profited handsomely. Of the nation's top 128 urban regions, those that grew fastest in 1914 and 1915 depended on wheat. They included Duluth, Fargo, Lincoln, Minneapolis, Omaha, and Wichita.[92] By 1915 and 1916 Southern agriculture, too, had begun to show the benefits of wartime exports. Tennessee, for example, had an offer to sell all of its surplus tobacco to a New York-based charity that wanted to give it away to Allied soldiers on the Western Front.[93] Kansas had enough of a wheat surplus to make money and provide charity to Belgium at the same time. The equivalent of more than fifty thousand barrels of donated Kansas wheat crossed the Atlantic with the state flag flying high above the merchant ships carrying it. Belgian women took the now-empty sacks that had carried the grain and embroidered designs on them before returning the sacks to Kansas as a way of expressing their gratitude. The artfully decorated sacks appeared in shop windows and government offices in Kansas towns, creating another tangible link between the United States and the victims of German oppression.[94]

John T. McCutcheon captured this widespread growth of the American economy in an August 1916 cartoon for the Chicago *Tribune* titled "War Prosperity Pudding." In it, a series of pudgy men dive into a pot while yelling statements like "This won't last forever and I've got to get busy," "I'm going to get my share or fight for it," and, simply, "More!" There are as many men in the cartoon wearing farmers' overalls as businessmen's suits, a reflection of the broad base of war profiteering.[95] The Des Moines *Register*'s J. N. Darling drew a similarly themed cartoon featuring an American merchant greedily eating like a child from a jam jar labeled "War Prosperity."[96]

In such circumstances, as Americans sought to maximize their profits as long as wartime conditions permitted it, they protested the infringements on their trade from both the German and the British blockades. At the end of 1915 Wilson had sent a letter of protest to the British government over the latter's expansion of the number of items it declared as contraband and, therefore, subject to seizure. But the letter did not demand that Britain stop its actions nor did it threaten retaliation. One recent scholar of the British blockade concluded that the letter had no effect whatever on British policy, nor did Wilson intend for it to do so. It was merely a "lawyer letter" written to satisfy those American firms complaining about British interference.[97] It did not prevent the British from listing eighty-five companies on a blacklist in July 1916, banning them from trading with Great Britain because they also did business with Germany.[98]

Although the United States and Great Britain bickered over blockade and commerce policy, they agreed on the basic outlines of their national strategies. Enough money was changing hands, moreover, to satisfy Americans even if the British blockade kept them from fulfilling some contracts with the Central Powers. The British, too, realized how much they needed American goods and American financing to win the war.[99] Thus although the United States occasionally grew angry at British seizure of American cargoes and the British grew angry at American willingness to stand aloof and profit from a war both sides wanted Britain to win, the two sides always found ways to compromise and smooth over rough patches, even Britain's brutal suppression of the Easter Rising in Dublin in 1916.[100] In short, little had changed since November 1914 when House had told British ambassador Sir Cecil Spring-Rice that American protests would largely be for show because American sentiment was sympathetic to the Allied cause.[101] As the election of 1916 would soon show, that sentiment would not change even as Americans contemplated changing who was in the White House.

5

No More Jerichos

JACOB MCGAVOCK DICKINSON HAD a fascinating life story. Sixty-three years old in 1915, a large man with a bushy mustache and a self-effacing demeanor, he had been born in Mississippi, had served in the Confederate Army as a cavalryman at the age of fourteen, lived in Leipzig and Paris, studied law at Columbia University in New York, became a successful corporate lawyer in Chicago, then went on to a remarkable (if today largely forgotten) career in public service. He served in many roles, among them Tennessee Supreme Court justice, assistant attorney general of the United States, president of the American Bar Association, and secretary of war under President William Howard Taft. Dickinson was among the first to understand that the war in Europe would sooner or later force the United States to make some unpleasant choices, even if Americans had played no role in its outbreak.

In June 1915 Dickinson gave a speech in Nashville that highlighted the two main topics then being debated around the country during the "Anno Diabolo" of 1915: Preparedness and Anti-Hyphenism. In the wake of the German sinking of the *Lusitania*, Americans had to realize, as Dickinson put it, that "it would be the blindest folly for us to regulate our conduct upon the assumption that there will be no more wars" for the nation to fight. Although he believed that the United States stood as the antithesis of the militarism then running amok in Europe, he saw in

France and Belgium's terrible suffering a reminder that in the modern world states had to do more than merely proclaim their love of liberty and desire for peace; they had an obligation to defend those ideals or risk losing them. Perhaps with a nod to his Nashville audience, he compared the fates of Belgium and France to that of the old Confederacy, quoting Robert E. Lee's assessment in 1865 that there were "sacred principles to maintain and rights to defend, for which we are duty bound to do our best, even if we perished in the endeavor."

Dickinson concluded that although the United States wanted nothing from the war except to help alleviate the suffering of the innocent and ensure a permanent peace for Europe, it nevertheless needed to prepare itself to fight or risk being dragged into the war on someone else's terms. He rejected utopian ideas of international government and binding arbitration, such as those that Taft and his League to Enforce Peace were advocating. Instead, Dickinson wanted the United States to arm itself in order to have its voice heard in the international arena. "A nation that has an armament to abandon," he argued, "will have a far more potential voice in a council of nations considering disarmament than one having none to abandon." Seeing the purpose of arming as the enforcement of peace rather than the acquisition of territory, Dickinson concluded, "It is no departure from our traditional advocacy of peace to inform ourselves as to our military status, or to prepare ourselves to resist invasion and to protect our citizens in their just rights of person and property."

In his Nashville speech Dickinson warned that the United States stood in no position to defend those rights. The American people needed to learn to treat questions of defense "in terms of sober earnestness and with a realization of what is involved." Speaking with the authority of a former secretary of war, he said that the militia and state National Guard units upon which the nation had traditionally depended were ill suited to defend the nation in a time of crisis. The world had changed too much in the past few decades to rely on a system of latter-day Minutemen or Andrew Jackson's Tennessee Volunteers. The modern world had grown too sophisticated and too dangerous for the nation to rely on amateurs. "There has been no time in our history," he concluded, "when a greater responsibility was imposed upon an administration," as Wilson sought a way to protect the nation from the ravages of war without actually fighting. A continued desire for peace at any price without preparing for war would, Dickinson argued, serve the nation poorly. The United States had to prepare to defend itself by force of arms if necessary because lofty ideals would not compel the belligerent powers of Europe to lay down their arms. "There are no more Jerichos to be demolished by a blowing of our horns," he concluded. The war had shown how much the world had changed, and how much the United States now had to change with it, whether its people wanted it to or not.

The second topic of Dickinson's speech, Anti-Hyphenism, centered on immigrants. He called on his audience to respect the rights and loyalty of recent arrivals to the United States. "Their minds and hearts are suffering intense strain," he told his audience, as they watched their homelands engage in a "death struggle" for their survival. Americans should take "special care" to remember that immigrants were now fellow citizens who shared the wider national desire for peace, security, and justice. No matter whether they were Irish-American, Italian-American, Swedish-American, or German-American, they too were part of the nation, and would be loyal to the United States in the event of any future crisis.[1]

The events of 1915 had increased Americans' anxieties about their security, internal and external, hence Dickinson's focus on these topics. On the issue of Preparedness, he was in tune with the country's mood. Most Americans in 1915 saw Preparedness as a way to avoid war through the creation of military strength that the nation would hopefully never have to use. The New York *Tribune* defended one plan to train all high school and college students in the rudiments of military science as "a plan by which the country is always prepared, but on a peace basis."[2] Preparedness also offered an avenue by which to impose an American-inspired peace on a rapidly barbarizing Europe. Such a peace could permit Europe to demobilize, disarm, and return to the pacific norms of the prewar years. In December 1915—looking back on the Anno Diabolos—Nobel laureate Elihu Root remarked that Europe had returned to "the moral standards of the Thirty Years' War." Only America could put Europe right not only for its interests but for America's own interests as well. Failure to do so would lead to a world permanently armed and mobilized.[3] One Iowa newspaper argued that Preparedness might help the United States atone for the shame of not having come to Belgium's defense at the start of the war.[4]

Preparedness would require major changes to the structure of the country's national defense. Prior to 1915, most Americans, especially those holding the purse strings in Congress, sought to keep spending on the military as low as possible. The war in Europe, however, threatened to change that tradition. Brooklyn minister Newell Dwight Hillis bemoaned that whatever the outcome of the war in Europe, Germany's aggression might compel the country to become "a military machine." If the Germans won the war or seemed likely to do so, the United States might have to "start in on a program of ten dreadnoughts a year instead of building ten colleges and universities for the same sum of money." To Americans in 1915, such a program would risk incurring massive debt and represent a fundamental change in the national self-image. Because America stood "at the other end of the universe" from German militarism and all that it stood for, ratcheting up defense spending meant running the risk of becoming the very thing that Americans claimed to despise.[5]

Facing few immediate threats, the nation had rarely seen a need for large numbers of soldiers in peacetime. The army, scattered mostly across isolated garrisons in the American West, had fewer than 5,000 officers and 102,000 soldiers. It had no field armies, no corps, no divisions, and no brigades. A standard regiment had (on paper) just four machine guns, although many regiments had no machine guns at all. Numerically, the United States had the seventeenth largest army in the world. Put another way, the French Army had had twice as many men killed and wounded in the first twelve days of the war as the entire American army had in its ranks.[6] The army was deficient in virtually every technical category, and in almost every single way it looked more like the one that had fought Spain in 1898 than the highly technical armies engaging in the murderous struggle on the Western Front in France in 1915 with machine guns, poison gas, long-range steel artillery, and airplanes.

Thanks to the efforts of the Theodore Roosevelt administration, the United States Navy was in better shape than the Army, but it, too, needed modernization. Because Congress was unwilling to put as much money into a navy as the Germans, British, and French did, the United States Navy had fallen from the heights of the Great White Fleet that Roosevelt had sent around the world in a demonstration of American might in 1907–9. The American fleet especially lagged in newer technology such as submarines and naval aviation. The navy did, however, possess modern battleships of the *Dreadnought* class, as well as a strong fleet of faster and more agile destroyers. The latter would soon prove their worth in escorting merchant ships and patrolling the seas for U-boats.

Before the sinking of the *Lusitania*, Preparedness had largely been an issue for defense and security specialists like General Leonard Wood and former secretary of war Henry L. Stimson. Their calls for continental-style universal military training for young men had fallen on deaf ears. Most tended to see such ideas as characteristic of European militarism and inconsistent with notions of American liberty. Plans for conscription called to mind images of the draft riots of the Civil War and proved to be especially unpopular in the rural South and Midwest where farmers feared a loss of agricultural labor. The American people generally did not show much interest in military matters in peacetime. The American Navy League, for example, had just seven thousand members (most of them retired naval officers) and an annual budget of just $15,000, while its German equivalent had one million members and an annual budget over $250,000. Nor did the American Navy League have much influence in policy circles. The league even failed to gain the ear of Wilson's secretary of the navy, Josephus Daniels, who consistently rejected their requests for higher naval appropriations and more sailors.[7]

Few political leaders had thought deeply about security issues. Wilson had campaigned almost exclusively on domestic issues in 1912 and upon his inauguration had remarked "it would be an irony of fate if my administration had to deal chiefly with foreign affairs."[8] He had chosen as his secretary of war a smart and efficient Episcopal priest and lawyer named Lindley Garrison, mainly to please party bosses. Garrison had expected Wilson to ask him to join the cabinet, but not as secretary of war, a position for which he thought himself completely unqualified.[9] As secretary of the navy, Wilson had chosen Daniels, a race-baiting North Carolina newspaperman who represented the rural and prohibitionist constituencies of the Democratic Party. Neither had any expertise in military matters; Wilson clearly didn't think such expertise might be necessary during his presidency. While Garrison proved to be innovative and popular with the army brass, Daniels infuriated navy leaders with his budget cuts, his centralization of power in Washington, and his decision to ban alcohol from ships.[10] Congress also lacked a reservoir of people informed about and interested in military matters.

The administration's inexperience with military matters produced a small scandal in the fall of 1915 when the Baltimore *Sun* reported that the Army General Staff had been preparing war plans in the event that the country might become involved in the European war. A furious Wilson, who saw even thinking about war as a non-neutral act, threatened to fire every officer on the staff. Assistant Secretary of War Henry Breckenridge tried to explain to the president that the staff had only been doing its job of preparing for any possible contingency. Wilson calmed down, but Breckenridge advised the Army Staff to "camouflage" its work more carefully in the future and to keep itself out of the public eye.[11]

Many of Wilson's critics on defense issues, mostly from the Republican Party, had begun to push for greater spending on defense. The sinkings of the *Lusitania* and the *Arabic* gave new life to the efforts of these Preparedness advocates and converted some former opponents to the cause. The *Wall Street Journal* editorialized that the sinkings had only happened because the Germans knew that they did not need to take American military power seriously.[12] In July, Secretary of State Robert Lansing warned the German ambassador to the United States that his country could not expect the United States government to limit itself to writing diplomatic notes forever in response to outrages, but, as Lansing surely knew, this was pure rhetoric.[13] Secretary of the Interior Franklin Lane wrote to a friend in August that America had to find a way to "make Germany understand that we meant business." Both officials had converted to the cause of Preparedness.[14]

The events of 1915 converted many other prominent Americans who had previously been skeptical or outright hostile to the idea of Preparedness. New York Democrat Perry Belmont, who in 1914 did not anticipate the United States having to take any active steps as a result of the war in Europe, had changed his mind by November 1915. In an article titled "An Armed Democracy," he argued for developing "an efficient military organization," and noted that support for such a concept "is now general throughout the country."[15] He wanted to see the country invest heavily in both the army and the navy, although he still did not envision either one having to fight in a European war.

A survey done by a newspaper in Dallas showed 5,612 city residents in favor of Preparedness and just 257 against. Both the local Rotary Club and the Chamber of Commerce came out in support of the idea. In rural Paris, Texas, near the Oklahoma border, a survey found 152 residents in favor of Preparedness and just 6 opposed. "Texas congressmen are hearing from home," reported one local newspaper, "and the ones against Preparedness are not so vehement or numerous as they were."[16] German-American statesman Charles Nagel (secretary of commerce and labor in the Taft administration) noted that all of the German-language newspapers in St. Louis were in favor of Preparedness. "I do not believe that any element has given the movement better support than has the German."[17] The Irish-Americans of the Knights of Columbus also enthusiastically backed Preparedness.[18]

Some advocates of Preparedness had a financial stake in the outcome, leading to charges that industrialists pushing for it sought to profit from increased spending on armaments (as indeed they would). The businessmen argued in return that no necessary contradiction existed between profit and patriotism; one could sit perfectly well alongside the other. *Manufacturer's Record*, a newspaper representing heavy industry, argued in October 1915 that the United States was "living in a fool's paradise because we are without an adequate army and navy" and that the nation must begin to invest in weaponry in order to "save ourselves from such overwhelming disaster as that of Belgium." US Steel offered to invest as much as $100 million of its own money into armaments factories and raw-materials production if the government would promise in return to contract for the weapons and transportation infrastructure that it argued the nation needed.[19] The Wilson administration reacted coolly to the offer, unwilling to allow a private corporation to determine government policy.

A similar blend of patriotism and profit motivated Powell Evans, president of the Schuylkill Railway, a Pennsylvania-based company that specialized in moving industrial goods from the Midwest to Eastern port cities like Philadelphia and New York. Evans urged corporate leaders to follow the Schuylkill Railway's lead and give employees paid time off to undertake military training. He also argued for increased taxation to fund a national army of five hundred thousand men. In an ideal world, these steps would protect the nation without forcing it to go to war. "We should not be Too Proud to Fight," he argued, but "Too Prepared to Have to Fight." Evans believed that the war in Europe made the United States a target for whichever nation or nations emerged victorious because America was simultaneously "the richest country in the world" and "the most unprotected." Whoever won the war would naturally and inevitably target America in order to recoup their wartime financial losses.[20]

If America did not prepare to defend itself, it might suffer the fate of China, carved up by rival powers eager to gain access to its raw materials and its markets. Evans thus urged America's corporate leaders to follow the Schuylkill Railway's lead and give employees paid time off to undertake military training. Only by taking such steps could America avoid the humiliation China had to suffer when Japan issued its Twenty-One Demands in January 1915. Those demands, delivered from a militarized nation to a defenseless one, gave Japan extended control over much of the Chinese economy as well as dominance in Manchuria. As one prominent American scientist noted, the demands proved that international law meant nothing as a way of protecting national rights. The world had become a "vast criminal's paradise" where the "wolves never were so bold and rapacious." America could not risk the fate of China. "If Japan were to put up such a document as that to any nation with a good army and navy, it would mean just one of two things: apology or war!"[21]

Even those uncomfortable with industry profiting from defense shared the general belief that Preparedness was necessary to deter another state from encroaching on American security. Chicago *Tribune* political cartoonist John T. McCutcheon, no great friend of profiteering industrialists, drew a rather simplistic but effective political cartoon on the subject titled "Nations Are Like Individuals." In the first panel, a well-dressed man is approached by a much larger, much shadier-looking, man. The well-dressed man says, "I want to go my way peacefully. I'm not looking for trouble with anybody." His words only make the bully approach more menacingly. In the third panel, the well-dressed man (obviously representing the United States) shouts, "BUT, I have my self-respect and certain rights to protect, and rather than yield them I'll FIGHT anybody, anywhere, and anytime." In the final panel, the bully shakes the man's hand and says, "Say, you're all right. Gee, I thought you wouldn't fight."[22] McCutcheon's folksy message could hardly have been more clear. If the nation prepared itself to fight and showed its willingness to fight, the European and Asian bullies would leave it alone.

Although Preparedness became a new national ideology, a vocal minority continued to speak out against it. Speaking for isolationists and socialists, William Jennings Bryan had said that "Preparedness provokes rather than prevents war" because more weapons could only lead to more violence.[23] Opponents also worried that Preparedness could militarize American society as it had militarized Europe. Socialists and religious leaders argued instead for a renewed emphasis on America's moral principles as a way of setting an example to Europe and being a latter-day City upon a Hill. To Bryan and others, America's obligation as a neutral power involved showing the world a better way, the American way.

The events of 1915, however, convinced even socialists and religious leaders to embrace Preparedness as the best route forward, however distasteful it might be. Charles Edward Russell, the well-known muckraking journalist and civil rights advocate, became a convert, as did Philadelphia's Reverend James A. Montgomery, who told his congregation that the sinking of the *Lusitania* had moved him to conclude that the United States lived in the shadow of "monstrous and damnable" atrocity yet sat "dazed, with the core of our virility wounded and stung" because the country lacked resolve and leadership. Anyone using Christian principles to argue against Preparedness was, he argued, making "an excuse for cowardice and indifference, a cloak for the indecision and unpreparedness for the battle of life."[24]

As the year went on, Preparedness drew more and more support from across the spectrum. Reflecting the split among British suffragists earlier in the war, American suffragist leader Carrie Chapman Catt led a group that came out in favor of Preparedness: "Let us build a fleet of airships and a school of submarines so numerous and wonderful as to stay the imagination of the most militarist; let us build great dreadnoughts to sail the ocean; let us establish conscription and train our men to march, to maneuver, and to kill."[25] Like most of her fellow Americans, she envisioned these forces as playing a deterrent role, forcing Asians, Europeans, and Mexicans to take American interests into account for fear of retaliation. The majority of Americans agreed with her and with Jacob McGavock Dickinson, who in October 1915 argued that worries of

America becoming a militarist nation as a result of Preparedness were "a groundless fear for a people who desire nothing belonging to other nations and whose only purpose in war is to resist unjust aggression." Preparedness, he argued, would not lead to militarism but would instead keep some outside power from deciding the terms of America's future.[26]

Such was the message of an October 1915 cartoon in *Life* titled "1920: If Germany Wins." In the cartoon, a doctor informs a man of the birth of his child with the words "Congrats, old chap. It's a soldier."[27] Debates about how to prepare for war or to avoid the grim future *Life* projected cut directly to the core responsibility of the nation to defend itself and to avoid the unpleasant fate of a future of permanent armament. But throughout 1915 the government had no strategic plan for producing the hundreds of thousands of soldiers (and their equipment) that modern war required. Americans had traditionally handled their defense needs either through volunteerism on the 1861 and 1898 models or through a mixture of the federal army and the various state-based National Guards and militias. Professionals criticized both methods as entirely inadequate to meeting the military conditions of the modern, industrial age. Still, proposals by the army and its advocates for some form of compulsory military service struck many as unnecessary and even antithetical to national traditions. The National Guard model, moreover, had the strong backing of state governors and those fearful of the extension of federal power at the expense of the states. Preparedness was therefore as much about domestic issues as foreign ones.

Furthermore, any changes to American defense policy and any attempts to modernize the military would take time that the nation might not have if another *Lusitania* incident forced it to fight. Preparedness therefore meant more than just authorizing more money for defense. The nation would have to make choices about the kind of preparation it wanted to make and the changes that that preparation might quickly impose on the nation's core values. Such debates would have been unimaginable in the American polity just a few months earlier. By the fall of 1915, however, Preparedness became a central issue, even if there was little consensus on the details; Americans agreed on the need to prepare far more than they agreed on how, exactly, to do it. Late in 1915, Progressive Republican A. P. Gardner of Massachusetts noted that "six months ago I should have been a mighty poor politician if I had preached about our lack of national defense. Today I should be a mighty poor politician if I were to drop the subject." Gardner provoked national (and almost uniformly favorable) news coverage for his demand for a congressional inquiry into the sad state of American defenses. He called for substantial increases in defense spending because, he contended, the navy could no longer protect American shores and the entire American Army "would just about garrison Paris" in a war of the magnitude of the one raging in Europe.

Editorials in the *New York Times*, which called the United States "a great, helpless unprepared nation," supported Gardner's efforts to get Congress moving on defense questions.[28] Experts testified about the sorry state of the American military. The army's adjutant general said that it was not even large enough to man the guns of New York City should the country enter the war. He also warned that America's past wars would look like "taking candy from a baby" compared to the industrialized mass murder occurring in France. At the same time, former secretary of war Henry L. Stimson told a group in New York that the United States Army had enough ammunition for about a day and a half of war on the scale of the Western Front.[29] From the army itself came a report that it was short four hundred thousand rifle cartridges, two thousand artillery pieces, and eleven million rounds of artillery ammunition.[30]

This lack of preparedness contrasted sharply with the news coming from Europe about the true costs of modern conflict. European armies continued to be parsimonious in giving out their own battle casualties, but they sometimes gave American journalists figures on enemy casualties. The French government announced in September that a remarkable 170,000 Germans had become casualties unsuccessfully defending a single hill in Artois.[31] The numbers correspondents reported were astonishing. A July article in the Washington *Star* told readers of lists at the Ministry of Defense in Paris numbering in the hundreds of thousands of Frenchmen killed in battle. The same article described French soldiers suffering from the "hideous fate" of being blinded by gas. The article shows them trying to learn new trades in order to make themselves useful after the war.[32] Letters home from Americans in Europe spoke, as nurse Caroline Duer did in October, of "countless millions" dead or permanently wounded with no end to the war in sight.[33]

Preparing for such a deadly war required an entirely new way of approaching military and diplomatic problems. Americans could no longer rely on morality and high-minded speeches to repel what Gardner called "the attacks of the effete monarchies of Europe and Asia." Lindley Garrison similarly warned that "because we have blundered through four or five wars we seem to think that we are possessed of a God-given inherent knowledge of the subject of war. Well, we are not." Thus did they both ridicule as unrealistic a statement from William Jennings Bryan that "the President knows that if this country needed a million men, and needed them in a day, the call could go out at sunrise and the sun would go down on a million men in arms." Even if such men could be found, they would have no weapons and would require two years of training to make them a modern army. The American political process was ill-suited to making the quick decisions needed to address the problem. As one magazine lampooned, "So it goes, dawdle, dawdle, dawdle, all along the line from voter to President."[34]

From outside the political process, Roosevelt continued to hammer away at those who sought protection in isolation and toothless international legal agreements, such as the Hague conventions of 1899 and 1907. With Wilson and Taft no doubt in mind, he wrote in November that "a year and a half ago, the argument of these pacificists [sic] was that the Hague Conventions removed all necessity for preparedness on the part of nations, because they gave a chance for international public opinion to express itself, by whatever means necessary, with such force that brutal wars of aggression and brutal wrong-doing were things of the past." Roosevelt saw such views not just as naive but dangerous to the very existence of the nation.[35]

Although more and more Americans had come to similar realizations by the middle of 1915, the political system moved slowly. Everyone familiar with the army and navy and their current state of readiness saw the problems. They acknowledged that the military was not up to the challenge of modern war. By the middle of 1915, moreover, most no longer argued that Preparedness was unnecessary because the war in Europe would end soon. The majority saw that war might well become the near-permanent condition of Europe, and recognized that the war could easily draw the United States into it at almost any moment. A national consensus formed around the idea that the nation needed to make some major changes. The consensus, however, ended there, mostly because Preparedness raised a series of hot-button domestic political issues that most politicians sought to avoid. One involved the debate between a national army managed from Washington and a defense system based in the state militias. The professionals saw the militias as "volunteer forces composed of entirely untrained citizens commanded in great part by equally untrained officers," as Assistant Secretary of War Henry Breckenridge termed it. He had served seven years in the Kentucky National Guard and dismissed it out of hand as a serious military force for the modern age. He also worried that state governors could resist any attempt to deploy their Guard and militia units outside their own borders, setting off a potentially disastrous constitutional debate in the middle of a war.[36] Federal officials wanted to force the militias to come under the control of the army, either by changing existing law to clarify the president's role as commander in chief over the National Guard or by giving federal defense dollars only to those Guard and militia units that agreed to federal control.

Secretary of War Garrison led the charge against the Guard and militia. In August 1915 he wrote a memorandum titled "An Outline of Military Policy" to Wilson, arguing that the current system for raising an army was wholly inadequate to the military challenges of the modern world. He wanted Wilson to advocate a federally controlled reserve system that could remove the need for the National Guard entirely. He also urged the president to begin discussing these issues with the American people to make them fully aware of its complexity. Wilson demurred on both scores, leading to a rupture between the two men that they never overcame. Their disagreement also led Garrison to take his ideas a step further toward a comprehensive solution to American military problems.[37]

Wilson resisted Garrison's advice in large part because the issue of replacing the militia and National Guard in favor of a larger federal army was simply too controversial and politically damaging. The National Guard and militia system had powerful supporters, most notably the governors who served as commanders in chief of the Guard and militia units. A national reserve commanded by the president would have undercut their power, and thus they resisted any form of control from Washington. The governors had powerful allies in both houses of Congress. House Armed Services Committee chairman James Hay (D-Virginia) proved a forceful advocate for local control. A 1912 proposal to replace the National Guard and militia units with a Federal Reserve had failed in its earliest stages in the face of Hay's determined opposition. So, too, did the idea of tying federal defense dollars for the modernization of equipment to the states agreeing to more control from Washington. Any changes to the American defense system in 1915 would therefore have to take into account the power of local officials and politicians like Hay. They remained the most dominant voices on the subject, even if military professionals recognized the ridiculousness of fighting a war with forty-eight governors acting as commanders in chief. Localism remained as strong as ever. As a navy quip went, the perfect number of battleships would be forty-eight: one named for each state in the union.

Defense debates also raised questions about the concentration of wealth and power, a key issue of debate in the Progressive Era. Senator Albert Cummins (R-Iowa), who planned to run for president in 1916, worried that arms manufacturing for the war in Europe had already had a deleterious effect by increasing the wealth of industrialists in the East. He testified in Congress in late 1915 that American companies had made $161,964,276 on arms from the start of the war to November 1915. Existing war contracts called for $432,056,500 more in profits, a sum Cummins called "appalling" for a neutral nation claiming that it only wanted to help end the war. Cummins noted that DuPont stock had risen from 58.5 cents a share at the start of the war to $1.04 a share by mid-1915. Westinghouse stock, too, had risen sharply, proving that the war in Europe was undermining economic equality (and therefore democracy) at home.[38]

Such arguments found supporters among labor leaders and socialists, most of whom had little problem with Preparedness per se but objected strenuously to a Preparedness system that would enrich the few at the expense of the many. Charles Edward Russell, as we've seen, surprised his socialist colleagues by speaking out strongly in favor of Preparedness in 1915, although Russell was careful to note his strenuous objections to private companies profiting from military contracts. He nevertheless argued that socialists in both Europe and the United States would suffer from the triumph of Prussian militarism. French and British socialists had come to the conclusion that they had to fight; American socialists should accept that possibility as well.[39] Similarly, the American Federation of Labor stated at its annual meeting in Bloomington, Illinois, in September 1915 that it opposed "peace at any price" and favored "Preparedness but not militarism."[40] Cummins and Russell wanted to build national factories for the manufacture of weapons so that there would be no private profit from war and the manufacture of armaments could become, as Cummins advocated, "exclusively a governmental function."[41]

The German press picked up on these tensions and tried to use them to stir up anti-American sentiment. In cartoons reprinted in the United States by *Literary Digest*, German newspapers lambasted what they called the American hypocrisy of making money from the war while simultaneously pronouncing a desire for peace. In a cartoon from the popular German magazine *Simplicissimus*, Uncle Sam is pictured selling war goods to a grim reaper. The caption, translated from the original German, reads, "Don't think for a moment, Mr. Death, that I wish only to make money. I sell you these things only because they will bring peace to the world." A cartoon from a newspaper in Stuttgart showed "Pious Uncle Sam as the Angel of Peace" worshipping a god called "Business."[42] Although these cartoons came from Germany, they reflected the discomfort many Americans felt about the money that they were making from the war. The financial aspects of Preparedness therefore exacerbated already bitter debates that had long characterized the Progressive Era, including over the balance between urban and rural America, as well as the fears of the concentration of wealth that William Jennings Bryan had popularized, most notably in his famous 1896 "Cross of Gold" speech in which he had used biblical imagery to argue that the fight against the concentration of wealth was "a cause as holy as the cause of liberty, the cause of humanity."[43] To alleviate these fears, US Steel talked of investing the bulk of its promised $100 million in the Midwest and South, in order to develop industry there and spread the wealth nationwide. Opponents interpreted the offer less as an act of largesse from the captains of industry and more as an attempt by industrialists to extend their reach into a predominately rural region.

Thus debates about Preparedness went far beyond questions about the need to defend the country's interests and values. On the need to be ready should the war come to America, people generally agreed. But working out the details further roiled an American political system already deeply riven by partisanship and expecting a close presidential election in 1916. Any argument for expanding the size of the army, moreover, led to the inevitable question of what that army might actually do with its new power. Few Americans in 1915 wanted it to go to Europe and fight in the trenches, which the Chicago *Day Book* depicted in March as a "stream of dead."[44] Yet an equally small number seems to have been genuinely concerned that the army might soon have to fight the Germans on the streets of New York, Pittsburgh, or Cincinnati. Most did not see the idea of increasing the army's size as giving in to the militarism of Europe or agree with Bryan's call for America to abandon all of its weapons programs and rely instead on the "Gospel of the Sermon on the Mount." The New York *World* admired Bryan's dedication to his pacifist cause, but noted that he increasingly spoke only for "certain backwoods Congressmen" who knew nothing of world affairs. "Theirs is the stupidity that the gods themselves battle against in vain."[45]

Increases to the navy's budget occasioned less rancorous debate than increases to the army did. Navies serve a more obviously defensive role, protecting the nation's coast lines, port cities, and overseas commerce. Constructing and outfitting ships, moreover, produced jobs for congressional districts, making shipbuilding an often popular and profitable way for politicians to stand up for defense. Ships were also out of sight and out of mind for Americans living away from the coasts, even if most were aware of their importance. The opening of the Panama Canal gave Americans a further reason to favor increasing the size of the navy. Thus did discussions of enormous naval appropriations bills begin to make the rounds in Washington with little controversy. By the end of 1915 estimates of projected expenditures as high as $500 million for ships and the sailors to man them were floating around the capital. So, too, were plans to invest millions more into a new ring of forts to protect the nation's harbors.[46]

But finding the money to pay for a substantial increase in the country's armed forces was going to prove a challenge. The war had led to a drop in tariff revenue from Europe. That may have been good news for DuPont and Westinghouse, but it was bad news for the United States Treasury. The War and Navy departments had also made major commitments to boost the fortifications of Hawaii, the Philippines, and the newly opened Panama Canal Zone. These investments would cost a great deal of money without materially helping to address any of the challenges raised by the war in Europe. Increasing taxes, even on corporations making money from war contracts, threatened to provoke nasty debates that few congressmen, even those who publicly favored Preparedness, wanted to refight.

The American people did not necessarily want to dig too deeply into their own pockets to pay for the very defense that they demanded. The government had to find new ways to raise money, import duties having fallen sharply since 1914 and corporations resisting a tax on war profits. In late 1915, Treasury Secretary William Gibbs McAdoo estimated that defense expenditures would require $112 million in new individual tax revenue in the next federal budget. He proposed to find the money with taxes that he promised would be "widely diffused and scarcely felt" including a new tax on gasoline and a reduction of the income exemption for the new income tax from $3,000 to $2,000 for individuals and $4,000 to $3,000 for families.[47] His plan attracted few supporters, despite the fact that many observers saw $112 million as far too little to meet the nation's defense needs.

Whatever their rhetoric, politicians were far from consistent in their support for Preparedness. When members of Congress discussed Preparedness, they mostly spoke either of ways to involve their district in any federal spending largesse or in terms of small measures rather than major ones. Speaker of the House Champ Clark, a Democrat from Missouri, advocated Preparedness in theory, but throughout 1915 he only supported minor reforms, such as calling for doubling the size of the United States Military Academy at West Point and introducing more military instruction into public schools. He did so, however, at prominent ceremonies such as the one that welcomed a touring Liberty Bell to San Francisco. Clark, a former presidential candidate, argued that Preparedness should have as its only aim preventing war from coming to America.[48] Like Clark, most politicians were content to trumpet platitudes about Preparedness without putting money where their

mouths were. Others criticized Preparedness in public while simultaneously supporting bills that would bring money to their own districts.

Given that the government was proving too sclerotic to take
Preparedness seriously, some organizations tried to take matters into
their own hands. Self-styled patriotic groups like one calling itself the
American Legion began to compile a list of the names and addresses of
volunteers so that men of military age could be quickly enrolled in a
future national emergency.[49] Theodore Roosevelt and General Leonard
Wood went a step further and supported the creation of voluntary
camps at which men could learn the basics of military service.
Approximately 160 men had volunteered for such camps in 1913, orga-
nized at Gettysburg in conjunction with the fiftieth anniversary com-
memorations of that battle. Roosevelt and Wood saw the Gettysburg
camps as a model for voluntary officer training and citizenship camps.
Other public figures saw it as an alternative to the unpleasant option of
introducing conscription, but only if the camps could be sustained at a
much higher level of participation. Four camps opened in the summer
of 1914 and trained seven hundred young men, almost all of them college students. Congress, however, failed to see the value in the camps
and refused to authorize money to help them expand. The War
Department largely dismissed them as well, seeing them as little better
than summer camps for rich boys. Nevertheless, what became known as
the Plattsburg Movement after the town in New York that hosted the
most prominent camps attracted 3,400 volunteers nationwide in 1915
and 16,639 in 1916.[50] Roosevelt himself spoke at the opening of the
camp session in summer 1915 and while acknowledging that it was a
small step, he argued that the movement would at the very least shame
Wilson into taking the issue of Preparedness more seriously.

Most of the men who volunteered came from elite private schools in
the East and saw themselves as America's future leaders. Many expressed
youthful idealism about the cause. One young man, an aspiring New
York journalist named Raymond Chamberlain, noted that his "wrath
rose at the outrages of Germany upon the world, upon our country,
upon our people." Those sentiments motivated him and his friends to
sign up for the camps. Recalling the military service of his ancestors in
the American Revolution and the Civil War, he went to Plattsburg and
later enlisted in the 26th Division in New England.[51] Another Plattsburg

veteran, a Yale football player whose attitudes were fairly representative of the participants, later recalled that for the men of his generation, in 1914 "our conceptions [of the war] were limited and our perspectives dreadfully short." By the fall of 1915, however, he and his friends realized "how much closer we were coming to it and how directly our own personal lives might be influenced and touched by the war." He volunteered both for a Yale Naval Aviation Unit training program and a thirty-day officers training course at a "citizens camp" in Monterey, California.[52]

Although mostly symbolic, these efforts seemed to show that voluntarism could play a key role in Preparedness, thus reducing the need to rely on the federal and state governments. Two-thirds of college and university presidents as well as an overwhelming majority of newspaper editors supported an increase in voluntary military training for (male) college students on the Plattsburg model. Volunteer groups such as the Navy League grew quickly, in this case to over eleven thousand members. By June 1915 the National Security League had chapters in twenty-five states and that month hosted a national meeting at the Astoria Hotel in New York.[53] Private groups such as these petitioned the federal government to take Preparedness more seriously and also looked for ways to assist in the national defense. One aviation specialist, frustrated with the government's sluggishness in providing the army and navy with airplanes, proposed buying them by public subscription, just as the French, German, and Ottoman governments had before the war. He helped the New York National Guard buy a Curtiss seaplane for $7,500 by public subscription with only one person donating more than $100.[54]

Businessmen such as Powell Evans saw industry as the key to Preparedness. A survey of 650 corporations with 100 or more employees conducted at the end of 1915 showed all but 5 willing to pay half or all of an employee's salary if he undertook voluntary military training.[55] Business leaders argued that American industry could build the weapons and fortifications the nation needed with minimal commitment from the federal or state governments, although they might require a relaxation of railroad regulations and increases in railroad rates in return for their patriotic service. Henry Joy, president of Packard Motor Company, also argued for letting industry take the lead. In an open letter criticizing his rival Henry Ford's isolationism, Joy wrote that given that the government had shown itself incapable of the task of Preparedness, industry had to take over, because "the ocean, instead of a barrier of defense, is the highway open to the invader."[56]

Joy, not Ford, represented the tone of American industrial views in 1915. In December, Ford hired a ship, the *Oscar II*, to go to Europe on a peace mission that he claimed could have the "boys in the trenches out of their holes and shaking hands with each other in pledges of never-ending peace" by Christmas. He told reporters that he and other noted American pacifists could convince the European powers to negotiate a speedy end to the war or, failing that, that he himself could inspire the troops to go on a kind of strike against their own nations. When asked how he would accomplish his goals, Ford told a reporter, "I can't tell you just how."[57] The trip met with ridicule and derision from the start. Wilson met personally with Ford but refused to lend his support to a mission he thought unlikely to accomplish anything constructive. Prominent Americans such as Thomas Edison, Jane Addams, and William Jennings Bryan also turned down Ford's invitation. The ship nevertheless left New York harbor with all the fanfare Ford and his publicists could muster. Almost as if to symbolize the futility of the mission, Ford caught influenza in Norway and took another ship quietly home from Europe, having spent $500,000 on his peace mission only to be ridiculed in the press. The episode, said one critic, provided nothing more than a "comic interlude" for the belligerents and an embarrassment for the United States.[58]

Americans dismissed Ford's attempt as crackpot because by the end of 1915 they had given up hope on Europeans reaching a compromise peace, with or without American help. The Chicago *Tribune*, in an editorial republished nationwide, called Ford's ship "The Good Ship Nutty" and Ford himself a multimillionaire anarchist, provoking a libel lawsuit from Ford that only made him seem more out of touch with the views of mainstream America.[59] The chancellor of Syracuse University, for example, called Ford's mission "grotesque" and said that it would "accomplish nothing but the ridicule of our country."[60] Still, despite this belittling of Ford's effort, the notion of private citizens rather than the government taking charge of the nation's destiny had widespread appeal. Pittsburgh-based physician Franklin Martin and Chicago-based physician Frank Simpson joined with the legendary Charles H. Mayo and twenty-five other notable medical specialists to form the Committee of American Physicians for Medical Preparedness. They worked to create a chapter in all forty-eight states and made connections to senior leaders in both the War and Navy departments. A Council on National Defense also formed to coordinate war-related scientific work. The Council had government representatives, but the real work was done by private citizens like financier Bernard Baruch, Sears chairman Julius Rosenwald, and Howard Coffin, an engineer from Michigan known as the "Father of Standardization." Thomas Edison had already helped to form the Naval Consulting Board to put into operation his grand plan, announced in the New York *Times Magazine* just weeks after the *Lusitania* incident, to develop national laboratories, stockpile modern weapons, and train young men in modern science and engineering techniques.[61]

Corporations responded by advertising their commitment to Preparedness as a public good. Bell Telephone ran an advertisement titled "We Are Prepared" in which Paul Revere making his famous midnight ride appears in one corner. The rest of the ad is dominated by a soldier on the telephone and a map on the wall behind him showing the national network of telephone lines that Bell owned and operated. The text reads, in part, "In its wonderful preparedness to inform its citizens of a national need, the United States stands alone and unequaled." The message was clear: Bell was the twentieth-century version of Revere, warning people from coast to coast of danger and, as the soldier symbolized, providing the nerve center for the military so that it could respond to any crisis.[62]

Universities, too, began to organize. In October 1915, Columbia's faculty held a general assembly to discuss "plans for the more effective organization and conduct of research in professional subjects" of interest to national defense.[63] A second assembly followed a few months later to propose ways to organize faculty research and align it with the Preparedness needs of the nation. Students and alumni participated as well, inviting Preparedness advocate General Leonard Wood to campus and voting unanimously to support Columbia students participating in the Plattsburg Movement. Wood and New York mayor John Mitchel drew "such enthusiastic cheering" from the students during their pro-Preparedness speeches that they could not speak for several minutes while waiting for the students to quiet down. The dean of the University of Michigan's graduate school wrote in a New York *Times* editorial that

Preparedness had become "the great question of the hour" on American campuses. He argued that Michigan, like the vast majority of universities and colleges nationwide, had come to see the need for military training and research support to the government "however much the need of preparation may be regretted, whatever shock and disappointment the people's better ideals have to suffer in these days of the great war abroad." Harvard students responded by voting in a special campus poll overwhelmingly in support of the voluntary military training of men on campus. Before the *Lusitania*, a group of Columbia students had opposed the nation arming with the words "War is the plaything of kings and the plaything of dynasties." Now, like students everywhere, they were arguing that preparing for it was patriotism itself.[64]

By the end of 1915, Preparedness had become much more than a watchword. It had become a way of life. One New York newspaper surveyed church sermons at Thanksgiving as part of an annual feature that explored what Americans were giving thanks for at the holiday. It found that churches were "well filled" nationwide as war fears grew. Sermons featured a "strong note of patriotism and pride of country together with emphasis on the necessity for adequate military preparedness." One minister likened Preparedness to taking out a fire insurance policy; just as insurance does not invite fire, he preached, neither does Preparedness invite war. Another compared Preparedness to making sure that the locks on the front door are in good order.[65] Insurance became a key metaphor for Preparedness; just as the average American spent 3.5 percent of his income on insurance, one advocate argued, so, too, should the country spend that same amount of its national wealth on its defense.[66] Building a larger army and navy would protect the country by deterring attacks and forcing the world's great powers to take American interests seriously. A former treasury secretary in the McKinley and Roosevelt administrations who called for two hundred thousand men in the active corps and another three million in a reserve corps wanted Americans to think of support for Preparedness like nurturing a porcupine, "a decent, law abiding porcupine, minding our own business, with not one cent for an attack on our neighbors, but millions of keenly barbed quills bristling for defense." The porcupine's quills, he noted, could protect it from German dachshunds, French poodles, English bulldogs, and Siberian bloodhounds alike.[67]

With a presidential election coming in 1916, and with the president and secretary of war at odds on the issue, Preparedness promised to be one of the key topics. So did Anti-Hyphenism, the second topic of Dickinson's speech evoked at the start of this chapter and a subject no less thorny. Anti-Hyphenism had some of its roots in nineteenth-century Nativism. At their most simplistic, Nativists divided the nation, as writer Arthur Gleason did, into a "historic America"—one that intuitively understood the debt it owed to democratic France and Great Britain—and "the various new Americas...a people of mixed blood [and] divergent ideals" who did not share the country's core value system. Gleason and other Nativists argued that successive waves of immigration from southern and eastern Europe had weakened the nation's moral fiber and "drown[ed] out the sharply defined character" of the American people.[68] Now in a time of existential crisis, Gleason and others argued, immigrants had to accept the values and norms of the wider society. They had, in effect, to become much more American and much less European. Many of the most dedicated Preparedness advocates also urged immigrants to assimilate more quickly, despite their rhetoric that what mattered most was behavior and loyalty, not place of origin.[69] To nativists like Gleason, "American" values included supporting France and Great Britain, with whom the country shared basic values, in their struggle against autocratic Germany and Austria-Hungary. That millions of immigrants to the United States in the decades before the war had come from those two states only seemed to make the problem more acute. The Irish, too, posed a potential problem by virtue of their Catholicism and their avowed mistrust of England. Nativists thus identified the "hyphenated American" as a potential threat to the nation in a time of crisis.

Despite their differences on almost every other issue, Wilson and Roosevelt agreed on the need to stamp out Hyphenism and press for what soon came to be known as "100% Americanism." In the eyes of Nativists, the issue fundamentally turned on where an individual placed his or her primary loyalty. Those espousing loyalty to the United States first and foremost were welcome wherever they had been born. Those who would not or who espoused socialist political ideals remained under a cloud of suspicion. Roosevelt delivered a widely publicized Columbus Day 1915 speech in which he revealed the essence of the Nativist views:

"The one absolutely certain way of bringing this nation to ruin, of preventing all possibility of its continuing to be a nation at all," he argued, "would be to permit it to become a tangle of squabbling nationalities, an intricate knot of German-Americans, Irish-Americans, English-Americans, French-Americans, Scandinavian-Americans or Italian-Americans, each preserving its separate nationality, each at heart feeling more sympathy with Europeans of that nationality, than with the other citizens of the American Republic." Simultaneously embracing and dismissing Nativism, he concluded, "There is no such thing as a hyphenated American who is a good American. The only man who is a good American is the man who is an American and nothing else."[70] Wilson, too, made the campaign against hyphenated Americans a central theme of his 1915 speeches, picking up where he had left off in the dedication of the memorial to John Barry in 1914.

For most Americans, the Anti-Hyphen campaign seemed just another episode in the messy and combative political process, as both Wilson and Roosevelt tried to equate patriotism with their own views of ethnicity, and as both parties competed for the core voting constituency of "unhyphenated" and "native-born" Americans. There was a strong element of fear and hypocrisy in the campaign. The same people Wilson tarred as hyphenated noted that the president himself spoke with pride about his own Scotch-Irish roots to show the inherent absurdity of the Anti-Hyphen campaign itself. The message, as everyone paying attention could see, was aimed predominately at Catholics and Jews. More specifically, it was aimed at those Catholics and Jews who had adopted "un-American" attitudes like Socialism, an ideology that both Roosevelt and Wilson despised. Those, like Hugo Münsterberg, who lived in the United States without ever seeking American citizenship also came in for suspicion.

The Anti-Hyphen campaign could be as vituperative as it was unnecessary given the unquestioned loyalty of the overwhelming majority of immigrants and their children. As both Wilson and Roosevelt recognized, most Americans, including most German-Americans, saw the nation's plight in the same general way that Nativists did. Still, the *Lusitania* incident and the campaign of sabotage in 1915 put Anti-Hyphenism at center stage in American discourse. At its more benign, the debate could demonstrate how far some groups and people had come in the traditional

American processes of assimilation and acculturation. The mere fact of immigration proved that Europeans had turned away from the hatreds of the Old World toward the peaceful sensibilities of the New. Roosevelt notably delivered his Columbus Day speech to the largely Catholic Knights of Columbus annual meeting at Carnegie Hall.[71] Rather than accuse them of a lack of patriotism, Roosevelt praised their willingness to put their American identity ahead of their Italian or Irish one. The Knights greeted his speech with thunderous applause because it confirmed in their own minds that they, too, had now become a central part of the mainstream by embracing their American identity in a time of national crisis.

Part of the popularity of Anti-Hyphenism among politicians was pure campaign rhetoric, and most knew it. The Harrisburg *Telegraph* praised the ideas and the rhetoric in Roosevelt's speech, although the editors did not see the reason for it in the first place. "We do not believe there is any dangerous proportion of potential traitors in this country," the paper noted. The editors took Roosevelt's speech as an occasion to urge politicians like Roosevelt and Wilson to stop playing "for the Irish Vote or the Italian Vote or the German Vote" because such categories no longer existed. Politicians aiming for cheap votes "have manufactured most of the hyphens" that continued to fall away naturally as the nation came to face the international crisis "with one voice."[72] The New York *Herald* similarly noted—with an unfortunate if intentioned choice of words—that the hyphen in "German-American" was "submarined with the *Lusitania*," and that the Germans in America stood side by side with their fellow Americans.[73] Roosevelt, too, recognized the difference. He introduced German-American newspaper publisher Edward Rumely to Charles Evans Hughes as "one of the unhyphenated Americans of German descent who is an American through and through." The distinction that Nativists drew thus had far less to do with national origin than political outlook and loyalty to the nation in a time of crisis.[74]

The notion of the war as fusing together Americans of varied backgrounds in the face of a common threat appeared throughout 1915 far more often than fears that the war would sow disloyalty or tear America apart along ethnic lines. In November, New York politician W. Bourke Cockran delivered a lecture on the war at the cavernous Chicago Coliseum to a house "packed to the roof" with people of all faiths and backgrounds. A Jewish judge named Samuel Alschuler introduced the Catholic Cockran (born in County Sligo, Ireland) to his mostly Protestant audience. Cockran took the occasion to remark that "We are here . . . not abating in any degree the fervor of our religious convictions, but remembering only that we are all Americans."[75] The key in this time of crisis, he told his multiethnic audience, was to focus on similarity not difference, even as each group retained the right to maintain elements of its own distinctive culture. The war therefore seemed to prove that the American experiment was working.

The lone major exception to this successful experiment—this example to the world—of course involved the African-American community. African-American leaders were sensitive to the perception among Nativists and even among many mainstream Americans that blacks stood outside the national consensus or would not stand with America. Community leaders therefore focused on the military service of African-Americans in past conflicts and the loyalty of the African-American community in times of national emergency. Thus in July 1915 did an African-American newspaper, the St. Paul *Appeal*, argue against the use of hyphenated terms like "Negro-American" or "Black-American." In an editorial titled "Eliminating the Hyphen," the newspaper wrote in terms similar to that of other communities that "colored citizens are native Americans with several generations of American ancestors and there is absolutely no reason why they should be differentiated in any way from any other citizen, native or naturalized. It is well to erase the hyphen." The editorial featured a picture of an American flag flying in a breeze.[76]

The German-American community also distanced itself from the hyphen. Charles Nagel, Taft's German-educated former secretary of commerce and labor, pled the case for neutrality and loyalty in an address to the Deutsche Gesellschaft of St. Louis. He argued against the use of the hyphen, saying that there was "just one platform upon which all the principles and traditions of all the races here represented must be assembled, and from which must be announced every rule for our guidance. That is the platform of the United States." Nagel argued for a complete freedom of trade for industrialists and farmers alike as well as a continued neutrality on all matters related to the war. In other words, he stood for the same goals that most mainstream American leaders sought in 1915.[77]

The American Jewish community, as reflected in an editorial from the Philadelphia-based *Jewish Exponent*, made a similar case, arguing that "the overwhelming majority of the people of foreign birth now in the United States would be loyal to the land of their adoption" in the event of any future crisis. "Their descendants would be almost unanimously so, no matter which nation happened to provoke the war." Turning specifically to the views of American Jews, the paper argued that they "stand for the nation that has granted to them and to all its people the blessings of civil and religious liberty."[78]

Members of the American elite also saw the trend. The historian William Roscoe Thayer, who wrote increasingly vicious screeds against Germany in 1914 and 1915, nonetheless took great pains to separate Germans in Europe from those Americans of German ancestry living peacefully in the United States. "When the show-down comes," he wrote in a book published in March 1916, "there will be a tragic surprise for those who have been banking on the disloyalty of any large number of persons in the United States." Taking note of the sabotage campaign in 1915, he noted that "the paid agents of the Kaiser do not represent the great body of German immigration." Thayer went further still, arguing that the war would lead to an acceleration of acculturation within the German-American community whether or not the country eventually fought in the war. "The hyphens will fall," he predicted and there would be "no mongrel citizenship to be used as a mask for treason."[79] The marked increase in German nationals seeking American citizenship in 1915 supported his case.

As with the issue of Preparedness, the Anti-Hyphen message was therefore not so much an anti-immigrant message as a political one. As the election year of 1916 was dawning, Americans from across the political and social spectrums had recognized that what mattered was less a place of birth than a willingness to come together with one voice should war come to the United States from any direction. Acculturation and the removal of the hyphen from public discourse did not mean that immigrant communities abandoned their traditional identities. It did, however, mean that they refused to accept any contradiction between their ethnic identity and their "American" one when it came to matters of national security.

Again as with the Preparedness campaign, the Anti-Hyphen campaign also coincided with a general sense of fear and anxiety about the future that had grown more pronounced in popular culture throughout 1915. *Scientific American* editor John Bernard Walker's popular novel *America Fallen!* depicted an Allied victory over Germany, which, thus constrained in Europe, decides to take over Latin America. Dismissing "this curious fiction which has come to be known as the Monroe Doctrine" as just another scrap of paper, the kaiser's navy then defeats the United States Navy, paving the way for the German Army to plunder a defenseless America and impose a $15 billion indemnity with which to pay off Germany's own indemnity to France and Britain. The Germans also collect $5 billion in gold by ransoming New York City. No less a military luminary than Admiral George Dewey, the hero of the Battle of Manila Bay in 1898, praised the book, which ended, "And that was how it came about that the United States, the wealthiest and . . . potentially the most powerful country on earth found itself, in the space of two eventful weeks, held fast in the mailed fist of a foreign foe."[80]

H. Irving Hancock's *At the Defense of Pittsburgh* presented the problem of Preparedness in fairly typical terms. In the book, aimed largely at a young adult readership, American soldiers prepare to repulse a German bayonet charge on American soil. One young man says to his comrade, "We have the satisfaction, at least, of knowing that we didn't start this one." His friend sharply retorts, "Oh, yes, we did, and in the most foolish and stupid fashion. We kept our country in such a weak military state that we fairly invited any ambitious nation to come here and conquer us. If we had had a real army a year ago no nation would have undertaken the job that the Germans are doing tonight."[81] These fears were not limited to popular culture. Thayer wrote that the Germans would do to New York, Boston, and Philadelphia what they had already done to Belgium. In language hardly more temperate than the teenage pulp fiction of H. Irving Hancock, Thayer wrote, "The most honored men of these cities will be taken as hostages, abused and murdered as if they were Belgian notables, and the women—let Belgium teach what will be their fate."[82]

As Charles Eliot noted, Americans did not seek war themselves, but for a number of reasons, including political ones, they had moved from neutrality to "heartily desire the success of the Allies, and the decisive defeat of Germany, Austria-Hungary, and Turkey." German atrocities in Belgium and the sinking of the *Lusitania* had sapped whatever sympathies most

Americans had felt for Germany in 1914.[83] Americans took heart from Italy's decision in May 1915 to join the Allies and therefore "the forces of civilization and justice." Writer H. Nelson Gay noted that as a result of Italy's decision "I have begun to feel again as if life might after all be worth living" as the world's neutrals began to line up against Germany. But even he did not argue for the United States to enter the war. He argued instead for breaking off diplomatic relations with Germany in the hopes of inspiring the European neutrals to join with the Allies. To most Americans, the war still remained someone else's to fight.[84]

A great change had nonetheless come over the country in the course of 1915. At the start of the year, "I Didn't Raise My Boy to Be a Soldier" had become a hit song:

> Let nations arbitrate their future troubles,
> It's time to lay the sword and gun away.
> There'd be no war today,
> If mothers all would say,
> "I didn't raise my boy to be a soldier."

But by the end of the year the national mood had shifted. Even the song's writer then claimed that he did not mean for the song to be an indictment of American preparation for war. Instead, he said, he had really meant it as an attack on German militarism. In a letter to a friend in November, Roosevelt noted the statement with some considerable satisfaction, but still sat confounded by the notion of fighting militarism with a song "meant to convert the hearts of German women and other women living in military despotisms to make them somehow or other, by song or otherwise, in manner unspecified, forthwith to procure the abandonment of militarism by the Kaiser and others."[85] Whatever its true meaning, the point is that by the end of 1915, the song no longer stood as an anthem of pacifism and idealism, but a symbol of the innocence that had so quickly faded in a few short months. However much American mothers (and fathers) still did not want to see their boys become soldiers, they needed an army to protect their families, and they knew that the soldiers in it would be the sons of mothers in their own communities.

6

Election Year Politics and National Defense
An Insoluble Dilemma

THE PRESIDENTIAL ELECTION OF 1916 revealed many of the uncertainties, ambiguities, and tensions that Americans felt toward the war in Europe, which was dragging into its third year. Although they tried to go on as normal and not make the war a priority as they decided on their next president, issues of war and defense continued to intrude into the political process. The two presidential candidates, reflecting the general mood, argued for staying out of the war in Europe for as long as possible while still using American power to help those suffering and bring the warring powers to peace. As the American people had also done, however, they had come to the conclusion that the United States no longer fully controlled its own fate. However much they preferred not to talk about it in 1916, the war, and the possibility of direct American involvement in it, was becoming ever more difficult to ignore.

Although political observers expected the presidential election of 1916 to be close, few thought that it would feature the high drama of the election of 1912. In that year, Theodore Roosevelt had shaken up the political system by forming a third party, the Progressive or Bull Moose Party. The ensuing split in the Republican vote had allowed Woodrow Wilson to build on the Democratic Party's base in the South and rural West, benefit from the division of the Republican vote in a few key contested states, and win an election he otherwise would not have. Roosevelt had pledged to come back to the Republican fold in 1916, so there would be no split in the party this time. With the Republicans reunified, and given the relatively poor showing by Democrats in the midterm election year of 1914, the incumbent Wilson appeared to be at risk of losing the White House in 1916.[1]

Both parties tried to allot the war in Europe a secondary role in the campaign, which, only hitting its stride in earnest after the conventions in June, took place in the relatively calm period after the Sussex Pledge. Voters were therefore making up their minds about the presidential candidates at a time when entry into the war seemed more unlikely than it had in many months. Moreover, the two main candidates for president, Wilson and Republican Charles Evans Hughes, generally agreed that they would uphold American rights of travel and trade, but would not involve the country directly in the war if they did not need to do so. Both, in other words, hoped to hold to the status quo, assuming that Germany continued to abide by the Sussex Pledge and the war did not take a turn that directly threatened American interests. With broad general agreement on the status quo as the best (or, perhaps, the least bad) approach to the war, there was little ground on which the two candidates could hope to gain votes over one another when it came to policy toward what many Americans were still calling the European War. The lack of clear policy disagreement over the war in Europe pushed foreign affairs to the background in 1916, further highlighting the persistent tensions of neutrality.

Throughout the summer of 1916, American political candidates calmed their pro-British rhetoric, pushing European affairs even further into the background. Although anger at Britain never rose to the level of American anger at Germany, British brutality in suppressing the 1916 Easter Rising in Dublin sat uneasily with the American people, even among those who generally supported the Allied cause. Americans across the political spectrum compared the heavy-handed British treatment of Ireland to Germany's atrocities in Belgium, and the summary execution of Irish rebels to the German execution of the British nurse Edith Cavell. British economic policy also continued to anger. Early in 1916 the British government had increased the number of firms it blacklisted as punishment for trading with Germany and added new items to the contraband list, including, most controversially, cotton. That action predictably drew fire from Southern politicians whose home districts depended on cotton exports. Senator M. Hoke Smith (D-Georgia), a former governor and secretary of the interior, led the charge against what he termed the "lawless" and "reckless" British contraband policy. He argued that the Germans were not using Southern cotton to pack munitions but for civilian pursuits only. Therefore, British contraband policy in his eyes was less about wartime exigency than about destroying American competition in anticipation of a postwar recovery for the British textiles industry. He also argued that the British ban on cotton sales had no precedent in history. Although neither argument had a basis in fact, Smith and other Southern senators wanted the United States to take a firmer line with the British over cotton sales. "Great Britain cannot continue the war without munitions from the United States. Great Britain cannot feed her population without foodstuffs from the United States and other neutral nations," Hoke thundered on the Senate floor. America, he argued, should therefore use its new economic power to force a change in British behavior. The nation should not suffer from what he called "indignities" from the British government and should apply the same forceful diplomacy to the British as it had to the Germans.[2]

Notwithstanding such anti-British sentiments in his own party, Wilson saw no reason to aggravate American disagreements with the British. Neither did the generally pro-British Republicans. The Southern states would vote overwhelmingly for Wilson regardless of his policy on British contraband, meaning that neither candidate could gain much on the issue.[3] The contraband on cotton therefore remained a regional issue largely kept alive by isolationist senators on the weaker wing of the Democratic Party in states unlikely to be close on election day. Moreover, several senior British officials, including Foreign Secretary Sir Edward Grey and Ambassador Sir Cecil Spring-Rice, urged their government to give in to the United States because they realized that, like it or not, Hoke Smith was right: the British could not win the war without the United States, which had, in a few short months, become the Allies' most important factory, banker, and food supplier. Britain simply could not treat it in the same manner it had before the war, and both sides knew it. In any case, except for the response to the Easter Rising,

American disagreements with Britain generally lacked the level of animosity that marked America's interactions with Germany. As the editors of *Current Opinion* argued, "The one [Great Britain] relates to property damage, the other [Germany] to a continuing menace to American lives."[4]

Issues of national defense briefly moved to center stage early in the year as the Preparedness discussions of 1915 became matters of political debate in 1916. In early February, Secretary of War Lindley Garrison and Assistant Secretary of War Henry Breckenridge both abruptly resigned their posts over the issue, making banner headlines.[5] Garrison and Wilson had never gotten along as well as a president and senior cabinet member should. Garrison did not hold Wilson in the exalted position that other members of his cabinet did, and he had grown impatient with Wilson's unwillingness to take the issue of the army's weakness as seriously as Garrison thought he should. He had begun to interrupt the president in cabinet meetings, leading Wilson to complain about Garrison in increasingly impolite terms to anyone within earshot.

The core of the disagreement between the two men revolved around Garrison's support for, and Wilson's opposition to, the Continental Army Plan. The most important aspect of that plan hinged on which body would provide the necessary reserves of manpower to supplement the regular standing army. Although almost everyone in the United States, outside William Jennings Bryan's isolationist circles and a few socialists, agreed that the United States Army was too small to meet the security needs of 1916, there was little consensus on how best to grow it without running political or financial risks.

Garrison and Wilson at least agreed on their shared desire to avoid the extreme measures of universal military training (UMT) and mass conscription that Roosevelt, Elihu Root, and many conservatives were then advocating. Not only did Garrison argue that UMT sat at odds with American traditions, he knew that it lacked the necessary support in Congress and among the American people more generally. He also rejected a detailed Army War College study that proposed a massive force of 574,000 Regulars, 500,000 Reserves, and 60,000 more men in a Harbor Defense Force, for a grand total of approximately 1,134,000 soldiers, an army far too large for either the American people to accept or Congress to fund.[6] That left just two options for providing manpower

Lieut. Col. Theo. Roosevelt and Richard Harding Davis.
Copyright 1898 by Strohmeyer & Wyman.

Theodore Roosevelt (left) and Richard Harding Davis together on Army maneu-vers. Davis was one of America's most trusted war correspondents, having covered virtually every global conflict of his age. He became an important anti-German voice in 1914.

Davis saw the German destruction of the Belgian university town of Louvain with his own eyes. He, like most Americans, saw Louvain as evidence of terrible war crimes committed by a dangerous German regime.

Like Davis, "The American Agatha Christie," Mary Roberts Rinehart, went to cover the war as a staunch neutral but soon became pro-Allied. She and Davis were both skeptical of British media accounts of German atrocities.

Heavyweight boxing champion Jack Johnson was in Europe when the war began. He arrived in Paris to an ecstatic greeting because of his promise to donate his vehicles to the French Army.

Harvard's Danzig-born Hugo Münsterberg was one of Germany's most eloquent defenders. But his views were out of step with those of Americans, even those of German descent.

This cartoon from mid-1915 shows the difficult position the war had created for the United States. It also shows that Europe was not the country's only worry.

This 1915 article reveals a growing interest in bolstering the nation's military, although it pledges to do so for defensive reasons only. Such ideas became commonplace in the United States in 1915 and 1916, although political wrangling often kept such ideas from becoming reality.

The suffering of the victims of the *Lusitania* evoked deep sympathy from the American people. Few Americans accepted any of Germany's justifications for the sinking.

Fred Spear designed this famous poster in June 1915. It reflected American anger at the German sinking of the *Lusitania* and also offered Americans a means of acting on that anger.

American volunteer pilots flying with the French became great heroes on both sides of the Atlantic. Tens of thousands of Americans served in the Canadian, British, and French armies before American entry.

Thousands more Americans came to Europe as volunteers. Here a daughter of former president Grover Cleveland and a granddaughter of former president Ulysses Grant care for blinded French soldiers.

Americans linked their problems in Mexico with Germany. Pancho Villa (here drawn as a snake) had bragged about the help he received from Berlin, and German spies were known to be active there.

Reporters kept Americans apprised of the human costs of the war in Europe. Most guessed that European armies were underestimating their casualties in order to maintain morale at home.

By early 1917 the war was less about Europe than about America itself. Following the release of the Zimmermann Telegram, these fears grew. Here the Kaiser is carving the country up to give some to Mexico and some to Japan in order to obtain their help.

Jewish-American singer Nora Bayes (née Eleanor Goldberg) sang one of the popular versions of "Over There." American Jews had undergone a remarkable transformation about the war since 1914.

in the numbers that Garrison believed the nation needed: relying on the state-based National Guard or creating a pool of men in a national reserve commanded, controlled, and equipped by the regulars in Washington.[7]

Garrison had come to the final and incontrovertible conclusion that to base the nation's security on the National Guard meant risking defeat on the battlefield, either in Europe or in North America itself. The state National Guards and militias, which Garrison called "utterly futile" and "the height of folly," had to be replaced if the United States wanted to be in a position to defend itself amid the many real and present dangers of the modern world.[8] The Republican-leaning Des Moines *Register* agreed, calling the National Guard "an 18th century idea fit for a pioneer country that had never heard of railroads, steamships, or percussion caps." Along the same lines, a Boston newspaper concluded that continuing to rely on the National Guard would mean defending America with "a thoroughly imaginary army, and leave us in the same helpless condition we are in now."[9] In the National Guard's place Garrison wanted a federal military composed of five hundred thousand Regulars and Reservists commanded and trained by officers answerable only to officials in Washington and completely out from under the control of the state governors.

Wilson proved unwilling to go that far, especially in an election year. He offered as a compromise an increase in the size of the regular army from just over 100,000 men to almost 186,000 men. He also proposed gradually increasing the size of the National Guard from 130,000 men to over 425,000 to create a reserve force. Under his plan, National Guardsmen would take a dual oath, to both their state governor and to the United States Constitution, thus eliminating the problem of National Guard units raising legal objections to serving outside their states. The National Guard would also agree to standardize its equipment with that of the regular army and more than triple the number of mandatory training days for its personnel.[10]

Wilson saw the compromise as a way to strengthen the National Guard and make it subject to control from Washington without challenging the powerful local forces that wanted to see the National Guard remain the backbone of the nation's defense. They included those who argued that National Guardsmen served the nation better because, in the words of one Iowa newspaper, they "live in the locality from which the men come and the locality where they must live after the war is over." In other words, being tied to the community would act as a check on military leaders overstepping their authority, knowing as they did that they had to return home after the war and face those same men in postwar civilian life. Local officers "know your boys and your boys know them," the Iowa editors argued, leading to a fairer, more democratic, and more egalitarian system for military service. Such people therefore saw Garrison's plan as nothing less than an attempt to destroy that traditional locally based system while pushing "a more or less transparent plan for a continental army on to an unsuspecting public." The author of the Iowa editorial did not even want regular army officers involved in training National Guard units. The two systems, the newspaper argued, should be utterly separate, although to Garrison's frustration, that desire for separation did not stop governors from demanding precious federal defense dollars in order to purchase expensive new equipment.[11]

This debate between central and local authority has a long history in the United States, dating back to an eighteenth-century debate between ideological groups later termed radical and moderate Whigs. The radicals had long seen the creation of a strong central army as a potentially dictatorial tool of central authority in the tradition of a latter-day Oliver Cromwell or George III. Their intellectual descendants in 1916 tended to argue that national defense should be the primary responsibility of local militias, not a single military answerable to a small number of officials in Washington.[12] The Continental Army Plan, they argued, flew in the face of American values and traditions. A divided system of military power, by contrast, fit in with the series of checks and balances built into the American political system more generally.[13]

The radical Whigs of 1916 supported either keeping military power vested in the state-based National Guards or the formation of local militias on the Swiss model, with all able-bodied men serving equal terms of military service.[14] Although Garrison condemned volunteer militias as an idea "that has utterly failed in the past [and] which menaces our safety now," the notion had broad support, mostly from local officials and those who shared the radical Whig ideology.[15] Wisconsin's Republican governor, E. L. Philipp, for example, opposed the Continental Army Plan because of his fears that it would create "militarism in the sense that it has existed in

Europe." He, too, favored a Swiss-style militia, as did Michigan congressman James McLaughlin, although McLaughlin at least proposed that the militia abandon its role in breaking strikes in an effort to make service in the military more palatable to miners and factory workers.[16]

Race played a role in the opposition to the Continental Army Plan as well. One Southern-born general argued that any large federal reserve would have no option but to enlist tens of thousands of African-Americans in order to find volunteer soldiers in the numbers that Garrison and the Army War College plan sought. Whites, he argued, would then see the army not as a patriotic institution that represented its citizens, but as an un-American institution composed of noncitizens. Thus would America's armed forces disproportionately "be composed of negroes," who he argued lacked the capability to serve in the role.[17] Several critical Southern politicians came out against Garrison's plan early on, often citing the potential for racial discord as a key factor in their arguments. They included Virginia's James Hay, the traditional enemy of army reform plans, and Mississippi's James K. Vardaman, who, in the euphemistic language of Jim Crow, said that the Continental Army Plan would constitute "a betrayal of the Democratic Party and a capital crime against posterity."[18]

By contrast, the African-American press greeted the Continental Army Plan with enthusiasm, hoping that it would take power out of the hands of the notoriously racist Southern governors, all of whom had banned blacks from serving in the National Guard. Although Wilson himself was by no means enlightened on issues of race, African-Americans hoped that putting national defense in a federally controlled system might promote the African-American bid for political equality, especially if a future president decided to enlist men into the Federal Reserve without regard to race. As the Philadelphia *Tribune* argued: "The National Guard is needed in every Southern State to uphold the bastard principle that 'white men can do no wrong and black men can do no right.'"[19] In some states in the North and Midwest, where men of all races served in the National Guard, the paper contended, it served the interests of the people, not one class or race alone. By taking power out of the hands of the National Guard, the Continental Army Plan could do the same for the entire American military. Supporters of military service under a centralized federal system contended that the

Continental Army Plan would benefit Americans of all races. As another African-American newspaper, the Chicago *Defender*, argued, under the federal system, the South would have to accept "the return of the [black] race to arms so that this group of people will be ready" to play a role in national defense in the future just as it always had in the past. Military training, the newspaper noted, would have the side benefit of providing discipline, physical fitness, and "stronger manhood" in those who served.[20]

Such qualities might have been exactly what opponents of federal military service for African-Americans most feared. They were not, of course, limited to the South. A New York State district court judge called plans to enlist African-Americans into the federal army in large numbers an "infamous suggestion." He made the self-serving and circular argument that because African-Americans were not full voting citizens in the sense that white Americans were, using them to fight the nation's wars would break the critical linkage between citizenship and military service. Because "the duty of military service must be co-extensive with the right to vote," arming African-Americans would amount to "hiring others to fight" the nation's wars. Because, in his view, the nation was not ready to give African-Americans the right to vote on par with whites, then the nation could not develop a military system that enlisted black Americans in large numbers.[21]

Although the race issue was secondary to him, Garrison could not tolerate Wilson's readiness to compromise on the fundamental issue of national defense just to secure a few votes in an election year. Nor could he stomach Wilson's unwillingness to take on the plan's opponents in his own party. Garrison sent the president a sharply worded resignation letter on February 10 that read, "It is evident that we hopelessly disagree upon what I conceive to be fundamental principles." With that letter, the man whom one Arizona newspaper called "one of the very strongest men in the executive's cabinet" was gone.[22] In his place as secretary of war came Newton Baker, a reform-minded mayor of Cleveland who belonged to what one general called the "pacifist of the capital P group." Baker's appointment "astounded" those who had supported the Continental Army Plan and Preparedness more generally. The new secretary of war would clearly not fight for the Continental Army Plan and other reforms that military professionals thought essential for the nation's security.[23]

The Democratic Party's division on the Continental Army Plan added further complications for Wilson. Speaker of the House Champ Clark (D-Missouri) favored a scaled-down version of the Continental Army Plan, but House Majority Leader Claude Kitchin (D-North Carolina) and Wilson's former secretary of state William Jennings Bryan opposed any growth in the Regular Army or any diminution of the authority of the National Guard. Kitchin claimed that even Wilson's halfway measures on defense and his support of a larger army were "menacing our peace and society and challenging the spirit of Christianity." He argued that Preparedness would only result in a series of pork barrel spending bills that would needlessly fritter away the nation's wealth. *Current Opinion* criticized this wing of the party's blithe avoidance of serious thinking on defense issues by saying that its policy for national defense amounted to three words: "rely on love."[24] In the unusual world of Washington politics, Wilson found more allies for his defense policy in the Republican Party than in his own party.

The predictable result of this debate was a political compromise that gave something to everyone without resolving the core issues. Passed in June, just as the presidential campaign began to heat up, the National Defense Act of 1916 gave the National Guard access to federal money for equipment and more days of training in exchange for its agreeing to federalization in the event of a national emergency. It pledged money for military aviation and increased the theoretical ceiling on the United States Army to 140,000 men. Crucially, it accepted the National Guard as the reserve force, and authorized a massive increase in it from 100,000 men to 400,000 men. It also created a Reserve Officers Training Corps to train men at colleges and universities in the basics of military service so that they might lead these new men. The ROTC program also served to bring together and organize the various Plattsburg-style movements, taking them out of the hands of well-meaning amateurs.[25]

With the help of James Hay and other political allies, the National Guard came out of the 1916 NDA the big winner.[26] The only real concession the National Guard made was the agreement to be federalized in the event of a national emergency, a provision that the Republicans in Congress demanded.[27] Theodore Roosevelt, General Leonard Wood,

Elihu Root, and other leading Republicans thought that concession far too little. Backed by the chambers of commerce in twenty-six states and many wealthy industrialists, they had initially sought national conscription but had agreed to support the Continental Army Plan as a compromise. Now they had neither, and they were angry at a piece of "destructive legislation" characterized by "weak compromise" that they thought failed to address the central problem of America's unpreparedness; the NDA, they argued, might even have left the country worse off than if Congress had done nothing at all.[28]

Iowa senator and Republican presidential candidate Albert Cummins (he finished fifth in the first ballot at the Republican convention in Chicago in June) also saw the 1916 NDA as insufficient because he had wanted to establish a network of national armaments factories. The government would thus have control over arms productions while at the same time limiting the ways that companies and individuals could profit from war. Nevertheless, the NDA only authorized money for one plant, a nitrates factory in Alabama. As its critics recognized, the NDA would take a long time to solve the nation's military problems. Should a major crisis strike, it would prove to be of little help, just as Garrison and his allies had feared. Roosevelt, noting that it took Prussia a century to build its military might, expressed his anger at the two-year spending limit that the 1916 NDA mandated. This was no way for a great power to defend itself.[29]

The political process had produced a compromise that solved an election issue more than a strategic one. Few people except the state governors and their congressional allies expressed any contentment with the NDA; almost everyone came away with more criticisms than compliments. As the *New Republic* noted, the Continental Army Plan "was a pretty little child, dressed to make a good appearance in public, but it was fatally anemic. Nobody was interested in keeping it alive."[30] *National Defence* was more blunt, calling the system the NDA created "a feeble infant more fit for the incubator than for normal development." The only cold comfort it could find lay in the hope that the system would prove so disastrous that the American people would demand major change.[31]

Life's satirists led the postmortem over the Continental Army Plan. The magazine featured a political cartoon with Uncle Sam standing amid a shell-torn Washington. A monument to Peace sits in rubble in the background and a small American soldier runs away from the battle with an iron ball labeled Congress shackled to his ankle. An empty box of ammunition lies at his feet, symbolic of the parsimony of military appropriations. Uncle Sam says to him, "See here, Army! You shouldn't let Honduras do this to me. You've had two weeks' training, eleven dollars in real money spent on you, and see what I get!"[32] Similarly, the New York *World* ran a cartoon showing Uncle Sam standing between two cannons labeled Europe and Japan (the latter a reflection of anxieties over the sharp growth of Japanese power since 1905[33]) both aimed directly at him. A figure labeled Congress, notably dressed in overalls as a swipe at Southerners with rural constituencies like Claude Kitchin and M. Hoke Smith, takes a rifle labeled Preparedness out of his hand. "Give up that gun, Sam," he says, "You might hurt yourself with it."[34]

The navy came out better from the 1916 legislative session than did the army. Congress authorized $315 million for new ships, including modern *Dreadnought*-style heavy battleships. Politicians like Kitchin had opposed that bill as well, based both on its high price tag and the belief that it marked another step on the road to American militarism. Kitchin had supported much smaller defense bills, hoping to reduce the combined $662 million of spending in Wilson's defense proposals, fearful as he was that military spending on that scale could destabilize the federal budget or require massive new taxes. Perhaps he recalled McAdoo's request only a few months earlier for what now seemed the small figure of $112 million in defense spending. Kitchin lamented that the new military expenses proved that "the war goblins and jingoes" had caught the president in their traps.[35] He also represented those Southerners who saw Preparedness as another scheme to concentrate wealth and power in the industrial Northeast.[36]

But however influential they were among their core constituents, Bryan, Smith, and Kitchin sat in the minority of American opinion. Americans agreed on the need to boost national defense, and increasingly saw the opponents of Preparedness as bordering on being unpatriotic. The status quo, they recognized, had become completely untenable. As Elihu Root argued, "We have not been following the path of peace. We have been blindly stumbling along the road that [if] continued must lead to war." More bluntly, the New York *World* ran a political cartoon showing Bryan and Kitchin goose-stepping past an admiring Kaiser Wilhelm.[37]

The NDA did, however, meet the needs of domestic politics in an election year by largely removing army reform as a point of debate between the two major parties. Local politicians on the campaign trail for their own reelections mostly avoided talking about defense and the war in Europe. Like politicians in the national parties, they kept the focus on domestic issues while making largely empty platitudes in support of peace and neutrality. Democrats ran not so much on being from the party of "He Kept Us Out of War," but, as Wilson himself said, as the party that had a domestic record "of extraordinary length and variety, rich in elements of many kinds, but consistent in principle." Secretary of Agriculture David F. Houston cited in particular the establishment of a Federal Trade Commission to regulate trusts and monopolies, the introduction of a progressive income tax to inhibit the concentration of wealth and to pay for part of the new defense appropriations, and tariff reform to take maximum advantage of America's recent growth in international trade.[38]

Although he liked to appear at Preparedness events, Wilson, too, kept to generalities and said little of substance about foreign or military policy. He had engaged in a late January speaking tour in Pittsburgh, Cleveland, Chicago, Milwaukee, Topeka, Des Moines, Kansas City, and St. Louis, all cities with high German-American populations. He spoke of the dangers of the situation in Europe, but avoided mentioning Germany by name. In fact, he said little of substance at all. Even the generally pro-Wilson *Current Opinion* had a hard time drawing any meaning from speeches long on clichés but short on substance. Wilson's speeches, the magazine note, "were singularly devoid of detail." The speeches usually ended with a call to build a larger navy, the one feature of Preparedness on which virtually all Americans agreed, as a large navy could protect commerce, secure American seaboards, and project American power worldwide.[39]

Wilson had his vulnerabilities on foreign policy issues. Not all Americans had accepted Wilson's "He Kept Us Out of War" at face value. Mary Roberts Rinehart noted with some sadness that the words were "only a statement of fact, not a promise."[40] Others had grown irate at Wilson's wartime leadership. Caroline King Duer wrote to a sister who shared her frustration, "I am so ashamed of the President's backing and filling, calling curses down on paper, and crawling out of his own position when anyone blusters back, that I can't bear to talk about it."[41] University of Pittsburgh chancellor Samuel B. McCormick similarly complained that restoring America to its former position in the good opinion of other nations would be "extremely difficult" because of Wilson's poor handling of the war. Although he saw it as "vitally essential" that America have a voice in the shaping of the postwar peace, he expressed "considerable skepticism" about any real progress with Wilson in the White House.[42]

The administration's pursuit of a careful neutrality had drawn its share of fierce critics who argued that the policy had made the country less, not more, safe. Most of these criticisms came from people sympathetic to the Republican Party. The African-American Philadelphia *Tribune* complained that the president's "high sounding diplomatic words," including the "He Kept Us Out of War" slogan itself, "weakened us in the estimation of other nations." It continued its criticism of Wilson, noting that "the weakness of our foreign policy, the record of broken pledges, the surrender of our rights, the useless expenditure of millions and the hypocrisy of Democratic legislation is so broad that the patience of the American people has been severely tested."[43] From a hospital in France where she was serving as a volunteer nurse, Caroline King Duer wrote home that she felt ashamed even to speak about America's role in the war to her French comrades. "How differently we might have appeared before the world with a President who behaved like a man!" She later scribbled a draft of a poem titled "To W. W.," which read in part: "Most eager Peaceman, had you but been taught / That Rights are not upheld by constant writing / If only in your youth some boy had caught / And shown you how to fight and love fair fighting / Perhaps in your head rises the generous red / Where that pale, cautious fluid creeps instead."[44]

Wilson at least understood that he did not control international events as much as the Duer sisters might have wanted him to. He knew that he could not guarantee America's continued neutrality in the ever more dangerous world that the war had created. He remarked to Secretary of the Navy Josephus Daniels that "I cannot keep the country out of war. . . . Any little German lieutenant can put us into the war at any time by some calculated outrage." For this reason, Wilson and many of his advisors came to dislike the "He Kept Us Out of War" slogan and campaign buttons with slogans like "War in Europe, Peace in America, God Bless Wilson."[45]

The president's supporters contended that he had kept America out of not one war, but two. A potential war against Germany sat across thousands of miles of ocean, but the possibility of war with Mexico hit much closer to home. In 1911, the collapse of the regime of Porfirio Díaz turned Mexico into what some today might call a failed state. Díaz had run Mexico since 1876, and the struggle to succeed him created danger-ous instability on America's border.[46] The popular writer and social jus-tice advocate Francisco Madero won the presidency in an election, but General Victoriano Huerta seized power in a coup and executed him. Wilson, who once said that he would teach Mexicans to elect good men, tried to weaken Huerta's regime through an arms embargo. When Huerta tried to get around the embargo, Wilson sent troops to Vera Cruz to take charge of the ports.[47] American forces occupied the town from April to November 1914; twenty-two Americans died in the operation.

Huerta resigned the presidency in the face of international pressure, but he lurked in the background as an enemy of the democratic order that Wilson was trying to establish in Mexico. American newspapers identified Huerta as "a mere German agent" and reported on the meet-ings he had with Germans such as attaché Franz von Rintelen, whose name had come up in connection with several of the sabotage plots of 1914 and 1915. American officials alleged that Rintelen was a German spy who had given Huerta as much as $30 million to "stir up Mexico for our embarrassment" and "to stop the export of arms and munitions to the Allies." Other reports warned that Germany was stashing arms and money in Cuba to help Huerta begin a war "that would keep the United States fully occupied and might stop the flow of munitions to the Allies."[48]

Wilson thought he might have found a solution to his Mexican prob-lems in Huerta's archenemy Venustiano Carranza, a former governor who became the head of a provisional "pre-constitutional" government in 1915. Carranza was in reality another Mexican strongman, but one with enough promise to attract the support of American Progressives like journalist Lincoln Steffens. In Mexico since 1914, Steffens knew the country as well as any American and, while recognizing Carranza's many shortcomings, thought him the best of the potential future leaders of Mexico. War correspondent Floyd Gibbons, sent to Mexico to cover the civil war for the Chicago *Tribune*, took a different view, seeing Northern Army commander and governor Pancho Villa as the best of the Mexican leaders. Gibbons spent a few months in northern Mexico with Villa, and, while not blind to his many faults, came to see Villa as the only leader who could hold the deeply fractured country together.[49] Gibbons supported American intervention in the Mexican conflict, while Steffens wrote that the United States had no more right to interfere in Mexico than the Germans had to intervene in Belgium.[50]

The United States remained deeply involved in the ongoing Mexican Civil War, which often spilled over the border. Wilson had decided to back Carranza in his efforts to destroy Carranza's main rivals, Villa and Emiliano Zapata, even allowing Carranza to use American railroads to move men and equipment. The publisher of the New York *Evening Mail* noted that although White House officials "do not like him [Carranza] at all, they are in such a position that they cannot do otherwise" but support him.[51] Villa, who had had the backing of the United States when he was governor of the northern state of Chihuahua, felt betrayed by Wilson and grew increasingly angry at the United States. In January 1916, his men killed fifteen American mining engineers living in Mexico. Villa then decided to raid the town of Columbus, New Mexico, on March 9 as a means of retribution and vengeance against Wilson. Columbus was also home to an arms dealer who had betrayed Villa. Villa's men burned the town and in the process of the raid eighteen Americans died.

Villa had become too serious a problem to ignore as indignation against him rose all across the United States. Villa was not only a threat to Wilson's Mexico policy. Americans saw the hand of Germany behind Villa's raid and his quest for control of Mexico. Perhaps because they held Villa in such low esteem, American officials discounted the possibility that he had acted without help from a major European power. Americans thus easily and naturally saw German agents secretly directing the raid on Columbus as a way of keeping the United States focused on North American security problems. Wilson himself told an aide that

"Germany is anxious to have us at war with Mexico so that our minds and energies will be taken off the great war across the sea."[52]

Support grew for sending the United States Army into Mexico to find Villa and perhaps to oust Carranza as well. Anti-Mexican riots in border cities added to the pressure building on Wilson. Even Senator William Borah (R-Idaho), normally opposed to foreign adventures, supported going after Villa. Theodore Roosevelt, recalling the war that made him famous, said, "There is a hundred times the justification for interfering in Mexico as there was for interfering in Cuba [in 1898]. We should have interfered in Mexico years ago." The Senate introduced a motion authorizing Wilson to order an expedition into Mexico as a way of prodding him into action, and newspapers across the country called for the president to take decisive measures up to, and perhaps including, war.[53]

Exactly how to chase Villa through the vast Mexican countryside he knew so well with an American Army ill-suited to the task and no reliable allies on the ground raised both questions and fears. The governor of Texas predicted failure and argued against a military expedition, saying that "in the present state of our Army and Navy it would be the wildest folly to attempt the pacification of Mexico by force."[54] The Omaha *World-Herald* bemoaned what it saw as American military weakness. "With almost our entire mobile army on the Mexican border, it takes one week to prepare to chase a second-rate bandit in a third-rate nation. The object lesson is so striking that nobody, not even the extreme pacifist, can fail to be impressed by it." Chasing Pancho Villa placed so much of America's army on the southern border as to leave it "practically defenseless" everywhere else. If the United States could not punish a single Mexican leader, what chance did it have against a modern foe like Germany?[55]

The situation in Mexico grew increasingly perilous. Carranza did not try to bring Villa's men to justice himself, although he gave his reluctant acquiescence to the so-called punitive expedition commanded by General John Pershing to find Villa. Carranza soon grew disenchanted with the Americans operating in his country and threatened to resist the expedition by force. A small clash between American forces and Mexican forces loyal to Carranza in June at Carrizal in Villa's home state of Chihuahua slowed down the American pursuit and raised questions about the wisdom of the entire expedition. Some newspapers reported that Villa had secretly watched the skirmish at Carrizal while laughing at seeing his enemies fight each other. He escaped justice and the United States stood humiliated.

As Garrison had predicted, the Villa operation showed the weaknesses of the National Guard. None of the units mobilized for the Mexican expedition had had more than one week per year of military training, which explained the poor results Guardsmen scored on their marksmanship tests. Approximately half of the men called up never answered the call, and almost one in five who did had to be rejected because of poor health. More than five hundred National Guard officers resigned rather than go to Mexico. The governor of South Carolina disbanded his National Guard rather than see it deployed outside the state and beyond his control, and Kentucky had to fill its quota with prison parolees. Clearly, the system was badly broken.[56]

America's Mexican problems continued, in part because the army was too small and ineffective to influence events there. Any growth in Mexican power, many Americans assumed, would also mean a growth for Germany. The punitive expedition had also raised fears in Mexico (likely in Carranza himself) that the United States sought to annex even more Mexican territory. Mexico was thus prime territory for German agents, and had been the logical landing spot for German saboteurs and spies fleeing the United States in 1915 and 1916. The thoughtful American general Tasker Howard Bliss reported that most of the anti-American propaganda in Mexico came from German agents, and Bliss knew that they had a receptive audience given past American avarice for Mexican land and America's repeated interference in Mexican politics. America, he recognized, had to do a better job of convincing Mexicans that the United States did not want to annex more of their land, but sought instead to help them develop a more stable future. Until they did so, Mexico would be the perfect launching pad for all manner of German intrigue.[57]

Links between Mexico and Germany appeared natural and obvious, even if the actual evidence for them remained largely indirect and circumstantial. Perhaps to boost his own credentials as a global player, Villa had bragged about the support he received from Berlin. His boasts backed up the work of American agents in Mexico, who had begun to make connections between German agents and some of Villa's closest aides. Americans felt the fear of a global plot, as the diary of C. Earl Baker, who joined the Pennsylvania National Guard after the *Sussex* affair, shows. Baker wrote that the Villa raid came "at Germany's instigation," the whole idea being to distract Wilson and keep him from joining the war. "The invasion, like nothing so much as a cockroach attacking an eagle, backfired on Germany in a big way."[58] Baker may have been influenced by media reports that publicized the links between the two thorns in America's side. Maud Hawkes, an American living in Mexico whom Villa had kidnapped then released, told reporters that Villa had bragged about the support he had received from both Germany and Japan. He had, she said, threatened to "kill everybody in the United States and would be helped by Germany and Japan."[59]

Suspicions of a global plot reaching from Mexico to Berlin (and perhaps to Tokyo as well) had wide appeal. Secretary of State Robert Lansing, American ambassador to Germany James Gerard, and Secretary of the Interior Franklin Lane all believed that Berlin had been behind Villa's raid, even if they could not prove any direct connection to officials in the German government. Lane wrote privately to the publisher of the New York *World* that he was "tired of having the Kaiser and Carranza vent their impudence at our expense because they know we do not want to go to war and because they want to keep their own people in line."[60] From Berlin, Gerard added that "Most Germans think that [America's] Mexican troubles are to their advantage. I am sure that Villa's attacks are made in Germany. Every night fifty million Germans cry themselves to sleep because all Mexico has not risen against us."[61]

As Maud Hawks indicated in her remarks to reporters, fears of a growing Japan added to this environment of concern, if not quite paranoia. Several senior American officials saw Germany's hands behind both Villa's raid into New Mexico and a more aggressive Japanese posture in the Pacific. The first issue of *National Defence* featured on its cover a cartoon of a Japanese official smiling at his country's new $278 million defense budget.[62] With Germany, Mexico, and Japan all becoming a problem, Americans had begun to worry about a tripartite alliance aimed at encircling them, as the map on *Life*'s cover for February 10, 1916, shows.

By the summer of 1916 Americans had begun to see a wide variety of global threats, and some Americans saw them as linked. Joseph Medill

Patterson, the publisher of the Chicago *Tribune*, thought that Japan posed the greatest threat to American security. Preparedness, he argued, should focus primarily on the "probable onslaught of the great military empire of Japan," which he believed was taking resources out of China in order to prepare to fight America. The "unmilitary and rich" United States was Japan's "next logical victim" because America sat defenseless to an outside attack.[63] Roosevelt agreed, writing to a journalist that "probably if this war results in a deadlock abroad (which will be a virtual triumph for Germany) we shall have to pay tribute to Japan in the end, as sure as fate; and by tribute, I mean the loss of Hawaii, the Panama Canal, and probably Alaska."[64] Patterson advocated holding up ammunition supplies to Great Britain until the British signed an anti-Japanese alliance with the United States. "Though we live in a flammable house and ought to take out fire insurance," he wrote, "we will probably prefer to chance it."[65] Not all Americans wanted to chance it. Harvard president Charles Eliot favored negotiating an alliance with France and Britain to fight the Germans and deter the Japanese and Mexicans at the same time.[66]

Japan, Germany, Villa's raid, and the American failure to find him temporarily energized the debates about Preparedness. Floyd Gibbons and other journalists reported not only on the sorry state of American military equipment in Mexico but also on the Keystone Cops-like marches through the desert by American troops; no matter how hard they tried, they failed to find one of the most famous men in North America.[67] That failure only underscored the national sense of embarrassment and humiliation at the ineffectiveness of the armed forces. Senator Reed Smoot (R-Utah) openly questioned how the nation had come to a place where it allowed the Mexican Army to be in better shape than its own, a concern that the skirmish at Carrizal underscored. Changes had to come. As *Current Opinion* noted, Villa had thus inadvertently managed to do what the kaiser, Roosevelt, and Lindley Garrison could not do: make American politicians take Preparedness seriously, at least for a few weeks.[68]

The dissatisfaction over the NDA only added fuel to the fire. In June and July, Preparedness supporters held huge parades nationwide. More than 130,000 people attended parades in New York and Chicago, and large crowds appeared at similar parades in cities nationwide. The twelve-hour New York parade featured two hundred bands, reunited squads of Spanish-American War veterans, and speeches from Elihu Root, Henry Stimson, Thomas Edison, and prominent clergymen.[69] These parades were not limited to the Northeast. More than thirty thousand people turned out in Montgomery, Alabama, on a July 4th "Preparedness Day" holiday to greet National Guardsmen en route to Mexico as part of the Villa expedition.[70] As that incident shows, the parades could be as much about Mexico (or even Japan) as about Germany, although in the minds of many Americans the three countries were becoming ever more closely linked.

Seeing a political opportunity, Wilson rode the bandwagon, launching the general election phase of his campaign at a Preparedness rally in Washington shortly after the conclusion of the Democratic convention in St. Louis in mid-June. He saw support for Preparedness as a way to insulate himself from the unpopular isolationist wing of his own party. The parades, in the words of the president of the United Press Associations, "served for a time to lift this nation out of the sordid, pot-bellied, fat-joweled state into which it is getting as a result of its orgy of money making," but they proved to be a temporary phenomenon that, having served their political purposes, largely faded by the time the presidential election entered its final phase in late summer.[71]

If Wilson's critics hoped that his Republican electoral rivals would develop a firmer stance on foreign affairs, they were soon disappointed. The one man who might have done so, Theodore Roosevelt, considered a run for the presidency, and he had wide support. A Texas railroad magnate willing to bankroll Roosevelt's campaign called him "the greatest American who ever lived" and believed that only Roosevelt could guide America through "the most critical epoch in the history of our country."[72] A Chicago *Post* political cartoon in April made a direct contrast between Roosevelt and the president by showing a timid Wilson as a baseball player at bat letting a fastball go by and saying, "I'm glad I didn't strike at that one. I might have missed it." The umpire calls out strike two. Roosevelt sits behind the dugout with his legendary big stick and says, "Don't put me in if you value that baseball—I'd wallop the cover off of it." Uncle Sam calls from the stands, "I want a batter in there who can bat!"[73]

Nevertheless, Roosevelt had burned too many bridges with the traditional wing of the Republican Party. He also had more success criticizing

Wilson than he had in developing serious alternative courses of action in an increasingly fraught international environment. He told Mary Roberts Rinehart, who came back from her trip out West to cover the party conventions, that if he had been president in 1914, "The moment the neutrality of Belgium was threatened, I would have sent for the German ambassador and told him that the United States would not stand quietly by while such a violation took place." Roosevelt argued that such a step would have stopped the war from starting. Rinehart was skeptical, although she accepted his basic point that a nation's neutrality and global influence depended on having the arms and political will to uphold them.[74]

Had the war and foreign policy been subjects where the Republicans thought they had a decided advantage over the Democrats, they might have chosen Nobel laureate Elihu Root as their candidate. A former secretary of war and secretary of state, he had a worldwide reputation in international security affairs based on his ideas on binding arbitration as well as his roles in the Algeciras Conference of 1906 and the Second Hague Conference in 1907. He had broken with Wilson's neutrality policy early on and had been one of the first prominent national figures to back the Preparedness movement. Still, his age (he was seventy-two years old in 1916), his anti-Progressive views, and his Wall Street ties made many Republicans, especially those outside the East Coast, wary of supporting him. He finished a distant third in the Republican balloting, an indication that the party was not ready to make the war a central issue despite its growing importance in the American consciousness.

The Republicans risked being trapped between the thundering Roosevelt-Root wing and the neutrality-supporting Robert LaFollette wing. Wanting to keep the focus on domestic affairs, they compromised at the convention, deciding after three ballots to nominate Associate Justice of the Supreme Court and former New York governor Charles Evans Hughes. Hughes had the advantage of being on the Supreme Court, and thus largely out of the public spotlight, during both the 1912 split in the Republican Party and the debates over American responses to the outbreak of the war in Europe. In fact, he had made almost no public pronouncement of any kind on the major issues of the day, including the war.[75] He could, therefore, stand above the party divisions of recent years and he had the additional virtue of having made no enemies among the top Republican brass. Hughes differed from the president much more in style than in substance. Sporting a closely cropped beard and a finely tailored mustache, he was dapper and well wired into the East Coast elite whereas Wilson was drab and more closely linked to the rural South and West. Privately, Roosevelt called Hughes a "bearded iceberg" and thought him worthless when it came to foreign policy issues, but he decided to support Hughes anyway, in the hopes of removing the even more offensive Wilson and his team of advisors from Washington. Uninspiring though many found him, Hughes might also have been the only politician in America who could have drawn the support of both Roosevelt and the German-American community.[76]

Neither Hughes nor the Republican Party leadership wanted to make the war a central part of the campaign. Despite the dangers that everyone saw as the war threatened to drag the United States in, Mary Roberts Rinehart did not hear a word spoken about it at the Republican convention in Chicago in early June. She did, however, hear the Democrats discussing it at their convention two weeks later. They mostly leaned on the Wilson campaign's "He Kept Us Out of War" slogan to remind the American people of Wilson's foreign policy successes. Kentucky senator Ollie M. James thundered from the convention podium that "every mother whose son is today safe in his home may thank God for Woodrow Wilson."[77]

The Republican Party really had no response, however much it recoiled from crediting Wilson with any foreign policy successes. Although they were generally united on the need to boost national defense, the Republicans did not want to make anti-German policies too central in the campaign because of their hopes of capturing the German-American vote in potential swing states like Wisconsin and Ohio. Even avowedly pro-Preparedness Republican candidates for election and reelection avoided discussion of the war in order to keep the focus on areas where they presumed they had a marked advantage over their Democratic rivals. As a result, Republicans stuck mostly to empty words on the campaign trail, leading the *New Republic* to argue in June that "if foreign policy is the failure of the Wilson administration, it is no less the failure of its critics. There is no Roosevelt-Root-Republican foreign policy at the moment. No man can say what they believe." Selecting Hughes as the nominee certainly did not make it any easier for American voters to see how a Republican administration would handle foreign affairs any differently than Wilson had.[78]

Several newspapers saw the Republican dilemma and argued that whatever the flaws in Wilsonian diplomacy, Hughes and the Republicans could have done no better. In July, the St. Louis *Mirror* compared Wilson's 1916 election campaign to Abraham Lincoln's 1864 campaign. Both were close wartime contests with a challenger falsely accusing the incumbent of bungling war policy without providing an alternative. Wilson, the *Mirror* claimed, had done all that voters could expect an American president to do. "His patience won his point with Germany. His patience has kept us out of war," an editorial read. "Would Mr. Hughes have had less or more patience with Germany, with Mexico? On either horn he must impale himself." Better, the *Mirror* argued, not to change presidential horses midstream on the basis of international affairs.[79]

The Republicans found themselves caught in a bind. On the one hand, Hughes and his team understood the disaffection among some German-Americans toward Wilson. By depicting himself as a moderate on the war and European issues more generally, Hughes might have a chance to win the votes of those in favor of continued neutrality. A softer line on the war, however, opened Hughes up to charges that his administration would give in to any future outrage like the *Lusitania* and the *Sussex*. Thus did Democratic newspapers depict Hughes as the "Kaiser's Candidate," with political cartoons showing Wilhelm putting up Hughes campaign posters.[80] George Sylvester Viereck's endorsement of Hughes in the pages of *Fatherland* made it all that much easier for Democrats to tar him with a pro-German brush.[81]

On the other hand, Hughes also had to deal with the bellicose Roosevelt, who set off on the campaign trail in support of his party's nominee. Roosevelt's daughter Alice noted that her father was always more anti-Wilson than pro-Hughes, in part because Roosevelt and Hughes disagreed on the correct approach toward the war.[82] Roosevelt claimed that American neutrality on Wilson's model made the United States "a partner in the crime of Germany."[83] Pulling no punches on the campaign trail, he made speeches like his "Shadow Lawn" speech, which referred to Wilson's summer house on the Jersey shore of the same name: "There should be shadows now at Shadow Lawn, the shadows of the men, women, and children who have risen from the ooze of the ocean bottom and from graves in foreign lands; the shadows of the helpless whom Mr. Wilson did not dare protect lest he might have to face danger; the shadows of babies gasping pitifully as they sank under the waves."[84]

Hughes, who, when he did mention the war, spoke far more moderately of "straight and honest neutrality" and "national self-respect," shrank from such harsh statements.[85] Even many pro-Hughes newspapers worried that Roosevelt was hurting the campaign much more than he was helping it.[86] Wilson partisans implied that a Hughes victory would lead to Roosevelt being named secretary of state or war, thus vastly increasing the likelihood of America entering the war.[87] As Charles Nagel told the Republican publisher of the New York *Evening Mail* shortly after the election, Republicans in the Midwest "were afraid of Hughes, because they concluded that his chief advisors during the campaign, and his prospective advisors in a Hughes administration, wanted war at any price."[88]

As the election campaign neared its conclusion, the war stayed mostly in the background, but occasionally the difficult position of the Republicans on foreign policy caused them confusion and embarrassment. Democrats continued to gain ground by contending that while Hughes had frequently criticized the president for his war policy, he had offered precious few details about what he might have done differently had he been in the White House. At a stop in Youngstown, Ohio, Hughes finally answered those critics. His supporters could not have been too pleased or too enlightened by what he said: "I was under the impression that when I said what I would have stated in advance as to what I would do everyone would know that I had stated in effect what I would have done." A week later in Evansville, Indiana, Hughes admitted in response to a question posed to him by a heckler that he agreed with Wilson in opposing both a ban on American travel into war zones and an arms embargo, further muddying any difference he might try to draw between his own proposed policies and those of Wilson. Hughes's views on the war were so muddied that in the span of just a few days two supporters wrote letters to the editor of the New York *Times* making diametrically opposed claims as to what a Hughes administration might do. One letter praised him for advocating a policy ending "Mr. Wilson's craven neutrality between good and evil; [Hughes] will be gloriously unneutral, to the aid and comfort of the Allies," while another conversely predicted that his election that would lead to a continuation of Wilson's neutrality policy and "a possible rupture with the two Allied powers, whose success is ardently wished by the vast majority of the American people." Note that both writers wrote about Hughes's views on the war with a pro-Allied bias, although they came to diametrically opposite conclusions. In an editorial on the election campaign, the dean of the graduate school at Cornell wrote that German-Americans "are a little confused, like the rest of us, regarding the position of Mr. Hughes."[89]

The election opened up cleavages in the American foreign policy consensus of 1914–16, as a number of prominent Republicans publicly broke with Wilson, even if many of them had their doubts about Hughes. Most members of the Republican elite had agreed in broad outline with Roosevelt since 1914, but, unlike Roosevelt, they had kept their criticisms largely private in the face of a national crisis. The election, however, created an opportunity for them to take these views public. Those views had hardened in the face of Wilson's "Too Proud to Fight" and "He Kept Us Out of War" statements, which they saw as insulting to national honor. Former secretaries of war Elihu Root and Henry Stimson both began a public campaign of criticism of Wilson in 1916.[90] Like most defense-minded Republicans and most conservatives, Stimson had supported Root for the nomination despite his age, but reluctantly backed Hughes in the general election.

In the end, the war played little role in the choice most Americans made on election day, in part because the two candidates agreed on the basic outlines of American policy toward Europe. Edward Rumely wrote a four-page letter to Hughes supporters in mid-October in an attempt to rally support for the candidate. The letter did not once mention the war or Europe. Rumely later blamed Hughes's defeat on his inability to attract independent Progressives. To cite another example, three New York newspapers, the *Times*, the *Evening Post*, and the *World* all endorsed Wilson despite having supported Hughes when he was governor of New York, but they did not mention the war as a reason for their change of heart. Instead, they argued that Hughes represented the "reactionary elite" of "Tories and Bourbons" that would set back both progressivism and democracy. As the *Evening News* argued, "All the forces of greed in the United States, all the forces of private interest, all the forces of plutocracy that seek to control government for personal profit, are allied with Mr. Hughes in this contest." Given that most Americans were not focused primarily on Europe during the election, what one pro-Hughes newspaper called Roosevelt's "wild war talk" hurt Hughes all the more, an observation shared by several Republican newspapers.[91]

Hughes nonetheless nearly pulled off a remarkable upset. On election night Wilson went to bed assuming that he had lost, telling his secretary "it looks as if we are licked."[92] Parisian newspapers the next morning reported a Hughes victory. But when the returns from California came in, they showed that Wilson had won this traditionally Republican state by the razor-thin margin of 3,773 votes (or .38 percent), giving him enough electoral votes to be reelected. Wilson's victory came in surprising fashion, as California had not voted for a Democratic presidential candidate since 1892; many observers blamed Hughes's defeat there on the cool personal relationship between him and California's irascible governor Hiram Johnson, who had run as Roosevelt's vice-presidential candidate on the Bull Moose ticket in 1912. Hughes and Johnson did not meet when Hughes campaigned in California; Johnson, taking it as a personal snub, refused in turn to help Hughes. Still, Hughes did not give up even after the election returns came in, hoping for some kind of a California miracle and waiting fifteen days to officially concede his defeat.[93]

Although the election had not turned largely on issues related to the war, it had clearly shown the ambiguity, ambivalence, and confusion that Americans felt near the end of 1916.[94] On home leave in Connecticut shortly after the election, Eric Bradley, an American volunteer in the British Army, found Americans "in complete ignorance" about the realities of war. He recalled that "it depressed me to hear people...blasting about when America was in the war we would show them how to do it, and that with all the material we would supply, and supply quickly, it would be only a short time before we defeated the enemy. This sort of thing rather spoilt my leave." Still, his community feted him as a great hero for having volunteered on the side they believed to be the right one. They invited him to speak to his home congregation about the war and hosted a gala farewell dinner for him before he returned to England. Poet Ella Wheeler Wilcox wrote a piece in his honor, leaving him a bit confused, but flattered nonetheless. "There is the mystery, that this lady who had written so much for the world should have written anything to a young man she knew only as a one-time neighbor [at the dinner] will always intrigue me."[95] Americans were willing to show their support for men like Bradley in no uncertain terms, but they were not yet ready to follow him into the fight.

In a similar vein, Gilbert Seldes read Wilson's electoral victory as a sign that the country remained trapped in an insoluble dilemma over its own security. On the one hand, he noted, even those "citizens who shrank from war in 1915 were prepared... to know that war was inevitable" by the time of the 1916 election. On the other, the American people had seen little reason to change administrations based on foreign policy issues because they knew that Wilson "trust[ed] the ways of negotiation and peace. He could therefore with more propriety than any other [presidential] candidate declare that the expedients of peace had failed." In other words, if another crisis struck shortly after the election, Wilson could face it with greater confidence from the American people than could Hughes because the nation "trusted [Wilson] not to go to war except when war was inevitable." Seldes also thought that Roosevelt's bellicosity on the campaign trail may have been enough to cost Hughes the presidency by making him seem more willing to go to war than Wilson.[96]

As Seldes's observations reveal, by the end of 1916, two trends existed side by side. On the one hand, many more Americans felt, in the words of Yale student Edward Clark, a "growing impatience to see our country line up with the Allies" in a war that most expected would eventually drag them in.[97] On the other hand, the international situation had calmed down, leading Americans to turn their eyes away from the problems of Europe and worry more about matters closer to home. Veteran war correspondent Frederick Palmer recalled the fall of 1916 as the low point of US-German tensions and the high point of optimism that the United States might somehow avoid the war.[98]

In that fall and in the winter of 1916–17 American newspapers and magazines reported far less frequently on the war as the odds of America being dragged into it seemed to decline. Seldes later wrote that these months were "an interval hard to describe." He was himself "heartbroken" with this shift in national attention, writing, "There seemed little likelihood that the United States of America would become a partner of

the Entente in the Great War. After two and a half years of war the liberal nations of the world still had to bear their great disappointment,
that the Democracy of the New World remained indifferent to the fate
of Democracy in the Old." Seldes thought that in some ways, appear-
ances could be deceiving, because support for the Allies remained high.
"The United States was not indifferent; but the fact was that it could not
bring sympathy to the sticking point."[99]

Others were more critical, believing that the problem had less to do
with circumstance than national will. In words that would have glad-
dened Roosevelt, Arthur Gleason bemoaned a nation "complacent in
our neutrality and fat with our profits" that lacked the courage to stand
up to Germany.[100] *Current Opinion* made a similar case, noting that
American per capita income had increased from $1,164 at the start of the
war to $1,868 in less than two years while Europeans were at the same
time "wasting the life-blood not only of their men but of their commerce and industry as well." Its editors asked readers, "Have we a moral
right to our present prosperity?"[101] At the end of the year, it seemed as
though the American dilemma would continue to center on the moral
question of profiting from the misery of others rather than the political
one of choosing sides.

But as 1916 turned into 1917, global events began to accelerate significantly. For reasons tied to both Europe and the United States itself,
more and more Americans were changing their views on the war and
what it might mean for them. Wilson's inauguration did not coincide
with continued American neutrality, as so many who voted for him had
hoped, but with the opening of a new chapter in America's relationship
to the war in Europe.

7

The Melting Pot, the War, and American Identity

SCHOLARS HAVE LONG PRESUMED THAT members of American immigrant communities supported their country's war effort mainly because of pressure from America's leaders to demonstrate "100% Americanism." The reality is in fact much more complex and involves patterns occurring within the communities themselves. Immigrants and their children may have disagreed about the right course for Americans to take in 1914, but by 1917 changes both at the global and domestic levels had combined to produce a remarkable amount of pro-intervention consensus both within these diverse communities and within society at large. The years 1914 to 1917 played a much more important role in assimilation and acculturation than most have recognized. We have also failed to see that the main agents of this transformation were the immigrants themselves and their children, not the United States government or Nativists.

The First World War occurred at a critical time in the history of acculturation and assimilation in the United States. By 1914, members of major immigrant groups like the Italians, Germans, Irish, and Jews had already "placed greater weight on the latter side of the hyphen," although throughout the war, there was much debate over how much children of immigrants born in the United States should conform to the wider American culture.[1] Randolph Bourne argued that they need not assimilate at all and that the so-called melting pot model would not work for the United States. In a 1916 article for the *Atlantic Monthly*, Bourne, a prominent intellectual of the age, explicitly linked acculturation in the United States to the outbreak of war in Europe, arguing both that excessive European nationalism had caused the war and that a dual identity in the United States could undercut it. Multiculturalism was a strength rather than a weakness, and even in wartime immigrants could maintain a dual identity without in any way undermining their primary loyalty to the United States.[2]

The Italian-American community seemed to prove Bourne's point. Italian-Americans were closely tied to the war in Europe from the moment Italy entered the war on the side of the Allies in May 1915. For Italians, as for other major groups, external pressures to conform to the general American desire for a pro-Allied position while maintaining a profitable legal neutrality undoubtedly existed, but dynamics within these communities proved far more influential than anything that Charles Evans Hughes, Theodore Roosevelt, or Woodrow Wilson said on the campaign trail in 1916. In the case of Italian-Americans, the needs of their homeland, the desires of their adopted land, and the exigencies of their local communities lined up rather neatly.

For other groups—(Catholic) Irish-Americans, German-Americans, Jewish-Americans, and African-Americans—the process was not quite as straightforward but resulted by 1917 in similar processes. By late 1916, all four groups had adopted a more pro-Allied position on the war, or at least came to identify their own position more closely with the pro-Allied position that by this point reflected the American mainstream. In each case, communal acculturation played a key role in changing their attitudes toward the war. Members of these groups were never homogenous and differences of political ideology, ethnicity, religiosity, and class always existed among them. No single "Jewish" or "Irish" view of the war ever existed. Still, by the end of 1916 a rough consensus had emerged within all four, and they all pointed toward a broader acceptance of, even outright support for, the cause of the Allies.

To the extent that they concerned themselves with wartime affairs in Ireland, most Irish-Americans fell into one of two groups.[3] In 1914, the majority hoped to see Great Britain extend more rights and autonomy to Ireland in exchange for the military service of the tens of thousands of Irishmen in the British Army on the Western Front and elsewhere. Irish men and women had also moved to England in large numbers to take factory jobs and to support the war effort in a wide variety of ways. A smaller, but quite vocal, group in both Ireland and the United States known as the Republicans sought total independence for Ireland and saw the war as a chance for Ireland to strike while Britain was distracted by its military campaigns in Europe, Asia, and Africa. Irish Republicans followed the old maxim that "England's difficulty is Ireland's opportunity."[4]

Most Irish-American political and religious leaders initially tried to remain neutral on the war, although they tended to share American outrage at incidents like the attacks on the *Lusitania* and *Sussex*. Their mistrust or outright hatred of England notwithstanding, Irish-Americans of all political leanings were loath to put at risk the progress they had made in the previous decades. America in 1914 was no longer a land of intensely anti-Irish sentiments, such as those expressed in nineteenth-century political cartoons or that followed the Fenian Raids of 1866–71.[5] Irish-Americans such as Massachusetts governor (and later United States senator) David Walsh, Montana senator Thomas Walsh, New York City alderman (and future governor and presidential candidate) Al Smith, and President Wilson's close aide Joseph Tumulty all symbolized the growing influence of Irish-Americans in politics. They had indeed come a long way in just a few generations and nobody wanted to go back.[6]

Many Irish-Americans also had relatives fighting in the British Army, linking them directly to the cause of the Allies. War correspondent Frederick Palmer spoke to some of these Irish soldiers during a 1915 visit to the Western Front. He found that the support of Irish-Americans for the war was crucial to maintaining the men's morale in the fight against Germany. After the Battle of Neuve Chapelle in March, Palmer asked Irish soldiers what they would want his readers to know about the war. "Tell them in America that the Irish are still fighting!" replied one man.[7]

The Easter Rising in Dublin in 1916 changed the relationship of Irish-Americans to the war, albeit in unexpected ways. During five days, April 24 to 29, a group called the Irish Republican Brotherhood seized power in Dublin and inspired smaller rebellions across Ireland.[8] As was true in Ireland itself, few Irish-Americans outside active Republican circles expressed much initial sympathy for the rebels. The influential

Irish-American lawyer John Quinn called the Rising "a horrible fiasco" and "sheer lunacy." Similarly, the Irish-American editor of the *New Republic* described the Rising as "wild and futile" and said that it worked against the interests of the Irish people on either side of the Atlantic. Both Irish-American cardinals also came out against the Rising, as did the majority of Irish-Catholic newspapers in the United States.[9]

Virtually all non-Irish newspapers in the United States condemned the Rising and refuted Republican claims that the rebels were following in the footsteps of America's own revolutionary heroes. Prominent journalists Walter Lippmann and Herbert Croly both condemned the Rising in no uncertain terms. Newspaper editors like those of the Memphis *Commercial Appeal* were appalled by the violence the rebels caused, and Southerners in general saw no link between Ireland's attempt at "secession" and their own attempt in 1861. Most important, Americans disliked the idea of an uprising against Britain while the British were fighting a war of necessity against Germany. Far better, most Irish-Americans had concluded, to allow the political process, flawed though it was, to work.[10]

The war greatly complicated Irish-American responses to the Rising and made it an international, not strictly an Irish, issue. Unlike the Pancho Villa raid, in which Americans only suspected German involvement, the German government had been intimately linked to the rebellion in Ireland. The Germans had provided most of the rebels' arms and had transported the Dublin-born former British diplomat Roger Casement in a submarine from Germany to Ireland so that he could play a leading role in the Rising. But Germany had turned its back on the rebels as soon as the Rising began to fail, and even the leaders of the rebellion themselves quickly came to see that Germany offered no reasonable alternative to Great Britain in the postwar world. Casement had written about the Germans after his arrest, "Why did I ever trust in a Govt such as this—They have no sense of honour, chivalry, generosity.... That is why they are hated by the world and [why] England will surely beat them."[11]

Americans also made connections between the Germans and the Irish rebellion. The New York *Evening Sun* ran a political cartoon featuring Kaiser Wilhelm leading a band consisting of Austro-Hungarian emperor Franz Joseph and the Ottoman sultan. They are playing the Irish

Republican anthem "The Wearing of the Green," and the caption reads "Irish Patriots." Similarly, the Chicago *Evening Post* ran a cartoon showing Wilhelm playing "Deutschland Über Alles" on an Irish harp over the caption "His New Instrument."[12] Americans initially tended to see the Irish rebels not as principled opponents of an unjust British occupation, but as naive dupes of a German government all too willing to use the rebels to cause chaos for England then leave them to their own devices.

Irish-Americans were sensitive to the rumors (and, indeed, the reality) that large sums of money for the purchase of weapons had come from the small but determined Irish Republican community in the United States. The rebels' Proclamation of the Irish Republic had specifically referred to the presumption that Ireland had the support of "her exiled children in America." On day five of the rebellion, the rebels had sent out a desperate message to the Irish people that read, "we have every confidence that our Allies in Germany and kinsmen in America are straining every nerve to hasten matters on our behalf."[13] Five of the signatories of the rebels' Proclamation of the Irish Republic plus the soon-to-be executed Roger Casement had spent significant time in the United States raising funds. One of the rebels, future Irish president Éamon de Valera, had been born in New York City; his American birth may well have saved him from being executed.

Undoubtedly, the rebels had the support of some Irish Republicans in the United States, but most Irish-Americans disliked being tarred alongside them with the brush of rebellion and mayhem. John Burke, an Irish-American lawyer and businessman living in New York, responded by saying that "we have a country—America, which is the land of our first and greatest love. Its interests are for us supreme."[14] The Irish-American community had to balance its sympathies for its homeland with a growing sentiment that that same sympathy might be at odds with American national security. The New York *Herald* reported that a global plot now linked Ireland, Germany, and Mexico to launch attacks against the United States if the United States got involved in the war. Newspapers used words like *seditious* and *treasonous* to describe any Irish-Americans living in the United States who might be tempted to help such plots either in Dublin or on American soil.[15] In such an environment most Irish-Americans, including poet and future war casualty

Joyce Kilmer, rushed to demonstrate their loyalty to the United States, while at the same time still expressing their sympathy for those who continued to suffer in Ireland and urging the White House to press for clemency for the captured rebels.[16]

Britain's brutal response to the Rising, which resulted in 250 Irish civilians killed and another 2,200 wounded, horrified Americans. The hasty execution of twenty rebel leaders in Dublin's Kilmainham Jail barely a week after the Rising angered Americans, including some of the most Anglophile. Even the avowedly pro-British Theodore Roosevelt condemned the British government's response in the strongest of terms. A protest meeting against the reprisals and Britain's refusal to offer clemency to those condemned to death led to a rally at Carnegie Hall that filled the seats and had as many as fifteen thousand people protesting the executions on the streets outside. A British subject living in the United States told the Foreign Office that before the harsh response to the Rising, 75 percent of the Irish in America had been pro-Allied, but after it virtually none of them would speak a kind word about Britain.[17] The violence in Dublin led to the virtual collapse of Irish-American support for the Nationalist plan of working with the British government on some version of Home Rule.[18] Republican organizations rose in membership and influence, as Irish-Americans increasingly gave their support to the idea of an independent Ireland after the war was over.[19]

At the same time, however, Irish-Americans recoiled from the idea that either their support for Irish independence or their opposition to British cruelty meant that they had become pro-German. The most complete case study of an Irish-American community in this period found no support at all for Germany, but did find deep support for Preparedness.[20] Statements of support for the United States and opposition to Germany were widespread. An Irish-American newspaper (which boasted about having begun publication on July 4, 1898, to honor the nation) went out of its way to praise Roger Casement's statement just before his execution that "I never asked an Irishman to fight for Germany. I have always claimed that he has no right to fight for any land but Ireland." As Casement himself did, most Irish-Americans saw the Germans as a false ally whose friendship had been narrowly based on a shared interest of reducing English power; in the wake of the Rising's failure, that shared interest quickly evaporated.[21]

Even those Irish-Americans who had no problem with the rebels working with the Germans rushed to pledge their loyalty to the United States. The *Irish World*, which took a firm anti-English line, urged its readers to show their fellow Americans that however much they sympathized with the Irish Republican cause, the Irish-American community would never rise in arms against the United States. The paper pledged that it was committed to "America and to America alone."[22] From the far more conservative end of the political spectrum, Cardinal James Gibbons, only the second American to attain that status, said after the Rising that all American Catholics had "to take an active, personal, and vital interest" in the welfare of the United States and that loyalty to America must take priority over any other national identity, including loyalty to Ireland itself.[23]

That the Easter Rising and its aftermath coincided with the start of an American presidential campaign only raised the stakes. Wilson and his Republican challengers drew distinctions between the majority of German- and Irish-Americans, whose votes they coveted, and those "hyphenated" Americans they saw as potentially disloyal. For example, when the American-born anti-English activist Jeremiah O'Leary sent Wilson a sneering "congratulatory" telegram after a Democrat lost his seat in Wilson's home state of New Jersey, the president retorted that he would be "deeply mortified" to have the votes of "disloyal Americans" like him. "Since you have access to many disloyal Americans and I have not," Wilson replied to O'Leary, "I will ask you to convey this message to them."[24] Trying to draw a line between "good" and "bad" German- and Irish-Americans proved to be another tightrope that both politicians tried to walk during the fall presidential campaign, largely without any great success.

The political map of the 1916 election contributed to the heated dialogue and the tricky political posturing for votes from both the nativist and the immigrant blocs. It did not, however, reflect the dominant patterns in the Irish-American community. Irish-American newspapers and leaders insisted that there was no monolithic "Irish vote," trying as they were to head off any lingering fears of a shadowy Catholic political influence reaching back to the Vatican. Voting patterns for Irish-Americans were indeed in flux. The Irish, who had voted heavily for Wilson and the Democrats in 1912, split their vote in 1916, with working-class Irish voters largely staying loyal to the Democrats and middle-class Irish voters largely switching to the Republicans. Cardinal James Gibbons himself disavowed any public discussion of politics, saying, "The Catholic Church is not in politics and I am not in politics."[25]

Demographics may also have played a role in deciding the Irish-American vote. The large waves of Irish immigration to the United States having slowed by the turn of the century, the vast majority of Irish-Americans were, unlike most Americans of Italian or eastern European ancestry, born in the United States. They included men like Gibbons, who used the fiftieth anniversary celebrations of his ordination in 1916 to praise his devotion to the United States, and California senator James Phelps who said in the same year that "in a contest of loyalties between the Old Land and the New Land," Irish-Americans would always "espouse the cause of the New." They also included the film and stage star Wilton Lackaye who said, "I should be the last person in the world to be in favor of hyphenated movements. . . . As far as I am concerned I would just as soon shoot an Irishman as a German if they came menacing New York."[26]

Even for those Irish-Americans who took a deep interest in Ireland, the Allied side paradoxically offered greater appeal by early 1917, notwithstanding Britain's brutal response to the Easter Rising. Wilson's steady march toward the concept of national self-determination seemed to hold out the best hope for the future of Ireland, but only if the Allies won the war. An Allied victory, with America as a member of the winning coalition, could put pressure on Great Britain to accept the idea of self-determination and apply it to Ireland.[27] That pressure might not solve all of the problems of the troubled island, but it seemed to many Irish-Americans to offer the best hope of gaining autonomy on the Home Rule model, or even outright independence, with a minimum of bloodshed. Tammany Hall politician and Democratic Party boss John Quinn bitterly opposed British policy in Ireland, wrote editorials denouncing the execution of Roger Casement, and pledged to resist any plans for the partition of Ireland after war. Still, by 1917 he also argued that only a shared Anglo-American victory over Germany could give Ireland the Home Rule it so badly needed.[28]

Paradoxical (and even tragic) though it might seem, therefore, by early 1917 Ireland's future increasingly depended on a British-American victory.

As William McKearney wrote in Cleveland's *Catholic Universe*, "There can be no such thing as hoping the United States wins but that England loses.... We are fighting the same fight and must win."[29] For Ireland to benefit at all from this war, the Allies had to win and the United States had to be in a position to help dictate peace terms not only to Germany but to Great Britain as well. In 1917, unlike 1914, a German victory no longer seemed to hold out any hope at all for Ireland; more important, England's difficulty no longer seemed to be Ireland's opportunity.[30]

Like Irish-Americans, German-Americans faced pressure from their fellow Americans to demonstrate that no contrast existed between their dual identities. The Anti-Hyphen and "100% Americanism" campaigns that were such a feature of the 1916 election season were aimed at both groups, but in the wake of the events of the previous two years, German-Americans felt their weight more heavily than any other single community. Although the process of acculturation was rapidly changing the nature of German-American communities, in 1910 German was still the second-most spoken language in the United States and the nation had more than five hundred German-language newspapers. St. Louis alone had five.[31] Still, the war occurred at the end of "a decades-long process of cultural negotiation and accommodation" that had made German-Americans in 1914 virtually indistinguishable from the dominant culture of their countrymen.[32] German-Americans thus saw pressure on them to conform to a culture into which they had already assimilated as an unnecessary slur on the loyalty of a people who had become as American as any other group.

In addition to being highly acculturated, German-Americans were a large and diverse population, representing more than eight million people and accounting for an estimated 16 percent of the American electorate. They saw themselves as fully American in every way. As Cardinal George Mundelein (whose father had fought in the Union Army in the Civil War) told an audience in September 1916, "It seems to me that it is rather late in the day to ask the German-American to prove his patriotism. He did that more than half a century ago."[33] What Hugo Münsterberg had noted in 1914 a British journalist also noted in 1916: those Germans born in Germany were likely to be sympathetic to the German cause and read German-language newspapers, but "the second generation is pro-American" in its attitudes and worldview.[34]

Exact data on the voting preferences of German-Americans in the election of 1916 is hard to come by, but qualitative data clearly shows a division of German-American opinion. German newspapers did not endorse either candidate in disproportionate numbers, and in what endorsements they did give, the war was rarely mentioned as a reason. The New York *Times* argued after the election that "not a single electoral vote was determined by the German-American vote" because, despite their raw numbers, German-Americans diverged in their voting patterns based on religion, class, and other factors unrelated to the war.[35] One quantitative analysis found that in the heavily German districts of Milwaukee, which Wilson won in 1912, the vote split in 1916. Wilson won just 26.8 percent of the vote in those districts (down from 45.2 percent four years earlier), while Hughes won 39.4 percent and the Socialist Allen Benson won 33.5 percent. Much of Benson's support may have been a protest vote against the two mainstream candidates, neither of whom had much to recommend them to a German-American electorate. Wilson had angered many of them with his Anti-Hyphen messages and Hughes suffered badly from his association with the vociferously anti-German Theodore Roosevelt.[36]

If they did not agree on electoral preferences at home, neither did German-Americans agree about the actions of their ancestral homeland. Non-Prussian Germans, which constituted the majority of German immigration to the United States in the nineteenth and early twentieth centuries, could be quite critical of the behavior of the Prussian-dominated government. Otto Kahn, a New York–based banker born in Mannheim in the western state of Baden-Württemberg and a former soldier in the Kaiser's Hussars, noted that the Germany into which he was born had disappeared under decades of Prussian domination. "From each successive visit to Germany for twenty-five years," he told a group in Pennsylvania, "I came away more appalled by the sinister transmutation Prussianism had wrought amongst the people and by the pretentious menace I recognized in it for the entire world." The Prussians, he argued, had worked to "pervert the mentality—indeed the very fiber and moral substance—of the German people, a people which until misled, corrupted and systematically poisoned by the Prussian ruling caste, was and deserved to be an honored, valued, and welcome member of the family of nations." While Kahn had hoped until the last minute that a war between the United States and Germany could be averted, he saw it as worth the sacrifices it would entail if it destroyed the kaiser's autocracy and gave the German people a chance to determine their own future.[37]

Kahn had obviously rooted his thinking in the Two Germanys thesis and saw the war in Europe not only as a contest between the Central Powers and the Allies, but a contest between Prussia and a democratic Germany as well. With America leading the world and Wilson setting the peace terms, the latter had a chance to reemerge if the Allies won and the war offered Germany a magnanimous peace based on friendship and democracy instead of one based on French, Russian, or British vengeance. In another public address given at about the same time, Kahn argued that the values he had once admired in Germany now found their greatest expression in the United States. Only American ideals, he argued, could form the basis of a postwar world because they stood for "the things of humanity, liberty, justice, and mercy, for which the best men among all the nations—including the German nation—have fought and bled these many generations past, which were the ideals of Luther, Goethe, Schiller, Kant, and a host of others who had made the name of Germany great and beloved until fanatical Prussianism, run amok, came to make its deeds a byword and a hissing."[38] Paradoxical though it might seem, Kahn argued that an American-led victory could therefore set not just the victors but a defeated Germany on the path of a future of peace and progress.

Another German-American saw the situation in the same way that Kahn did, although perhaps with a greater sense of tragedy. He wrote, in an article first published by the Chicago *Tribune* but soon republished in newspapers nationwide, "It sickens my soul to think of this Nation going forth to help destroy people many of whom are bound to me by ties of blood and friendship. But it must be so." The war was like "a dreadful surgical operation." And as for the "fear of the hyphen"— and what the German-Americans would do—he was clear: "No such thing exists." German-Americans were united in the cause of war against Germany, for "the lion and the lamb can not lie down together. One or the other must perish."[39] Of course, not all German-Americans took their case this far, but these and the statements of other German-Americans showed that they saw no conflict between their German ancestry and their American citizenship.

What German-American politician Charles Nagel called the "perfect amalgamation of our people" played a key role in this process. No group in the United States had reached such a level of acculturation. To Nagel, this high level of assimilation meant that no distinct German-American identity any longer existed. Germans had become Americans in every sense, including disagreeing among themselves on political issues.[40] The German-American newspaperman Edward Rumely saw in positive terms what Hugo Münsterberg had seen in negative terms. Whereas Münsterberg bemoaned the fact that "German-Americans are placing the American interest above [that of] Germany," Rumely saw it as a positive milestone marking his community's acculturation into mainstream society.[41] Cardinal Mundelein agreed, supporting Preparedness campaigns in the Midwest and pledging the unwavering patriotism of German-Americans, as he noted in September 1916: "This [America] is the land of their adoption; the land where their children were born; the land where they have lived their lives and where their bones will rest."[42] As a final example, the head of the German department at the City College of New York wrote the following month that after many years of teaching German-American students he had concluded that Germans born in the United States seek "as a rule to break all contact with Germany and to become as Anglo-Saxon as possible" with the consequence that they rarely saw the world as people in Germany did.[43]

Imperial Germany's supporters continued to make arguments in its defense, but these arguments became less and less convincing the longer the war ground on. When George Sylvester Viereck bet most of his remaining credibility on his assertion that the aforementioned Zimmermann Telegram was a British hoax, only—as we shall see—to have the German foreign minister himself confirm its authenticity, Viereck largely faded from influence. He had already come under fire for his increasingly inchoate and bizarre ramblings. The New York *Herald* tired of Viereck's constant accusations of hidden plots and secret treaties between the British and American elites. The newspaper called him a false prophet and his newspaper a book of false faith.

In the summer of 1916, Viereck published one of his strangest stories. In it, Woodrow Wilson awakens from a dream and speaks to George Washington, who makes a case for Germany, telling Wilson that

America's old nemesis the British are to blame for the war, and that the Germans had acted legally in sinking the *Lusitania*. Only after Wilson is convinced by his interlocutor's speech to forgive Germany does the figure reveal himself not as George Washington, but George Viereck. The implication that Washington himself would have supported the German cause drew anger from American readers, as did Viereck's statement that only the Germans and Irish had their adopted homeland's true interests at heart. The rest of the American people, he implied, were dupes of Wilson and the man Viereck described as "the very devil" himself, Theodore Roosevelt.[44]

Hugo Münsterberg's speeches also became more extreme throughout 1916. He was no longer content with touting the superiority of German culture to Slavic culture, but to American culture as well. In October 1916 he gave one of his most controversial (and one of his last) speeches in Hoboken, New Jersey, in which he predicted that American individualism would disappear forever as German values came to dominate over degenerate democracies like Britain, France, and the United States. Just as Napoleon had spread the ideas of the French revolution, so, too, would the armies of Kaiser Wilhelm II lead "the earth to be Germanized." That process would force "the subordination of the individual to the national ideal" in the United States just as it had in Germany. This speech led many of his Harvard colleagues to demand that he be dismissed from the university and, in the words of one professor who had previously defended his right to speak, "sent out of the country."[45]

The more mainstream German-language press had long given up the extreme positions of Viereck and Münsterberg. As 1916 came to a close, it continued to urge that, whatever their feelings about the war in Europe, Americans should urge that their nation remain neutral. It also continued to blame the English media for its negative portrayals of Germany, criticize the behavior of the British in Ireland, and excoriate Russia for a host of real and alleged atrocities.[46] Together these events seemed to many German-Americans to prove that neither side had a monopoly on either justice or wickedness in wartime. The problem, they argued, lay less with Germany than with (in the eyes of socialists) the nature of capitalism or (in the eyes of middle-class Germans) the threat that Russia posed to Germany and all of civilized Europe. They urged above all that the United States not tie itself to the goals of the

British but to enter the war, if entrance became an absolute necessity, for strictly American goals, such as self-defense.

A number of prominent Americans were eager to differentiate between Germany and German-Americans. Noted Brooklyn Congregationalist minister Newell Dwight Hillis preached against Germany in a fiery sermon, but reminded his listeners that German-Americans, having "escaped conscription and years of military service, with heavy taxation" saw the world as Americans did.[47] The Chicago *Day Book* told its readers not to pay much attention to the extreme positions of German newspapers like *Fatherland*. Readers of those papers, the *Day Book* noted, were older people eager to read the news in their native language and more susceptible to the propaganda that the German embassy gave Viereck to print under the guise of "news." The younger generation of Germans "was educated in [American] public schools and read newspapers printed in the English language." They therefore behaved and thought as their fellow Americans did.[48]

Ultimately, even as anger toward Germany continued to rise, most Americans failed to see any conflict between German ancestry and American citizenship. A Minnesota newspaper in a heavily German community reset the terms of the hyphen controversy by defining "German-Americans" as "American citizens of German blood, who are first for their country, America."[49] Their fellow Americans could therefore count on them to defend the United States no matter what foreign crises came their way. The war bore out this argument in the military service of Americans with German ancestry such as John Pershing, Dwight Eisenhower, and one of America's biggest wartime heroes, aviation ace Eddie Rickenbacker.[50]

As with the Irish, several German-American religious leaders prevailed upon their communities to pledge their loyalty to the United States first and foremost. They included the influential theologian Reinhold Niebuhr, who changed his Detroit congregation's language of worship from German to English as a statement of patriotism.[51] German Catholics called on the warring parties to support German overtures to the Vatican at the end of 1916 as a means of making peace. They also argued that the overture itself showed Germany's willingness to come to a compromise peace.[52] Others, like Cardinal Mundelein, believed until the very end that war between Germany and the United States could never happen. If it did, however, he pledged the loyalty of the German-American community "from the little drummer boy in the orphan asylum to the aged veteran in the Old Folks' home."[53]

Despite all this, it would be fair to conclude that German-Americans became the group most skeptical of going to war and also of American foreign policy more generally. During the 1916 election, they saw themselves trapped between Wilson, whose pro-British stance they mistrusted, and Hughes, who, while not personally objectionable, had objectionable men supporting him. One German-American supporter of Wilson gave a speech to a heavily German audience urging them to reelect the president. A Hughes victory, he warned, would mean that Theodore Roosevelt would have the dominant voice on foreign affairs in the new administration and J. P. Morgan, "the practical financial agent of the Allies in this country," would control American economic policy. "Are there any German-Americans in this country who wish to see this state of affairs? An answer to this question is unnecessary."[54] What German-American votes Wilson did win likely had less to do with issues related to the war than his party's sustained opposition to Prohibition, the one issue that unquestionably united German-Americans. Sixteen governors, all Republicans, were running for election using Prohibition as a central plank of their platforms.[55] In this sense, even for German-Americans the election likely turned more on domestic issues than foreign ones.

When they did discuss the war, most German-Americans hoped to hold on to neutrality for as long as possible. On a trip through Missouri, Wisconsin, and Minnesota—the heart of German-America—during the election campaign, Ray Stannard Baker found German-Americans "unconvinced" by the arguments of Roosevelt, Root, and other Republicans that war was imminent, but not necessarily hostile to the notion of national defense should American relations with Germany take a turn for the worse.[56] They argued that America should go to war, if at all, for American interests, not British ones.[57] Whatever happened, however, they would show their loyalty to their adopted homeland and hope that German-American relations would somehow take a turn for the better. Should war come, however, they had made their choice clear: they would stand with their fellow Americans and hope that the United States could, through war, establish a just peace for Germany, Europe, and the world.

Of the four groups, American Jews probably represented the least homogeneity. They were divided along class lines, ideological lines, even linguistic lines; as with the Germans and Irish, in 1916 no single "Jewish vote" existed.[58] Jews, moreover, fought in all of the armies of Europe, and therefore the American Jewish community had no single country to which it felt any ancestral allegiance. Indeed, few Jews felt any link to the Old World at all, having escaped pogroms and violence to make new lives as far away from the *shtetls* of eastern Europe as they could.[59]

They did, however, agree on one subject in 1914: the hope that the war might lead to the destruction of the notoriously anti-Semitic regime of Tsar Nicholas II in Russia. Rabbi H. G. Enelow of one of America's most influential synagogues, the Reform Temple Emanu-El on Fifth Avenue in Manhattan, called the name of Russia "a synonym of nothing so much as Jewish suffering."[60] As a result, most Jews tended to favor the Central Powers when the war began. Although anti-Semitism surely existed in those countries as well, Austria-Hungary and Germany had reputations as far more tolerant of Jews than either Russia or France. Russian-born Abraham Cahan, editor of the most influential Jewish-American newspaper, New York City's *Daily Forward*, based his paper's initial stance on the war almost exclusively on his hatred of Nicholas II's regime. So, too, did the leading Jewish socialist newspapers, which hoped for a German victory over what one of them called "Nicholas' pogromists." Still, this support was largely passive. Most Jewish newspapers in 1914 and 1915 argued for American neutrality, even after the *Lusitania* and *Sussex* incidents, blaming them not on Germany but on "the politics of war" more generally.[61]

Both domestic and international events began to change that pro–Central Powers preference. Most Jews, especially the younger generations, had undergone a process of acculturation similar to that of the Irish and the Germans. They preferred to speak English instead of Yiddish, and began to dress, act, eat, and vote more like other Americans. Whereas the Irish and Germans had their governors and senators, Jews also had prominent public figures in American political life, including the Bavarian-born governor of Idaho Moses Alexander; the Austrian-born Felix Frankfurter, on the faculty of the law school at Harvard; and Louis Brandeis, nominated to the Supreme Court in January 1916, as evidence of Jewish acceptance into the broader society.[62] Even *Life*, not normally terribly sympathetic to immigrant issues, praised the nomination in terms flattering not only to Brandeis but to Jews more generally: "Mr. Brandeis is a Jew, and up to now there has never been a Jew in [*sic*] the Supreme Court. Perhaps it's time we had one" because "to serve mankind . . . [is] the Jewish mission."[63] From Springfield, Massachusetts, Rabbi Samuel Price picked up the acculturation theme in an address he gave to a high school graduating class in August. "You are no longer Polish or Russian or even Jewish by nationality," he told them. "Remember your duties as American citizens. It matters not where you or your parents came from. You are at all times first and foremost Americans. Show your unstinted and unlimited loyalty to the flag and the country which has given you all the opportunities in the world and has elevated you to the high and exalted position of American citizen."[64]

As American attitudes toward Germany grew harsher, the attitudes of the country's Jews moved with them. This shift by no means equated to support for Russia, but it did mean a much closer alignment of Jewish voices with mainstream American ones. In February 1916 the first American Jewish Congress met in Philadelphia. Rabbi Stephen Wise, one of the most influential Jewish leaders in America and a prominent Jewish leader during World War II, noted that they chose the word *Congress* intentionally because "its American associations have endeared it to us native and adoptive children of the Republic." Chicago's Judge Hugo Pam further noted that the Congress chose to meet in Philadelphia because "in every nation the world over" Philadelphia stands as a symbol of freedom and democracy. Both speakers noted the easy congruence and shared values between American and Jewish identity.[65]

In the early months of the war, American Jews had focused on sending relief and aid to Jews suffering all along the Eastern Front. The war there, more fluid and more destructive of civilian property than the static Western Front, moved back and forth across Russian Poland, Galicia, Belarus, and other areas of high Jewish populations. Much of that aid never reached the people who needed it, as the German, Austro-Hungarian, and Russian governments alike stole it to give it to their own people. Rabbi Price noted in late 1914 that although "American Jews are doing a great deal to relieve the suffering, it seems that the calamity is so great that we can never do enough."[66] In June 1916, Isaac Siegel, who represented New York in the House of Representatives, delivered a lecture at Carnegie Hall on his trip to German-ruled Galicia and Poland in late 1915. Siegel told his audience that under German rule, eastern European Jews were living in "heartbreaking" agony, with 750,000 of them at risk of starvation. While he certainly did not want to see the region go back to Russian control, he also recognized that life under Germany did not offer the hope of a better future that many American Jews had anticipated for them in 1914. "The suffering and poverty that I have seen and which I did not have the means of alleviating," he told his audience, "caused me many tears."[67]

As soon became obvious to Siegel, Price, and others, life for Jews under German dominance offered little cause for optimism. The kaiser had made positive statements about the loyalty of German Jews at the outset of the war, but the behavior of German armies in the eastern regions they conquered suggested a far less hopeful future. The German Army forcibly relocated tens of thousands of Lithuanian and Polish Jews from their homes, sending some back to Germany as laborers. American observers reported that German policy in Poland after 1916 was introducing a system of proportional representation that would isolate Jews from any say in Polish politics. Jews had also become victims of anti-Semitic riots in Krakow and elsewhere.[68] In Berlin, anti-Semitic Reichstag deputies made accusations that Jews were evading their duty to Germany. The calls grew so vituperative that the German War Ministry ordered a *Judenzählung*, or Jew Census, in October 1916. When the census showed that Jews were, in fact, serving in numbers proportionate to their share of the population, the Reichstag suppressed the report, allowing the allegations to remain unanswered and become a key feature of right-wing discourse throughout the war and after.[69]

The Jew Census and the rise of anti-Semitism in the Central Powers more generally shifted American Jewish support away from Germany and Austria-Hungary. Russian advances into Austrian Galicia in 1914 led to an influx of rural Jews to Austrian cities, which in turn led to a rise in anti-Semitic attitudes as the cities could not easily absorb the new arrivals.[70] Attitudes in Germany seemed to show, moreover, that the modern version of anti-Semitism was, according to the *American Hebrew and Jewish Messenger*, "made in Germany," even if it had temporarily disappeared in 1914 in the interests of creating a united front to fight the war. Under the increasing pressures of war, however, it had shown its ugly face for all the world to see.[71] The Boston-based *Jewish Advocate* reported in January 1917 that the anti-Semitism in Germany since the start of the war had changed American Jews to a pro-Allied position, notwithstanding their abiding hatred of the tsarist regime in Russia. "We believed then [in 1914] that the Jews could afford to be neutral. Today we feel there is something of shame, the folly of stupidity, in any such selection of our friends." Germany, the paper chillingly argued, planned to "grind the Jews into powder" in the areas they occupied, especially Romania and Poland.[72] Another Jewish newspaper predicted in the same month that Germany would use Jews as scapegoats if they lost the war. European Jews, it sadly noted, "are playthings in the hands of strangers."[73]

The Allies (other than Russia) had meanwhile moved to a position of support for allowing the Jews displaced by the war in east Europe to resettle in Palestine. News about British and French support for a Jewish homeland reached the United States in the war's opening months. From Massachusetts, Rabbi Price first made mention of the idea in his diary entry of November 7, 1914, noting that the move "is an appeal to the Jews for support."[74] Such support was not long in coming from American Jews. In 1916, Israel Zangwill, a popular British humorist and author of *The Melting Pot*, a hit 1908 play that Roosevelt had praised, published *The War for the World*. In it, he told his readers that the rise in German anti-Semitism and Germany's brutal treatment of Belgium and Poland showed the bleak future that the Jews of eastern Europe would face if Germany won the war. He argued for siding with the Allies in the hopes that the British and French would in turn fulfill their promises of creating a Jewish homeland. The pro-Zionist Zangwill toured the United States later in the year with his wife, speaking to audiences mostly about theater, but often proffering his opinion that a British-French victory offered the best hope for the salvation of the Jews from the traditional oppression of Jews in eastern Europe.[75]

Despite the continued horrors inflicted on Jews by the Russians, the increasing support that the French and British gave to the idea of Zionism led to greater Jewish support for the Allies. French attitudes seemed to have come a long way from the anti-Semitic depths of the Dreyfus Affair, leading Rabbi Enelow to write that France knew how to "right a wrong." Dreyfus himself, Enelow noted, was back in a French uniform and, in contrast to Austria and Germany, the war had led to "a cessation of anti-Semitism in France," proving that "a long history—full of heroism and honor—links the Jew with France."[76]

The position of the British government underwent perhaps the most profound change. Herbert Samuel, a Zionist secular Jew, accepted the position of home secretary in the British cabinet in January 1916, seemingly showing the assimilation of British Jews at the highest levels of society. Samuel helped to influence the publication the following year of the Balfour Declaration, famously promising the Jews "a national home" in Palestine. These events led Rabbi Enelow in New York City to proclaim that the cause of England and the cause of the Jewish people shared a dedication to democracy and "the liberation of the Jewish soul" from oppression. "As long, I say, as England remains true to democracy," he wrote, "so long will Israel be safe under her flag."[77]

American Jews, as much as if not more than any of the hyphenated groups, professed their loyalty first and foremost to the land of their adoption, and well they should have, aware as they were that the United States had saved them from pogroms and the horrors of the Eastern front. Samuel Price warned in a Rosh Hashanah sermon he delivered in September 1916 that the war might lead to the destruction of European Judaism, meaning that "the preservation of Judaism and of Israel's future will henceforth devolve upon us, American Jews."[78] Even American Zionists argued that their support for a refuge for eastern European Jews did not in any way stand in contrast to the life that Jews had built in the United States. As the *Maccabean*, a leading Zionist newspaper, noted in March 1917: "Our love and loyalty go out to America, not only because it has been a haven of refuge for our oppressed people, but because we have derived inspiration and strength from the ideals and enthusiasm that are America's contribution to modern civilization." Jews, it pledged, would "be among the first to come forward prepared to make our personal sacrifices for American national interests should the efforts of the President to avert war be unsuccessful, just as we have done in the past in moments of national crisis."[79]

Jewish interests and American interests more generally came into even greater harmony with the abdication of the tsar in March 1917. For Wilson, the abdication meant that he could now depict the war as one of democracies against despots, thus clearing the way for the most important American slogan of the war, "A War to Make the World Safe for

Democracy." For Rabbi Samuel Price in Massachusetts, the abdication meant nothing less than "*Freedom for Jews*," the words he wrote in unusually large letters in his diary when he heard that the tsar had abdicated. The abdication brought with it the hope of a new government that might safeguard Jewish rights in post-tsarist Russia.[80] From Cincinnati, the *American Israelite* thought the abdication so momentous that it proposed adding a new holiday to the Jewish calendar. "The Romanoff dynasty, the wickedest the world has ever known [and] the whole tyrannous Russian autocratic fabric has tumbled into ruins.... Let us praise God that He has allowed us to live to see this day."[81]

A German victory under these circumstances would destroy what Rabbi Enelow called the "marvelous change" in Russia from anti-Semitic autocracy to an open and free democracy. Should the Germans win, they would likely impose an autocratic government in Russia and return to some version of the tsar's anti-Semitic policies. Should the Allies win, Britain and France could help make the seeming Russian turn to democracy permanent. Jews now had to support the new Russia and its democratic leaders as they began to redeem Russia "of the past and its sins," including its notorious anti-Semitism. The cause of America, the Allies, and the Jews had now merged into perfect accord. "If we would help the Jews, we must do what we can toward the help of Russian democracy," Rabbi Enelow said in a sermon at Temple Emanu-El. "Let democracy triumph in Russia, and it will mean the triumph of the Jew."[82] The *American Israelite* further noted that it was "happy that we can join with all others of our fellow Americans in welcoming the new Russian regime which marks the entry of Russia among the civilized nations."[83] That war for civilization had now become as much a war for American Jews as for any other group.

Like most white Americans, African-Americans raised their voices in outrage at the German invasion of Belgium and the sinking of the *Lusitania*. In a book titled *The World War for Human Rights*, Howard University dean Kelly Miller called the Germans "ungainly, acrimonious and obdurate, part Saxon, part Hun, part Vandal and part Visigoth, a creature of blood and iron."[84] Germany's behavior struck most African-Americans as dangerous to world order, even if they tended to see Germany less as standing apart from a civilized Europe than as merely an extreme example of the worst aspects of the European-dominated world imperial system. The African-American newspaper *Iowa State Bystander* was among those that blamed Germany for the outbreak of the war in 1914 and criticized the espionage and sabotage networks that the Germans and Austrians had developed in the United States.[85]

African-Americans saw the war in terms broadly congruent with those of their fellow Americans. But they also tended to see the war's outbreak as a function of "the global color line."[86] They did not forget that Belgium, the object of so much American sympathy and charity, had brutalized African subjects in its colony in the Congo as part of Europe's general history of racism, imperialism, and slavery. The same white Americans who volunteered their time and money to alleviate Belgian suffering had mostly stood silent in the face of widespread Congolese suffering at the hands of those same Belgians.[87]

Of course African-Americans could hardly forget that Americans were preaching law and order in the international arena while largely turning their backs on disorder at home, most notably in the form of Jim Crow laws and the nation's failure to pass anti-lynching laws.[88] The United States averaged fifty lynchings per year during Wilson's presidency. There were five lynchings in Louisiana alone the week that Europe went to war in 1914 and five more in a single night just outside Gainesville, Florida, in August 1916.[89] Nevertheless, Wilson still refused even the largely symbolic step of forming the National Race Committee that the NAACP recommended to study ways to improve racial justice in America.[90]

Little wonder, then, that many African-Americans wanted the United States first to clean up its own record at home before trying to solve the problems of Europe. Or, as Alabama native Joseph Manning wrote in the Washington *Bee*, "It is not consistent to advocate government with the consent of the governed, and democracy for other lands without applying the principle everywhere in our own land." The Baltimore *Afro-American* was more blunt: "Let us have a real democracy for the United States and then we can advise a house cleaning over on the other side of the water."[91] The newspaper further argued that black Americans would be hard pressed to find any moral difference at all between Germany's "ruthlessness on the high seas" and the "ruthlessness in my home town."[92] African-Americans were therefore as likely to see hypocrisy as high ideals in United States foreign policy, especially coming from the administration of the deeply racist Wilson. The New York *Age* found little substantive difference between the Ottoman Empire's murder of Armenians and the lynchings at home. If the United States could not prevent atrocities at home, it asked, how could it arrogate to itself the right to stop them in Belgium, Armenia, or Poland? The *Afro-American* invoked the kaiser's words upon invading Belgium when it suggested that the United States Constitution itself was a mere "scrap of paper" as long as lynchings went not only unpunished but largely uninvestigated as well.[93]

Differences on the domestic front notwithstanding, African-Americans, like their white compatriots, generally wanted their nation to remain neutral for as long as possible. They also shared white America's generally pro-Allied sympathies. Most of these sentiments focused on France, whose citizens, the New York *Age* argued, "have less prejudice against Negroid people than Germany, and have been more generous in their treatment of West Indian and African natives of their colonies than Germany, or any country." France had, indeed, made extensive use of African troops, especially the Tirailleurs Sénégalais, who quickly established a reputation as some of the French Army's most elite soldiers. Their exploits on the Western Front so terrified the Germans that they objected to France using African troops on European battlefields, calling their presence inappropriate in a war between civilized states.[94] African-Americans might also have recalled the warm reception that boxer Jack Johnson had received in Paris in 1914, as noted earlier. By contrast, Germany had recently fought a brutal war against the Herero in southwest Africa that killed seventy thousand Herero soldiers and civilians between 1904 and 1908.[95]

France was certainly no racial paradise, but it struck many African-Americans as far ahead of most of the rest of the "civilized" world and quite ahead of racial views in their own country.[96] In the United States, Jim Crow laws were at their height in 1914, and the blatantly racist film *Birth of a Nation*, released in March 1915, drew praise from across the country, including from the White House itself. Wilson had recently resegregated the federal civil service and had named Josephus Daniels as his secretary of the navy despite Daniels's open endorsement of white supremacy. Postmaster General Albert S. Burleson, who led the movement to resegregate the civil service, also had outspoken white supremacist views, as did Treasury Secretary (and Wilson son-in-law) William Gibbs McAdoo.[97]

Despite the racism prevalent in the country from Pennsylvania Avenue to Main Street, most African-Americans nevertheless supported Preparedness. They opposed any form of Preparedness that shut them out, however, arguing that the defense of the nation should be the responsibility of all its people. As the Savannah *Tribune* succinctly argued, "The Negro believes in Preparedness, but not in any Preparedness which does not take him into account."[98] The African-American community saw an opportunity to use Preparedness and the threatening approach of war to demonstrate their reliability, equality, and loyalty to the nation. As the NAACP's Kathryn Johnson noted, the war "carried in its wake a wonderful opening of opportunities for the American negro." Or, as an Atlanta minister told his congregation on April 2, 1917, "The black man has nothing to lose and everything to gain" from demonstrating loyalty to the nation. Even W. E. B. Du Bois came to support the war, although he noted that "this is our war and not Woodrow Wilson's." He hoped that African-Americans would earn the respect of white America from the war and acquire the skills to propel a new generation forward toward increased political and economic opportunities.[99]

African-Americans demonstrated their support for the nation by offering to put their own lives on the line. They generally supported the Continental Army Plan as a way of allowing African-American men to serve their country and, when that failed, responded by joining National Guard units in states that permitted it. The Illinois African-American community took great pride in the opening of the 8th Regiment Armory, the only entirely black National Guard armory in the country. Thousands of people came out to see its opening and the parade that accompanied it.[100] In the summer of 1916, the 15th New York National Guard Regiment opened a recruiting station in Harlem, hoping to attract African-American men. The governor of New York himself presented the unit with its brand new colors and the regiment ended up turning people away because of the massive interest.[101] Enlistees into the unit included African-American celebrities, such as musician Jim Europe; baseball star Spottswood Poles (known as "the Black Ty Cobb"); and boxer George "Kid" Cotton, who came from Pittsburgh to sign up. Most of the regimental officers (including political scion Hamilton Fish III[102]) were white, but the 15th did give a few officer commissions to African-Americans.[103]

African-American newspapers across the country hailed the New York regiment and saw it as a model for other states to follow. The regiment proved to one editor that "there is no question as to the soldierly qualities of the race," and that black military service could undermine many of the claims of white supremacists while at the same time proving that African-Americans merited full citizenship. Even the South, the paper argued, should look to African-American soldiers as a means of meeting the current Preparedness emergency.[104] At least some Southerners agreed. In a positive, if patronizing, tone, the Atlanta *Constitution* argued that military service had already inspired "Aryan courage and restrained discipline" in African soldiers fighting in the French Army; it could do the same for African-Americans in the United States Army.[105]

The service of African-American soldiers in Mexico underscored the point.[106] Major Charles Young, one of the few African-American graduates of the United States Military Academy at West Point, led a squadron of the 10th United States Cavalry into Mexico, on one highly publicized occasion routing enemy forces and rescuing trapped American soldiers without losing a man. The Kansas City *Sun* praised the "brilliant" officer, undoubtedly the most famous African-American soldier in the country, as "one of the best tacticians" in the army. African-American troops, it noted, were "doing wonderful work" in Mexico. It also lauded another black soldier, George Prioleau, as "one of the most active, intelligent, and popular men of the race," a man who "is idolized by the men of the army." African-Americans had clearly proven their worth in Mexico and could do so in Europe as well if the need arose. "Colored troops," the newspaper's editor noted after a trip to the border, were "both respected and feared by Mexicans."[107]

An Arizona newspaper also implied that African-American military service in Mexico could translate in a war against Germany, noting that black troops were "among the first heroes" of the punitive expedition against Pancho Villa. In typically paternalistic tones, the paper supported the formation of more black regiments because "the negro in most cases possesses a capacity for personal devotion and loyalty to his leaders that make[s] him a blithe and willing fighter." Racialized though such images usually were, they nevertheless seemed at least to open an opportunity for African-Americans to prove wrong the assertions of some whites that black men had no place in the defense of their country.[108]

The war might do still more for the African-American community. Noting the way that the Civil War had begun over the issue of states' rights, but eventually became a struggle to end slavery, the Chicago *Defender* even dared to hope that the war in Europe might help lead to the end of imperialism and perhaps mark the beginning of the end of racism as well. "If the twentieth century is to be the high noon of the white races who dominate all other peoples through their might, un-mindful of right and justice, HOW SOON will the CLOCK of TIME STRIKE the hour of SUNSET when their DECLINE will have been ordained?" Recalling the ways that the fortunes of war can change quickly, the editorial ended, "Napoleon's sun rose at Austerlitz but it set forever at Waterloo." Perhaps the same might happen to the European colonial empires.[109]

As the United States approached war, step by step, African-Americans saw a link between the nation's goals and those of their own community. Thus, although the Philadelphia *Tribune* noted at the height of the Preparedness fever in the summer of 1916 that "the Federal Union ex-pects more of Afro-American citizens in war and peace than it gives, or is willing to give them, in return," it also argued that the community should nevertheless stand with their fellow Americans in a time of na-tional crisis.[110] The Baltimore-based *Afro-American* argued that for the black community, Preparedness would bring with it "industrial and civic" gains as well as military ones. "We can show Germany that we can strike preparedness by aiming at citizens. Citizens make the best sol-diers."[111] In other words, African-Americans were willing to trade their military service to the nation in a time of crisis for promises of greater equality, although many doubted that white America would in the end live up to its share of the bargain. The newspaper therefore joined in the Anti-Hyphen campaign, arguing for mandatory English classes for all immigrants and debating changing its name to the *American* in order to take the hyphen out of its title.[112] Perhaps most dramatically, the Richmond *Planet* ran a cartoon showing an African-American soldier planting an American flag in the Deep South. A paper behind him reads "52 Negroes Lynched in 1916." The caption nevertheless states proudly, "Though *you* have slain *mine*, yet you may trust me."[113]

By the end of 1916, like the majority of their fellow Americans, members of these four groups did not actively call for joining the war in Europe. For the most part, they still hoped that the nation would find a way to project its positive values and protect its interests short of belligerence. Still, as 1916 turned into 1917 their views had come into sharper focus and had, for reasons dealing with both their "ethnic" and their "American" identities, come to conform to those of the nation more generally. As the year turned, it had become ever harder to find sharp divisions on the war among groups of Americans. Thus, for reasons having little to do with coercion or propaganda, the goals of most members of these four groups came to overlap with those of Americans more generally.

This process sparked the development of what one scholar has called a "tri-faith America," although he locates this process in the Second World War, not the First. The evidence shows, however, that the events of 1914–17 played an enormous, and largely unrecognized and underappreciated, role in forging this new America. It also helped to produce the rough American consensus on foreign policy that broadly held until the 1960s.[114] Even before the country's entry into World War I therefore, the war played an enormous role in catalyzing a decades-long process of acculturation, especially in regard to American views on the nation's relationship to the rest of the world.[115] As 1917 began, few Americans knew the direction that American foreign policy might take. War with Mexico, war with Germany, or a continued shaky neutrality were all possibilities. But whatever was to come, Americans of every group were prepared to face an uncertain future together.

8

Awaiting the Overt Act

HIS SECOND TERM AS PRESIDENT assured, a newly re-elected Woodrow Wilson decided to make another attempt at negotiating an end to the war in Europe. As the leader of the most powerful remaining neutral nation, Wilson believed himself the only world figure who could start the two warring sides on a road toward peace.[1] In December 1916, just a few short days after Charles Evans Hughes officially conceded defeat, Wilson sent a series of diplomatic notes to the belligerent powers, asking them to state their war aims. He hoped to find areas of potential compromise as a basis to promote peace talks. The idea was well intentioned, and it did show the American people that Wilson wanted to explore all options short of war for his country. Still, his efforts found little purchase in Paris, London, and Berlin because the warring powers were just too far apart in their basic strategic positions. The rise of David Lloyd George as British prime minister and Georges Clemenceau as French premier, moreover, put in power two Allied leaders who had no intention of compromising with a German regime that they blamed for the suffering of their peoples since 1914.

Although it was unlikely to succeed, Wilson and his supporters knew that they could use the mere existence of his peace initiative to demonstrate that he had tried to use the influence and the power of the United States to end a war that seemed destined to go on for many more months, if not years. He could also tell the American people that he had done all that he could to end the war peacefully. The only option left to secure the country's future might well be to enter the war. As Wilson himself had said on the campaign trail in Cincinnati in October 1916, "I believe that this business of neutrality is over, that war now has such a scale that the position of neutrals sooner or later becomes intolerable."[2] The central problem, of course, lay in figuring out exactly when that "intolerable" moment had arrived.

While Wilson's efforts at peace never really had much of a chance at bringing an end to the war, the American people generally supported his outreach. They also generally agreed on why they believed that his proposal had failed. A January 1917 review of American newspaper editorial opinions in the *Review of Reviews* praised Wilson for his efforts and put the blame for the failure of the peace talks almost entirely on the German government. The punitive "peace of the sword" that the Germans had imposed on Romania in 1916 and appeared ready to impose on Russia proved the basic insincerity of the German government.[3] Most Americans, the review noted, thought that "it would be wholly wrong to negotiate at this time with a Germany still too arrogant to confess her sins and plead for mercy." The Germans appeared to be using Wilson's benevolent overtures as a way to buy time to improve their military and diplomatic positions. Or, worse still, they would only accept peace after the complete conquest of their enemies, thus imposing a peace of the sword on Belgium, France, and Britain as well as Romania and Russia, leaving Germany the unquestioned masters of continental Europe.

After Belgium, Armenia, Poland, Mexico, submarine war, sabotage, and many more examples of German wartime behavior, few Americans trusted the German government or wanted it to emerge from the war one bit stronger than it had been in 1914.[4] Its reaction to Wilson's peace efforts did the German government few favors, at least in America's eyes. Not only did it set impossible conditions for peace in its response to the president, it showed a remarkable arrogance while doing so. The German government told Wilson that it was only willing to accept the conditions that the Germans themselves would set. "If, in spite of this offer of peace and reconciliation, the struggle should go on, the four Allied powers (meaning in this case Germany, Austria-Hungary, the Ottoman Empire, and Bulgaria) are resolved to continue to a victorious end, but they disclaim responsibility for this before humanity and history."[5] In other words, if Britain and France did not accept German terms in their entirety, Germany would consider itself to have a free hand to set even harsher conditions of peace after it won the war. This position was so prima facie unacceptable that few Americans could take it seriously or expect the British and French to do so either.

Moreover the Germans showed little remorse for their past crimes. In an interview with the German press at the end of 1916, Wilhelm had said that the terms offered by the Entente to Wilson would "stir Germans to Holy Wrath" if he revealed them; in reality Wilhelm did not even know what those terms were.[6] For their part, neither the French nor the British had shown much interest in negotiating an end to the war on the terms Germany had offered, but they had managed to be diplomatic enough to avoid exhibiting the arrogance that Germany had displayed. The American people, moreover, generally approved of the Allied un-willingness to negotiate with a German government that still insisted on annexations of Belgian, Polish, French, Romanian, Russian, and even neutral Dutch territories as a minimum condition for peace. To allow Germany to come out of the war with such annexations would be akin to allowing a burglar to keep the jewels he had stolen.[7]

In its survey of American opinion, the January 1917 issue of the *Literary Digest* concluded that most Americans believed that Germany had acted in bad faith in its reactions to Wilson's peace efforts. Instead of seeking peace, the German government was stalling the United States in order to attain further conquests, which it could then claim at the end of the war that it had won with German blood and, therefore, had a duty and a right to keep. The United States could not, the magazine argued, "ask Great Britain and France to enter a peace conference beaten and blindfolded, to learn in the dark what terms a Germany conscious of victory is prepared to impose." Germany's behavior in the face of America's honest attempts to end the slaughter, its editors concluded, meant that the "door to peace is closed."[8]

At the very moment that they rejected Wilson's proposals, the Germans seemed to be gearing up for a new round of war. In mid-January American newspapers reported that Germany planned to build a fleet of one thousand submarines for the prosecution of a "ruthless sea war." Having failed to win the war on land, Germany would try to win it at sea. "The German people are ready to bear the consequences," said one report, "for the entire Prussian people were solidly behind their king." This new phase of the war would inevitably lead to greater tensions in Germany's interaction with the United States and halt whatever small amount of momentum remained from Wilson's peace efforts.[9]

The pressure on Wilson was similarly increasing. On January 22, he delivered a speech calling for a "peace without victory," words of which most Americans disapproved, given German behavior. The Hartford *Courant* went as far as to say that if Wilson believed in such a victory then he no longer spoke for the American people. Wilson's defenders made a halfhearted attempt to argue that a peace without victory need not mean a peace without vanquished, but such spin failed to win the president much support. By this point American attitudes had become too hardened against Germany for anyone to want Germany to come away with any gains.[10]

Deciding what, exactly, America should do remained as elusive as ever, from the White House on down. Most Americans had concluded that continued neutrality made war more, not less, likely. That realization certainly made it no easier to decide on specific policy options, however. Most public officials were confused and exasperated, trapped between a desire to do something and a continued reluctance to see war as a desirable option.[11] Michigan governor Woodbridge N. Ferris threw up his hands in exasperation, writing privately to Edward Rumely that he had no idea what steps the president could or should take in the face of the new crisis. "If I had anything better than a guess to offer," he wrote, "I would most cheerfully present it."[12] One prominent Princeton neurologist even argued that for America's leadership to remain officially neutral in a great "moral test" while most of its people supported the Allies could lead to a kind of national neurosis. Continued neutrality under such conditions, he contended, could cause a "sacrificing at least for a generation to come [of] many of the elements essential for clear vision, honesty of purpose, and the strength of mind necessary to face critical situations successfully." As a result of three years of inactivity in the face of danger and evil, Americans might "continue to repress our feelings until we are capable of making only impulsive and irrational efforts to meet actual conditions."[13]

Most Americans feared that the war might go on indefinitely. With Germany dominant on land and Britain still dominant on the sea, neither side had proven capable of delivering a knockout blow to the other. At the beginning of 1917 the only foreseeable route to victory seemed to involve a naval blockade, a strategy that would mean the intentional starvation of millions of Germans, as well as the Poles, Ukrainians, Romanians, Belgians, and other peoples whose lands the Germans were pillaging in an attempt to make up for the shortages they were suffering from the British blockade. A successful strategy of mass starvation would still leave Europe devastated, hardly a solution that anyone saw as ideal. Even absent a deliberate strategy of starvation, millions of Europeans would suffer terribly from famine if the 1917 harvest turned out to be as bad as many experts had begun to predict. For three years, the war had taken millions of men away from their farms, destroyed markets, and led to military control over vital road and rail networks. Massive food shortages, and the public health risks that came along with them, were a real possibility.

Unless the last great neutral power came to the rescue, the war might well mean the final destruction of European civilization. The New World, many felt, now had little choice but to come to the rescue of the Old. If it did not, *Literary Digest* noted, then the war would continue to threaten to "drag this nation into the vortex" on terms not of its own choosing.[14] Should the United States manage to avoid belligerence, it would nonetheless need to stay permanently armed, investing more and more of its own treasure into peacetime defense—an idea odious to Americans of 1917. Heavy military expenditures, mass conscription, and persistent insecurity all seemed to loom if the United States did not help Europe to set its house right, by force if absolutely necessary.

By early 1917, Americans had concluded that they could no longer stand aside as Europe, the world, and the United States itself seemed to be at the breaking point. As one mainstream magazine editorial argued in March, "When war is clearly the one remedy that will rescue the weak from the strong, that will secure justice otherwise unattainable, that will promote righteousness, truth, and peace in the world with the least relative sacrifice—[then] let war be invoked as a remedy and as an instrument for specific achievement." The status quo, with many years of suffering ahead, would likely result in the deaths of more people than those killed by American intervention.[15]

All of this was theory, however. Exact American war aims remained far from clear in the minds of most. Newspaper editorials generally made the argument that honor alone was not worth risking what the *Review of Reviews* called "the terrible business of war" and the attendant threat to hundreds of thousands of American lives.[16] Led by Theodore Roosevelt, many Americans wanted at the very least to see the German government forcibly replaced in a policy of regime change *avant la lettre*, and Germany itself greatly reduced in power. To Roosevelt, once commissioner of the New York City Police Department, after all, the problem did not in its essence differ much from crime. Germany (or, more specifically, the German leadership) had been the guilty party and must face punishment for the rule of law, domestic or international, to have any meaning. Only by meting out the appropriate punishment could the United States send a clear message not just to Germany but to any state that dared to upset the global order.

This police action would not be unilateral, of course, and not all Americans wanted to see France and Britain emerge from it in too powerful a position. For those still suspicious of British motives, the problem was not only Germany, but imperialism and militarism wherever it existed. America should help to promote democracy, reestablish markets, and (maybe) adjust the borders of Europe; the final peace should not crown winners and punish losers, but focus first and foremost on the problems common to all of the warring powers. Militarism did not exist in one state alone; its malicious influence had spread across the continent. Thus did Samuel Dutton, a leading American educator and the founder of the New York Peace Society in 1906, say that "there can be no safety for free institutions, much less for lasting peace, unless this hydra-headed monster of militarism is destroyed."[17]

Consensus emerged, however, on what the nation's war aims should *not* be. Almost no one in 1917 envisioned a permanent role for the United States in a postwar Europe. They did not, moreover, see American goals as overlapping too closely with those of the British and French. Wilson later refused to sign the 1915 Treaty of London that formed the legal basis of the Anglo-French-Russian-Italian alliance. He also insisted on referring to the United States as an "associated power," not formally one of the Allies. The key to Americans of this way of thinking was to solve the problems of Europe more generally, in large part so that they no longer threatened the future peace and prosperity of America.

No American leaders, even those most in favor of military engagement, spoke of acquiring land or imperial possessions from the war. Rather, they took great pride in fighting (should fighting become necessary) for ideals instead of territory. In stark contrast to the recent wars with Mexico and Spain, this war would not result in adding European, Asian, or Mexican territory as a way of compensating the United States for its efforts. Such territorial dealing was part of the very worst aspects of the old European way of diplomacy. Having rejected territorial or monetary concessions, Americans could go to war confident that they were doing so for the most just reason of all: to make the world a more peaceful place and to stop the suffering of millions of innocent people. As one politician noted, the war "is a world calamity, indeed, but a calamity, since it has to come, to be spiritualized and utilized for the benefit of the future society of mankind. It must be made to serve a purpose."[18]

The war had finally become impossible to ignore. It would not end soon or on its own, and its effects would eventually engulf America. A German victory would impose a European and global order unacceptable to the American people. University of Chicago professor Andrew C. McLaughlin, lecturing shortly after entry into the war, noted the impact of what a potential German victory meant to America. It meant "the enthronement of might; and it meant that we must henceforward live in a world of struggle—we and our children after us." Without joining the war in Europe "there was little hope for relief from the crushing weight of war and the almost equally burdensome weight of ever-increasing and armed preparation." It was a grim choice but a necessary one. The United States would abrogate its place as the City Upon a Hill and the model for the world to follow if it ignored the German challenge to global order. "A German victory would mean the victory of *Machtpolitik*—a victory for the very forces which pacific idealism decries." The American and German ideals could, in effect, no longer coexist. "If we wished to see a world we could live in, it was necessary in time of trouble to do our part."[19]

Still, however much Americans may have believed in the necessity of action, the consequences had become far more clear than they had been three years earlier. The battles of Verdun and the Somme by themselves had inflicted more than two million combined casualties. Aware of the scale of death on the Western Front, Americans understandably remained anxious about the step the nation was on the verge of taking. If millions of Americans had ruefully concluded that war was no longer the worst of all possible options, millions more remained trapped in what Seldes had called "the interval hard to describe." Their fundamental belief that Germany was, as Walter Lippmann described it, "an enemy of international order" and a prosecutor of crimes "against the bases of faith at which the world must build or perish" had not changed.[20] Neither had the division in their own minds between the autocratic German government and the essentially decent German people.

Two nearly simultaneous global events in early 1917 shook the United States out of the "interval hard to describe" and changed the nation's perception of the necessity of war. The seemingly more important event involved Tsar Nicholas II's abdication on March 2. As we have seen, American Jews received the abdication as kind of divine deliverance. But Americans of all faiths welcomed the change in Russia and held out the hope that it would herald a future of democracy and progress for a nation so central to both European and Asian security. The radical Bolshevik phase of the Russian Revolution, which Wilson eventually sent American armed forces to try to contain, came later in the year. In March, the Russians established a relatively democratic provisional government that seemed to hold out the hope of Russia finally joining the family of modern nations. It also held out the promise of re-energizing Russia's war effort by giving the Russian people something to fight for other than the glory of the Romanov dynasty or imperial possessions in faraway lands. As Alexander Kerensky, the politician who led the provisional government, told Russian soldiers, they would thereafter fight for themselves and their own freedom rather than the maintenance of the tsar and the aristocracy. Both Britain and France welcomed the new government and lavishly funded it, in the hopes that Kerensky could maintain Russian military pressure on the Germans in the east.

Americans similarly embraced this first Russian Revolution with tremendous enthusiasm. Images of the Russian people as a kind of latter-day Gulliver breaking free from his chains were commonplace. The New York *Tribune* featured one such image, with a colossus labeled "Russia" breaking out of restraints placed there by smaller figures labeled "Plutocracy." The caption reads "Breaking His Chains."[21] More than half a century after the emancipation of the serfs, Russia appeared at long last ready to enter the modern, democratic age. The change seemed to show that the war could indeed produce positive reform and even freedom for formerly oppressed people. A telegram from the administration of Columbia University to the American ambassador in Russia praised the revolution as nothing less than "the ending of the last great attempt of the dark forces of the world to exploit and oppress humanity."[22] The revolution seemed to prove the case of those that argued that this war, while harsh, could produce positive changes for mankind.

Freed from their retrograde and backward autocracy, the Russian people might at long last be ready to fulfill their destiny as a peaceful and productive part of the family of nations. The *Review of Reviews*, in its monthly summary of newspaper opinions, noted that before the massive changes in Russia, Americans were "content to aid the Allies with supplies of foodstuffs, munitions, and other materials, and with the necessary credit in the form of loans." But with Russia on the road to democracy and liberty and "doing her full part" behind "an honest and efficient government," the United States had a moral obligation to take a more aggressive stand in regard to the war. The tsar's abdication truly made the war one of democracies against autocracies. The revolution was therefore nothing less than "the most hopeful indication for the world's future peace and welfare that any country has given since the outbreak of the war. With the new Russia dawns a bright era."[23]

A democratic Russia promised not only gains for the Russians themselves but for the whole world. Americans presumed that a representative and democratic Russia would pose no threat to Germany, Turkey, or China, thus allowing those states to develop peacefully if similar governments also came to rule there. A liberal Germany would in turn pose no threat to its neighbors and would allow Germans to "secure the respect and influence throughout the world that naturally belongs to the German people."[24] Thus could this one change of government vastly improve the prospects for peace in Europe and the world.

The miraculous transformation of Russia eventually allowed Wilson to publicize his justification of the war as the "war to make the world safe for democracy," a phrase that began to appear in American newspapers within a few days after the abdication. A democratic Russia changed the global strategic calculus almost overnight. Walter Lippmann noted when the tsar abdicated that the United States could, if necessary, now enter the war "with a clear conscience and a whole heart" because the lines between democracy and autocracy had suddenly become crystal clear. Lippmann further argued that the United States now had a responsibility to help a fellow democracy survive the crucible of its birth and undergo the long process into maturity, much as the United States itself had. "When Russia became a republic and the American Republic became an enemy," Lippmann wrote, "the German Empire was isolated before all mankind as the final refuge of autocracy."[25] Bringing democracy to Germany and Austria-Hungary could complete a great European political project and redeem the sacrifices of millions.

Lippmann's comment about Germany making the United States an enemy referred to the other major event of early 1917: Germany's declaration that it would resume unrestricted submarine warfare (USW). Fearful that they were approaching the end of their resources, the Germans decided in late January that they could no longer afford to allow their submarines, arguably their best weapon for defeating Great Britain, to sit harmlessly in their bases. The decision certainly came with its share of risks. Most German diplomats opposed the idea, knowing that it could drag the American giant into war. But the German military leadership argued that it could not allow the navy to sit idle while the army continued to bear the burden of combat and Germany's allies showed increasing signs of fatigue. By January 1917 most Germans thought of America as a de facto member of the international coalition lined up against them in any case, at least in economic terms. German strategists had calculated that they could starve Great Britain into submission by submarine before the somnolent Americans could build an army and make a decisive impact in Europe. If, moreover, the Germans could deliver a knockout blow to a Russia undergoing massive political turmoil, they could achieve their long-standing goal of a single-front war; with Russia out they could send hundreds of thousands of soldiers from Russia to the Western Front to break the stalemate in Belgium and France, and do so long before American manpower could tip the scales against them. An occupation of large swaths of eastern Europe would also allow the Germans to subsist on the food of the region and thereby survive the British blockade while Britain's own food supplies dwindled under the renewed pressure of German submarines.

Secretary of War Newton Baker knew that the Germans made their USW decision because they wanted to target Great Britain, not the United States, but he also knew that the decision would likely leave the United States with no choice but to declare war. For the United States not to respond forcefully would mean giving "Germany a license to kill all Americans in the future." Baker and many others were especially angry at the German decision's timing, coming so soon after Wilson's attempts to make peace. The contrast led many Americans to conclude that the Germans had not really wanted peace all along, but had instead sought a victory of conquest. Within a few days of the USW announcement Wilson had broken off diplomatic relations with Germany, calling it "a madman that should be curbed." The United States had at long last come to the final realization that each side was fighting for a total victory; neither side was at all interested in a compromise peace of the sort Wilson had been promoting.

The American media saw German resumption of USW as the practical equivalent of a declaration of war. The Philadelphia *Inquirer* wrote that it made American involvement inevitable. A staff editorial by the Associated Press argued that "it can hardly be necessary to say that the United States cannot acquiesce for a moment in the conditions thus to be created, that it cannot upon any ground or for any consideration excuse or condone or tolerate the heinous and abhorrent course which Germany has decided to pursue." An Albany newspaper put its case more directly: "There should be but one reply to such a message, and that need not be in writing."[26] In practical terms, giving in to Germany would mean banning overseas travel and curtailing the commerce that had sustained American economic growth. It also meant leaving the French and the British at the mercy of German Army.[27] Almost no one in the United States wanted to continue neutrality on those terms. Stating that "the Evil Day Has Come," the Greensboro (North Carolina) *Daily News* argued in February that the return of submarine warfare gave the United States just two options: war or national humiliation.[28] As an example of the humiliations the Germans planned to impose, the German government said it could allow one American ship to cross the Atlantic per week if its hull were painted with red-and-white stripes (so that submarine commanders could easily identify it), had its course pre-approved by Berlin, and permitted German naval officers to inspect its cargoes for contraband.[29]

Wilson had complete support from the American people for breaking off diplomatic relations, and he likely could have gotten a declaration of war at this stage had he sought one. The Senate quickly voted seventy-eight to five to support the decision to break off diplomatic relations, and the House of Representatives just as quickly passed a bill authorizing $368,000,000 to build new warships.[30] Former president William Howard Taft wrote that the resumption of USW had created "an exhibition of patriotism that we have not seen since the days of the Civil War."[31] Newton Baker wrote that tensions had risen so high that "war remained undeclared but certain upon the arising of an appropriate incident."[32]

The USW crisis nonetheless came as a shock because it followed several months of relative calm between the United States and Germany. Edward House told the German ambassador that "it is too sad that your Government should have declared the [sic] Unrestricted Submarine Warfare at a moment when we were so near to peace."[33] The sense of shock was widespread. In a letter written to a friend "in case I ever wish to remind myself of what transpired," Secretary of the Interior Franklin Lane wrote that Wilson received the news of the German USW declaration as "an astounding surprise," especially given the German ambassador's promises just ten days earlier that his country would keep to the terms of the Sussex Pledge and therefore not return to submarine warfare. The decision led Wilson to tell Lane that "Germany was to turn 'mad dog' again, and sink all ships going within her war zone." America would have no choice but to respond forcefully.[34] The USW announcement caused Rabbi Samuel Price to return to the war in his diary for the first time in many months. Writing from Springfield, Massachusetts, in early February, he noted that "the country is in tumult about the war clouds that are pending in the air.... Everyone is excited. It looks like war with Germany unless the latter changes her submarine policy."

Gilbert Seldes's "interval hard to describe" was now definitively over. Price wrote in his diary on February 4, "The country is filled with war fever. Everyone is enthusiastic over the pending war." Price thought that Wilson would ask for a declaration of war against both Germany and

Mexico, and he assumed that Congress would give it to him.[35] Price's observations support the notion that the American people would almost certainly have backed such a declaration of war had Wilson desired one. But at first he did not, still hopeful that breaking diplomatic relations might push Berlin to revoke the USW proclamation just as forceful diplomacy had resolved the *Lusitania* and *Sussex* crises. He would wait, as he said in a speech to Congress on February 3, for the "overt act" by Germany that would finally pull America into the war. He held out the hope that Germany would not actually sink ships despite what it had stated. "I cannot bring myself to believe that they will indeed pay no regard to the ancient friendship between their people and our own," he said.[36]

The phrase "overt act" was in newspapers across the country starting on February 7, just a few days after the United States had broken off diplomatic relations with Germany.[37] The overt act might be a ship sinking, a new act of sabotage on American soil, a German-inspired attack against American interests by the Mexican government, or something totally unexpected. Not knowing when, how, or where the overt act might happen, of course, only increased national anxiety. But wherever and however it came, the government would not respond to it with more diplomatic notes or by turning the other cheek yet again.

Domestic sabotage incidents continued as well, further stirring up anxieties. A massive fire and explosion at the Canadian Car and Foundry plant in Kingsland, New Jersey, in January had destroyed 750,000 artillery shells bound for the Allies. People as far away as Long Island heard the blast, which put at risk the plant's monthly production of three million shells. An Austrian national, found to be a veteran of the Austro-Hungarian Army, later admitted responsibility but claimed that he had been careless rather than malicious. Lacking evidence to prove otherwise, federal authorities could not press charges.[38] On the West Coast, German Consul Franz Bopp and five other German nationals were arrested in San Francisco for plotting sabotage.[39] Neither these incidents—nor even the USW declaration itself—however, amounted in Wilson's mind to an overt act. They did, however, lead to the closing of the ports in and around New York for fear of sabotage.

Wilson's February 7 decision to break diplomatic relations with Germany came as no surprise. "No sane person will question the

President's decision as to his conduct towards Germany," read an editorial in the *Jewish Advocate*, ominously titled "Is it Armageddon?"[40] On February 27 the House of Representatives passed a bill authorizing American merchantmen to carry weapons (effectively making them instruments of war) and to shoot on sight if they saw a German submarine. Twelve senators, led by Republicans Robert La Follette and Henry Cabot Lodge, filibustered the bill in the Senate, leading Wilson to call them "a little group of willful men who represent no opinion but their own."[41] Most Americans supported the president. The Fayetteville (North Carolina) *Observer* boldly called the filibustering senators "enemies of their country" and the New York *Sun* accused them of "petty political obstruction" at a moment of national crisis.[42]

Crises seemed to be multiplying faster than the American people could react to them. On February 25, two days before the armament bill, the Germans fired two torpedoes into the *RMS Laconia*, a Cunard liner carrying almost three hundred people, including many women and children. Twelve people died, including two Americans, a mother and daughter from Chicago who were acquaintances of First Lady Edith Galt Wilson. Chicago *Tribune* reporter Floyd Gibbons was also on the ship en route to Europe in anticipation of being the first reporter in France to greet American troops when they eventually arrived. After sitting in freezing lifeboats and surviving the ordeal of the sinking, he arrived at Queenstown (today Cobh), Ireland, wet and cold, but alive. A fellow survivor, a Briton whom Gibbons had befriended when the *Laconia* had left New York, approached him. Slapping him on the back, he asked Gibbons, "Well, old Casus Belli, is *this* your blooming overt act?"

Gibbons had to admit that, as much as he hoped it might be, he did not know how the president or the American people might react. He did, however, immediately write a powerful dispatch on the sinking for the *Tribune* "to put the question to the American people for an answer."[43] They evidently answered in the negative because the sinking of the *Laconia* failed to generate the kind of anger that the *Lusitania* or the *Sussex* had. The announcement of USW weeks before and the breaking of diplomatic relations that ensued had reduced any sense of shock.

Or perhaps people were distracted from the *Laconia* incident by a story that hit the newspapers at almost the same time. On March 1 came reports of a telegram, written in code and transcribed by the British, sent from German foreign minister Arthur Zimmermann to the German legation in Mexico. It is worth reprinting here in full:

> We intend to begin on the first of February unrestricted submarine warfare. We shall endeavor in spite of this to keep the United States of America neutral. In the event of this not succeeding, we make Mexico a proposal of alliance on the following basis: make war together, make peace together, generous financial support and an understanding on our part that Mexico is to reconquer the lost territory in Texas, New Mexico, and Arizona. The settlement in detail is left to you. You will inform the President of the above most secretly as soon as the outbreak of war with the United States of America is certain and add the suggestion that he should, on his own initiative, invite Japan to immediate adherence and at the same time mediate between Japan and ourselves. Please call the [Mexican] President's attention to the fact that the ruthless employment of our submarines now offers the prospect of compelling England in a few months to make peace. Signed, ZIMMERMANN[44]

The full history of the telegram, including its transmission to the United States and the Wilson administration's handling of it, became clear only many years later.[45] More immediately, Zimmermann himself soon verified the telegram's authenticity, thus putting to rest any lingering suspicions among a minority of Americans of a British ruse.[46] The telegram immediately heightened the fears of global anti-American conspiracies as expressed in the *Life* cover of a year earlier. It also struck at the American South and West where the war had sometimes seemed much more distant than it had on the eastern seaboard. In places like Texas, Arizona, and New Mexico the telegram led newspapers to demand war against Germany, both to punish the Germans and to warn the Mexicans and the Japanese against taking up Zimmermann's offer. Others called for war against both Germany and Mexico if the latter showed any interest in taking up Germany's offer (in the end neither Mexico nor Japan did).[47]

Calling the Zimmermann Telegram "an unpardonable sin," the *Review of Reviews* saw it as precisely the "overt act" that Wilson had

feared. "Far more than the submarine policy or any of Germany's violations of neutral rights, this [Zimmermann] note," the journal wrote in
April, "had the effect of making the American people feel that Germany
had put herself beyond the hope of keeping America in a non-combat-
ant position." Most important, the telegram convinced Americans that
they could now enter the war safe in the knowledge that Germany, and
Germany alone, had caused it: "German diplomacy has cleared the
American atmosphere. If Uncle Sam goes fully into the war, it will not
be with hatred toward the German people, but to aid in their early
emancipation" from their own deceitful government.[48]

By itself the telegram did not lead the United States into the war, but
it certainly confirmed in the minds of many Americans, including those
who had recently been ambivalent, that declaring war was the only remaining choice. Knoxville, Tennessee, author Roy Myers wrote in his diary
that the telegram was akin to a formal declaration of war and was the
event that finally convinced the few remaining doubters in his community to support war as the sole remaining option.[49] In Springfield,
Samuel Price noted that the telegram had had an identical effect in his
community. "The people are frantic with the war fever," he wrote on
March 1, the day news of the telegram hit American newspapers.[50] Or,
as one man in Indiana wrote, the time had at long last come to "quit
TALKING and DO!"[51]

Across America, people argued that the nation had done all it could
have to avoid war, but now it had no choice. The Seattle *Post-Intelligencer*
ran a cartoon with a spent candle on top of a candleholder labeled "U. S.
Patience." The caption reads "Used Up."[52] Similarly, the Philadelphia-
based *Jewish Exponent* contended that Wilson's foreign policy had been
pacific but had now run completely out of options. "It is plain to see
that the President has sought no quarrel with Germany and will seek
none," its editors wrote. "A war forced on America would be a crime
against the very spirit of human liberty."[53] War had thus become a viable
option, but Americans could believe themselves to be fighting a defensive war. As one North Carolina newspaper noted in late March, "War
is not ours to choose, but has been thrust upon us."[54] As the month wore
on, tensions continued to build, making the national mood increasingly
anxious. With his usual insight and intelligence, as well as an awareness
of the failures of the Preparedness movement, the army's assistant chief

of staff, General Tasker H. Bliss, noted that "by the middle of March, no one who had any knowledge of the movements of great public passion through personal experience or historical reading might doubt the certainty of the event for which we were preparing ourselves in spirit if not in force."[55]

Even former isolationists and pacifists had finally had enough. The Iowa-born and Brooklyn-based minister Newell Dwight Hillis, once a firm pacifist, had said in February that he would forgive the Germans "just as soon as they were all shot." He later supported forced sterilization for German militarists. Other former doubters about the wisdom of war such as Reverend Billy Sunday, Lyman Abbott, and Gifford Pinchot now advocated American entry into the war instead of another round of presidential diplomacy. By the end of March, North Carolina's Reverend Randolph McKim could say in a sermon that the "voice of a just God summons us to this war and that it is in the highest sense of the word a Holy War." Reaching for historical parallels, he concluded that the "Crusades shrink into insignificance compared with the crusade to which we are summoned at the present moment."[56] Mississippi senator John Sharp Williams, who described himself as a "peace fanatic" and who had voted repeatedly against conscription and Preparedness bills, had by March come to accept the need for war. "We submitted to having written notice served on us that we were going to be kicked again," he noted that month in reference to the German USW policy. "There are some things in this world that men must fight for." Andrew McLaughlin used a similar logic, noting that "war is horrible and demonically ridiculous." He nevertheless now argued that it was necessary to "save our own real selves, our own essential character" by destroying German military power.[57] Finally, the time had come when Americans had to face up to the reality that they had no choice but to face up to Germany— and to do so with armed force, rather than moral suasion or economics, as the main instrument of power.[58]

A willingness to go to war was widespread by March. So, too, was the belief that the country had no other viable choice if it were to preserve its own safety and security. Nearly three years of neutrality had made the nation less, not more, safe in the face of a global total war that seemed to grow more terrifying by the month. Surveying the attitudes of formerly antiwar politicians in the American West, Franklin Lane concluded on April 1 that "they don't want war to be sure—no one does. But they will not suffer further humiliations." Lane told Wilson that despite their previous ambivalence about belligerence, the president could count on their support for a war to defend Western values and American sovereignty.[59] The presidents of eight northeastern women's colleges wrote to Wilson in early April, saying that "although we believe that the settlement of international difficulties by war is fundamentally wrong, we recognize that in a world crisis such as this it may become our highest duty to defend by force the principles upon which Christian civilization is founded."[60]

Progressive, socialist, and labor leaders saw matters in much the same way. Despite the lingering suspicions of many in the labor movement that the war was serving to enrich capitalists, the American Federation of Labor officially lent its support to any future decision for war. Samuel Gompers, its president, noted in terms similar to those of Williams and McLaughlin that his organization was "convinced that peace cannot come until the militarist and imperialist policy of Prussia and of the German government shall have been put an end to for all time."[61] *Pearson Magazine*'s A. W. Ricker made the case for Socialist Party support for the war, citing the Russian Revolution as a defining moment. "Democracy, real democracy," he argued, "is beginning to come to power in every one of the Allied nations, and when democracy attains influence in the Allied governments, then the war indeed becomes democratic in plan and purpose." To further oppose such a war would, he concluded, be "ridiculous."[62] John Dewey made a similar case for those Progressives who had come to see entry into the war as a necessity. Arguing from a platform of both Progressive values and American Exceptionalism, he called pacifism noble in principle, but said that peace had to mean something more "than the mere absence of military war." Although he noted his own hatred of war, he called his support for entering this war an "atypical case" because American entry held out the promise of re-making the postwar world based upon a "progressive world settlement" and the imposition of democratic values worldwide. Under such circumstances, American entry into the war became not a symbol of militarism but "a needed thing" for both America and the world.[63]

German-Americans also rallied to the cause, even though many of them had voted against Wilson just a few short months earlier. After

Germany announced its resumption of USW, more than one thousand German-Americans took oaths of American citizenship on a single day, with tens of thousands more doing so in the ensuing weeks. The once pro-neutrality German-American National Alliance, representing three million people, wrote on February 8 to support Wilson's decision to break off diplomatic relations. Its president said that in case of war "we will organize German-American regiments, and, in case of a call for volunteers, we mean to show the American people with what readiness and patriotism we will answer a call to arms for the defense of the flag and the country." Five hundred prominent German-Americans signed a pledge of support, "to which," the *Literary Digest* noted, "the best native American could not object."[64] Former cabinet official and German-American politician Charles Nagel wrote in support of war that "for those who are clear with themselves as citizens of the United States, the problem virtually answers itself," and the Chicago *Tribune* ran a cartoon showing a smiling Uncle Sam watching a German-American worker stoke the fires of Patriotism, Allegiance, and Honor.[65]

Wilson had in fact lagged behind his country's increasingly bellicose mood, still believing that he could find a way out of the crisis without war. When Wilson had said in a cabinet meeting on February 25 that "the country was not willing that we should take any risks of war," a frustrated Franklin Lane replied, "I got no such sentiment out of the country." He, Secretary of Agriculture David Houston, and William Gibbs McAdoo grew so frustrated with Wilson that Lane thought all three might resign their cabinet posts rather than remain in a rudderless administration unable or unwilling to do what they thought obviously had to be done. Lane suspected that Republican arguments in favor of war made Wilson more obstinate than he would otherwise have been, and Lane also grew frustrated by the president's continued public pronouncements in favor of neutrality. The German media picked up on these stories and told its readers that America would not under any circumstances declare war. "Thus does the Kaiser learn of American sentiment!" Lane wrote to his son in frustration. "No wonder he sizes us up as cowards!"[66]

Some of Wilson's senior advisors did not seem to sense the full gravity of the situation. In a private letter, Baker told a friend in Pittsburgh on February 25 (the same day as the cabinet meeting discussed above) that he expected to be able to get away from Washington for a month-long trip out West. Although he recognized that the "international situation is very perilous and uncertain," he seemed prepared to wait out the crisis calmly and deal with other issues in the meantime. Baker wrote that he looked forward to the quiet that would follow Congress's scheduled adjournment on March 4, and most of the letters to his friend thereafter dealt not with the war, but a subject both men had an interest in, bridges. Little wonder, then, that Franklin Lane had been willing to consider resigning.[67]

More representative of American opinion was one of Baker's predecessors as secretary of war, Jacob Dickinson, who took to the stage in Chicago in late March to urge Wilson to declare war. "Our ships have been sunk and our citizens have been ruthlessly put to death by the German government on the high seas.... What deeper wrongs are we waiting for to stimulate us to action?" Reminding his audience that the country had already lost precious time by failing to take Preparedness seriously, he warned that further inaction will "invite despoilment of our hoarded wealth, the destruction of our cities, the devastation of our country, the desecration of our national monuments, the violation of our women, and the deportation of our children into captivity." Criticizing the anti-militarist views of William Jennings Bryan, Claude Kitchin, and other isolationists, he noted that an America that had produced George Washington, Andrew Jackson, and Ulysses Grant had nothing to fear from militarism. It did, however, have everything to fear from "the professional militarism of Europe," especially as practiced by the Prussians.[68]

Predictably enough, the sharpest criticisms of Wilson's reticence came from the Roosevelts. When she first read about the resumption of USW, Alice Roosevelt Longworth assumed that Wilson would at long last act decisively and declare war. "Obviously," she recalled her state of mind in February and March, "temporizing was over—it became a question of knuckling under or war." Instead, Wilson came up with the "overt act" speech, which Longworth laconically dismissed as "another of his phrases."[69] Not surprisingly, her father was just as direct, calling Wilson "yellow all through" when he did not declare war in February.[70] Upon hearing about the Zimmermann Telegram, Roosevelt publicly threatened to march on the White House and "skin him alive" if Wilson did not at long last declare war.[71]

With or without Wilson, war was declaring itself. Charles Nagel, for example, wrote on March 9 that "to all intents and purposes...a state of war now exists, and it is well for citizens to govern themselves accordingly." One week later, the Charlotte *Observer* declared in a headline that a "virtual state of war with Germany exists" and argued that the sooner the United States legally began the war, the better.[72] On March 25, Massachusetts mobilized its militia and Samuel Price wrote in his diary that "the whole country is in a state of war."[73] Treasury Secretary William Gibbs McAdoo warned Wilson on March 20 that he had to declare war soon or he would surely lose the support of the American people.[74]

State and city governments often responded before the federal government did. On March 17, the governors of Pennsylvania, New Jersey, Delaware, New York, and Maryland met in Philadelphia to discuss common approaches to the global crisis, and, notably, to demand emergency money from Washington in order to modernize the equipment of their National Guards. Philadelphia then put out a call for twenty thousand volunteers for the National Guard and seven hundred more for a Naval Militia. The city also began to enroll women volunteers to serve as nurses, telephone operators, and clerks.[75] Offers of help in the nation's hour of need came from every corner. Citizens of Tennessee flooded the governor's office with pledges of support. They ranged from the entire Boy Scout troop of Knoxville volunteering its services to the twenty-five thousand members of the Tennessee Equal Suffrage Association who volunteered en masse "for the purposes of recruiting, work in munitions factories, hospitals, and in any field that might be left vacant by the men at the front." Two Tennessee Spanish-American War veterans offered to raise, train, and lead companies of soldiers, and one woman offered the governor two of her horses "on account of trouble with Germany."[76]

In New York, officials worried about their exposed coastlines and almost completely unguarded infrastructure. Given incidents like Black Tom and the virtual absence of both sea and air defenses around the city, New Yorkers had good reason to be concerned. In early March, the mayor and governor hastily arranged for militiamen to guard the bridges and patrol the harbors. Clearly, they were in no mood to await action from the White House or Congress, the latter of which tried hurriedly to find money for emergency defenses. Columbia University had already sprung into action without waiting for word from Washington. On February 6 the university faculty met "for the purpose of considering ways and means by which the University might be of service to the nation, the state, and the city in the present critical situation." The faculty created eight divisions modeled on an army general staff system: Staff, Medical, Legal, Technical, Economics, Home Instruction, Language, and Military Training. The university administration asked all faculty to determine which of the divisions their skills could best assist. Columbia's president then wrote to Wilson to pledge "the unanimous support of Columbia University" after the breaking of diplomatic relations with Germany.[77]

The country still faced the prospect of a war for which it was not prepared and which Americans were uncertain would make them more secure. All they knew for sure in March 1917 was that isolation and neutrality had both incontrovertibly failed. Three years of well-intentioned policies had put the nation in its most dangerous position yet. As the *Review of Reviews* solemnly noted, "the plan of sending arguments ably written by authorities in international law" to the German government had manifestly failed given that the United States was facing the threat of worldwide "German terrorism." Looking back, it argued that America's policy toward the war had been wrong all along, a sad realization that the resumption of USW had starkly revealed.[78]

Mary Roberts Rinehart's journey since 1914 perhaps best represents the mood and the moment of April 1917. She had been one of the first Americans to urge a more assertive posture toward the war. Two years earlier, Rinehart had written that although she supported the United States taking a more active pro-Allied stance in the wake of the *Lusitania* tragedy, she was glad that her sons were then too young to fight if it came to war. She had hoped then that the war would end before she had to face the prospect of a son going off to fight the war that she had advocated. Now, in 1917, her older son was old enough to fight, and Rinehart took to the pages of the *Saturday Evening Post* to explain not just her support for a war that nevertheless terrified her, but why she would not want her son to try to evade the military service that might kill him. "If in this war we allow the few to fight for us, then as a nation we have died and our ideals have died with us," she wrote. "Though we win, if we all have not borne this burden alike, then do we all lose."

Although her article was ostensibly about the roles of citizens and motherhood in time of war, it highlighted many of the themes that had been running through American thoughts on the war since 1914. Writing in late March 1917 she told her readers, "We are virtually at war. By the time this is published perhaps the declaration will have been made." America, she believed, was "the last stand of the humanities on earth, the realization of a dream and the fulfillment of an ideal." Britain and France both shared parts of that ideal and had had a foundational role in creating it. Since 1914, they had been fighting for "the ideal on which my country was founded." Under the domination of the Prussians, imperial Germany now threatened those values, not only in Europe but in America itself, for it "had broken loose something terrible, something that must be killed or the world dies."

America should have awakened to these realities in 1915, but it did not. Now it had to face them under far more adverse conditions, having lost two precious years to get ready. Since the sinking of the *Lusitania*, the American people, she noted, had gone to church on Sundays and given thanks to God that "we were out of it" when they should have been listening to the warnings of those saying that the United States had to get ready for the looming crisis on the horizon. Instead, Congress had "refused to listen to talk of preparation" and the American people had refused to force them to do so. As a result, millions of young men, including her own son, would now go into history's most devastating war without the training and equipment that they needed.

Rinehart concluded with two more observations based in America's experiences since 1914. In the first she reiterated her belief from her tour of the Western Front that the United States must make war on the German government, not the German people. "There is no great hatred of the enemy, however much we abominate the things the German government has driven an acquiescent people into doing." The United States should therefore not fight to destroy Germany, but to liberate it from the brutality of a regime that threatened to destroy civilization itself. Second, she wrote that she had no worries at all about the loyalties of the Germans living inside the United States. German-Americans "are not Huns or Vandals. The German we know has come here to escape the very thing that has wrecked the Old World.... In coming to this Land of the Free he has followed an ideal as steadily as back in the Fatherland his kindred are following the false gods of Hate and War."[79] The war itself, however, would put such views to the test.

No one put the American experience of 1914–17 into sharper focus than Rinehart had, perhaps not even President Wilson in his eloquent declaration of war speech on April 2. As millions of Rinehart's fellow Americans understood, the United States had drifted to "the verge of war, in an uncertain attitude" that was neither enthusiasm nor resignation.[80] It was rather the acknowledgment that they no longer had a better choice and that by failing for so long to confront reality they had put themselves in an even more dangerous position. Noble impulses like charity, neutrality, and mediation had all run their course and war stood as the only option remaining. What Samuel Price called "the beastly passions for blood" would now put an end to the indescribable interval of uncertainty.[81] The nation, and the world, would never be the same.

CONCLUSION

IN THE SUMMER OF 1941, with America's entry into another world war looking increasingly likely, an article in the *Atlantic* by journalist and political commentator Stewart Alsop drew an unfavorable comparison between his generation and that of a generation earlier. "To fight the war we will sooner or later be called upon to fight," Alsop wrote, "we need a crusading faith, the kind that inspired the soldiers of 1917, setting forth the war to make the world safe for democracy."[1] History will likely not be kind to crusading wars, but the point to note is the contrast Alsop drew (just a few months before Pearl Harbor) between the animating spirit of the First World War and what he saw as American apathy toward the Second. Today, of course, we tend to remember just the opposite; or, if we think of the First World War at all, we think of something akin to F. Scott Fitzgerald's 1926 line about "country boys dying in the Argonne for a phrase that was empty before their bodies withered."[2]

To Fitzgerald and his generation the war nonetheless mattered—and mattered a great deal. In the 1920s, Fitzgerald often felt ashamed that the war had ended before he could go to France. Ernest Hemingway and John Dos Passos—both of whom had volunteered to drive ambulances—teased him about it, leading Fitzgerald to inflate his war service and even to hang his unused trench helmet in the bedroom of a house he had rented. Fitzgerald made sure that both Nick Carraway and Jay Gatsby had proven their worth on the battlefield, Gatsby in the Argonne itself. Readers who have gone back to *The Great Gatsby* since high school might recall that Gatsby won a medal from "little Montenegro" that he proudly showed off to Nick to establish his masculine bona fides. Tom Buchanan (in the space of one paragraph Fitzgerald describes him as "supercilious," "arrogant," and "cruel") also spent a year in France, but, as Nick reminds us, Tom did so "for no particular reason."[3] While Nick and Gatsby were fighting in France, Tom was in Louisville, sealing his faithless courtship of Nick's cousin, Daisy, with an expensive string of pearls. Nick reminds Daisy that he had to miss her wedding to Tom because he was at war.

Nick is his generation's conscience, reminding them of the price of war and of "empty phrases." Since then there has been amnesia about the First World War, the memory of which is today entirely eclipsed by the Second. Nowhere is this more obvious than on the National Mall in Washington. In 2004, the United States opened a gigantic seven-and-a-half-acre memorial to World War II that cost more than $200 million dollars to build. All but $16 million of that money came from private donations. The memorial sits in what was then the most prominent piece of open ground in the nation's capital, at the end of the Reflecting Pool roughly halfway between the Lincoln Memorial and the Washington Monument. The location itself is symbolic of the centrality of World War II in national memory. An estimated four and a half million tourists visit it each year. Its triumphal quality stands in the starkest of contrasts to the Vietnam War Memorial, with its black stone face cut into the ground, and the Korean War Memorial with its much more ambivalent symbolism. Indeed, those contrasts are very much the point. World War II is, to Americans, the moment of the nation's greatest victory and the people who fought it both at home and abroad are now unquestionably, as Tom Brokaw famously labeled them, "the greatest generation."[4]

The World War II Memorial stands in stark contrast to the Washington, D.C., World War Memorial, built in 1931 and located close to the new Martin Luther King Memorial. It commemorates only those men from the District of Columbia, but given that there is still no other in D.C., it has effectively become the official memorial in our nation's capital.[5] Years of neglect had caused the memorial to become dirty, strewn with trash, and structurally unsound. Neither the National Parks Service nor the District of Columbia wanted to spend the $3.6 million (less than 2 percent of the money spent on its World War II counterpart just a short walk away) needed to keep the Washington World War Memorial from crumbling off of its pedestal.[6]

The point is not to denigrate the memory of other wars. Nor is it even to argue, as some have, for building a memorial on the Mall to what was once called the "Great War for Civilization" in our nation's capital.[7] Kansas City, Missouri, already hosts the impressive Liberty Memorial (dedicated in 1921), home since 2004 to the National World War I Museum. It has become the nation's most important site of memory about the war, as well as a center for study and academic exchange.[8] In any case, Americans don't need to travel to Kansas City or Washington to see memorials to the war. Thousands already exist across the United States. So-called Doughboy statues grace parks and squares in hundreds of communities nationwide whose street names, such as the Boulevard of the Allies in Pittsburgh and Victory Boulevard on Staten Island, also keep alive the memory of the war.

A lack of memorials is therefore not the reason for amnesia about World War I. There may in fact be more memorials to the war in the United States than to any other event in American history expect, perhaps, the Civil War; some of these memorials, like San Francisco's War Memorial Opera House, are quite striking. One art historian has found more than ten thousand memorials to the First World War in America, located in big cities, small towns, and rural communities alike.[9] The New York City Parks Department is responsible for an amazing 122 of them in the communities of the five boroughs.[10] Fans flying from Boston to Los Angeles (connecting in New York's La Guardia airport) to see a sporting event at the Coliseum have visited three landmarks either built or named for veterans of the war. Dozens of cities created "living memorials" designed to keep the memory of the war ever-present. To cite just a few examples, New York City has Pershing Place (so named in 1923) to greet commuters and visitors arriving into the city from Grand Central Terminal; Chicago has Soldier Field (opened in 1925); and Indiana University has a Memorial Stadium, a Memorial Hall, and a Memorial Union (all conceived in 1921).[11] Residents of, and visitors to, places as diverse as Provincetown, Massachusetts; Syracuse, New York; Lincoln,

Nebraska; and Waikiki, Hawaii, walk past prominent memorials to the war every day.[12]

Yet as a nation we have largely forgotten the meaning of these memorials, and the world war they were meant to commemorate, in part because of the one that followed upon it. We see World War II as, in the phrase Studs Terkel used, "The Good War."[13] Terkel used the words ironically (he spoke to dozens of people for whom the war was anything but "good") but our love affair with World War II has led those words to become the phrase that we, as a society, use as a shorthand for a conflict that killed as many as fifty million people worldwide. Part of this remembrance has, of course, to do with the nature of the evil that the United States helped to defeat in 1945. Part of it also has to do with the ambiguity and the frustration of the limited wars in Korea and Vietnam that followed and thereby made World War II seem all the more dignified and "good" by contrast.[14] We see the First World War as a mistake, if we see it at all—despite the thousands of monuments.

Rather than separate them, we would be well served to begin to see the two world wars as one long conflict. Many of the American leaders of the second had their worldviews set in the first. They include, most famously, Franklin Roosevelt, assistant secretary of the navy in the First World War, and Capt. Harry Truman, an artillery officer in the Missouri National Guard. They also include millions of men born in the shadow of the war's first phase of tense neutrality as well as those who, after it was over, thought that their work was not finished. As one veteran from Illinois noted, "I can truthfully say that without egotism we, the soldiers of World War I, predicted that within twenty-five to fifty years this war would be fought again. For we had a premonition that it was not entirely settled as it should have been."[15] That the United States had to fight another world war a generation later seemed to prove the essential failure of Wilsonianism and, by extension, the entire First World War. Thus to millions of Americans it became something hard to understand. By contrast, the memory of World War II allows for far less ambiguity, removing the need to deal with complexities and allowing Americans to forget the persistent wartime racial discrimination Terkel highlighted as well as an alliance with Joseph Stalin's murderous regime. Americans have done a much better job at confronting the Japanese internment, but even that gets treated as a "bad" asterisk to a "good" war.

The two wars also ended very differently, in part because in 1945 the country's leaders made a quiet conscious decision not to follow Wilson's model. Instead, they devised new instruments of American power, first in the form of the United Nations, the World Bank, and the Bretton Woods international financial arrangements, and later in the form of NATO, the Marshall Plan, and the garrisoning of American troops on European soil. None of these decisions could have come about had the leaders not been shaped by the experience of the First World War.[16]

It is long past time that we take a fresh look at the First World War and the ways it created modern America. Ignorance and the simplistic contrasts between the two world wars badly distort a complex and fascinating history. In part, we have only ourselves to blame for remembering this war as a tragic mistake committed by Woodrow Wilson, egged on by the power of modern propaganda and abetted by the financial interests of J. P. Morgan.[17] Such views, moreover, remove agency from the American people, seeing them as pawns to their government or the financial elite.

As I hope this book has shown, they were nothing of the kind. The American people had their own reasons for reacting to the war as they did, when they did. Part of a large and diverse society, they did not always agree on those reasons, but by March 1917 they had reached a remarkable degree of consensus on a few fundamental points. First, they recognized that although the war in Europe was horrific, they felt that they had no choice but to enter it to secure Europe's future, and their own as well. Europe may have been over there, but it was also close to home. During the course of three years, the two had become more connected as the safety once provided by the Atlantic Ocean vanished. Second, they collectively believed that they themselves had had little role in starting the war, hence they were acting in self-defense and in the wider interests of mankind against a German imperial government that had, in Wilson's words, gone "mad dog." Third, they agreed that their disparate ethnic identities meant less than their common identity as Americans. The war galvanized assimilation as nothing had done before.

The American people did not go into the war blind to its costs. The New York *Tribune* ran a front-page banner headline in October 1916 that read "The Butcher's Bill—What the War Has Cost in Life." Readers learned that according to official statistics from the warring powers

4,500,000 people had already died, equivalent to the prewar populations of Chicago, Cincinnati, Detroit, Boston, and Cleveland combined. Germany officially claimed four million men as casualties of war (meaning killed, wounded, or captured), half of whom they expected would never return to the army. *Tribune* correspondents questioned the official numbers, suspecting that governments might be lowering their estimates to avoid harming morale on the home front. Frank Simonds, who had been covering the war from Europe for the *Tribune*, guessed that the true number of total war casualties across Europe might have surpassed eighteen million soldiers and civilians (equivalent to the 1910 populations of New York, Pennsylvania, and California combined). At this rate, he guessed that the war might end in a few months' time because one or more of the powers would simply run out of young men.[18]

To ignore or misrepresent the history of this era is to misunderstand a foundational event in shaping the modern United States and its entrance onto the world stage. Most scholars recognize in a vague sense that the First World War stands as a watershed of American social, political, economic, and diplomatic history, but few have taken a serious look at how and why that was the case.[19] Although Wilson and a small group of public officials may have believed in lofty goals and high-sounding ideals, the majority of Americans fought the war to ensure their own national security, to confirm their place in a rapidly changing American society, and to place themselves at the center of the new world order taking shape across the globe. Their president may have thought he could motivate them with words, but the American people knew that his phrases had become empty long before Fitzgerald's country boys died in the Argonne. Once the guns fell silent in November 1918, the American people believed that their work was over; we therefore mark the anniversary of the end of the war on November 11, the day of the armistice, rather than June 28, the anniversary of the Versailles Peace Treaty.

The war became an American war. It is therefore fitting to end this book by returning to the words of someone who fought it. Raymond Chamberlain, like millions of his fellow Americans, was "engrossed" by war news from the moment the war began in 1914. As his father later recalled, "his wrath rose at the outrages of Germany upon the world, upon our country, upon our people." Chamberlain volunteered for military training in 1916 at a Plattsburg-style camp and later left behind a fiancée and a promising career in journalism to fight on the Western Front. It was, he noted, "the only thing for a man to do . . . in the war for the defense of civilization."

By the time of his death on the Western Front in September 1918, Chamberlain seemed to have realized how difficult it would be to translate the imminent military victory of the Allies into the permanent peace he and so many others so earnestly desired. Or, put another way, he knew already that the Wilsonian phrases would not inspire Americans to sacrifice or struggle once the Germans surrendered. Yet he had no regrets in risking his life, even if he had already guessed that that decision might soon come under intense scrutiny. "If another generation can prevent wars," he wrote home shortly before his death, "it will be entitled to its scorn."[20] If for no other reason than that no generation has found a way to prevent wars, we owe it to his memory to understand them on their terms and to learn what we can from their decision to go Over There.

ACKNOWLEDGMENTS

I think I have accumulated more debts in working on this book than any other I have ever written thanks to the incredible generosity of so many people. I have thanked many of them in the footnotes for their help in finding sources, but some people went far above and beyond the call of duty and I'd like to thank them here. I'd like to start with Maartje Abbenhuis at the University of Auckland in New Zealand. Maartje was a friend on social media and a fellow scholar of the First World War whom I first got the chance to meet in person in Seville at a 2014 conference on neutrality. I'd like to thank her both for sharing some ideas with me in Spain and for taking the time to read this entire manuscript. It is so much better for her comments. Thanks also to Chris Capozzola at MIT who took time out of a busy schedule to read parts of the manuscript. I'd also like to thank Carolina Garcia Sanz and Inmaculada Cordero Olivero for hosting the Seville conference on neutrality in the First World War and inviting me to speak. I'd encourage anyone interested in this topic to read the conference proceedings.

I also had the benefit of attending two other European conferences that helped to shape my thinking. Gearóid Barry, Róisín Healy, and Enrico Dal Lago gave me the chance to speak at a conference on small nations at war at the National University of Ireland at Galway. Those proceedings, too, should be of great interest to scholars. NUI-Galway also granted me a Moore Fellowship that gave me a few weeks to discuss this project with the terrific people there. Thanks as well to Jean-Noël Grandhomme for the chance to speak at a conference at Saverne, France, on the 1913–14 crisis there.

I feel very fortunate to have such a wonderful international network of colleagues and friends on whom I can draw for advice and support. Geri Thoma once again helped to shepherd a manuscript into a book. John Milton Cooper, Richard Immerman, Jennifer Keene, and Dennis Showalter all provided support and encouragement.

Thanks also to Tim Bent, Susan Ferber, and the staff of Oxford University Press for seeing the value in this book. Erin Hochman, Andrew Graybill, and the faculty at Southern Methodist University gave me great feedback during a symposium in Dallas. Closer to home, I have some wonderful people at the US Army War College to acknowledge. My thanks go out especially to Rob Citino, Tami Davis Biddle, Paul Rexton Kan, and Craig Nation for letting me bounce some ideas off of them. Lance Betros, Richard Lacquement, George Teague, and Leah Hohn also deserve my thanks for all of their help.

I'd also like to acknowledge Tim Haggerty and Steve Schlossman for the invitation to come home to give a talk at Carnegie Mellon University. Thanks to Heath Lee, Leo Landes, and the staff of the Iowa State Library; to Kurt Piehler and Susan Contente at Florida State; to Andrea Ciccarelli, Michelle Moyd, and Julia Roos at Indiana University; to Lisa and Mike Mundey at St. Thomas University in Houston; to Susan Gordon and Bob Hunt for their help in working in the Tennessee State Library and Archives; to Susan Saidenberg and Alinda Borell of the Gilder-Lehrman Institute of American History and the New-York Historical Society; to my friend Kristine LaLonde and her husband, Claudio Mosse, for their hospitality in Nashville; to David Rosenberg for his invaluable help at the Center for Jewish History; to the staffs of the New York Public Library, the Boston Public Library, the Newberry Library in Chicago, the National Library of Ireland, the British Library, the Carnegie Library of Pittsburgh, Barnard College Special Collections, the Rare Book and Manuscript Library of Columbia University, the Manuscript Division of the Library of Congress, Florida State University Library's Special Collections Department, the Lilly Library at Indiana University, Iren

Snavely of the Pennsylvania State Library in Harrisburg; and to all my friends at the United States Army Heritage and Education Center. It is a real treat to have a world-class facility right down the street. For help with finding sources, let me single out Louise Arnold-Friend, Steve Bye, and Thomas Buffenbarger. I should add, as always, that any errors in here are mine alone and that the views herein are mine, not those of the United States Army, the United States Army War College, or any part of the United States government.

Last but certainly not least, let me turn to my family. I need to thank my wife, Barbara, and my daughters, Claire and Maya, for their never-ending support of their husband and father. The World War I centennial has kept me away from home much more than I would like and their understanding has been critical to both my productivity and my sanity. Our parents, Larry and Phyllis Neiberg and Sue and John Lockley, were immensely supportive, as always. I also want to extend my deep thanks to my New York City family. Moving back to the Northeast has given us the chance to reconnect with them, and that has meant a great deal to me and to my family. So thank you to Rory, Jeremey, and Zoey Tahari; Barbara and Brittany Portman; and Josh Green and Lindsey Kottler. I would like to dedicate this book to them and especially to my new cousin, Josh and Lindsey's son, Noah Benjamin. Maybe one day when he gets older, he'll stroll down Fifth Avenue at 67th Street (passing Temple Emanu-El on the way) and pause at the 107th Infantry Regiment Memorial on the edge of Central Park. And maybe he'll bore his mom and dad about what those men did and why it matters.

NOTES

Introduction

1. Roosevelt said that people who approved of the song would also approve of a song called "I Didn't Raise My Girl to Be a Mother." He then said that women who admired the song should live "in a harem, not in the United States."
2. *The Little American*, directed by Cecil B. DeMille (Hollywood: Mary Pickford Company, 1917). My thanks to my friend and graduate school classmate Jeff Hinkleman for calling my attention to this movie.
3. Chapter 8 covers the Zimmermann Telegram in detail. In short, the Germans used it to offer Mexico the return of territory in the American Southwest it lost in 1848 in exchange for Mexican entry into the war.
4. Charles Fremont Taylor in *Equity*, January 11, 1916, in Rumely MSS, Box 7, January 1–14 folder, Lilly Library, Indiana University.

Chapter 1

1. See Pierre Vonau, *L'Affaire de Saverne, 1913* (Saverne: Société d'histoire et pays d'archeologie de Saverne, 1993).
2. The Dreyfus Affair is far too complex to introduce here. For a short introduction to it, see http://www.telegraph.co.uk/news/worldnews/europe/france/9045659/France-is-still-fractured-by-the-Dreyfus-Affair.html. For a longer analysis, see Louis Begley, *Why the Dreyfus Affair Matters* (New Haven: Yale University Press, 2009).
3. Forstner died on the Eastern front in 1915.

4. Colorado Springs *Gazette*, December 28, 1913, 13; New York *Tribune*, December 6, 1913, 1–2.
5. Michael Neiberg, "L'Affaire de Saverne vue des États-Unis," presented at L'Affaire de Saverne Conference, Saverne, France, February 5–7, 2014.
6. That push, led by Émile Zola and Georges Clemenceau, resulted in a new trial and an acquittal for Dreyfus, who was back in a French uniform and a member of the Legion of Honor by 1906.
7. "Kaiser Transfers Zabern Garrison," New York *Times*, December 6, 1914, 3:1.
8. "May Demoralize German Politics," Montgomery *Advertiser*, December 31, 1914, 3. In November, 1918, Erzberger led the German delegation that accepted Allied armistice terms in the forest of Compiègne.
9. Frederick Palmer, *My Year of the Great War* (New York: Dodd, Mead, and Company, 1915), 7–8.
10. David Starr Jordan, "A War of Dishonor," *New York Times Current History* 1 (1915); 503.
11. Charles Seymour, ed., *The Intimate Papers of Colonel House*, vol. 1 (Boston: Houghton Mifflin, 1926), 252; and Godfrey Hodgson, *Woodrow Wilson's Right Hand: The Life of Colonel Edward M. House* (New Haven: Yale University Press, 2006), 96–101.
12. Burton Hendrick, ed., *The Life and Letters of Walter H. Page*, vol. 1 (Garden City, N.Y.: Doubleday, Page, and Company, 1922), 300. Emphasis in original.
13. The other two were the Austro-Prussian War of 1866 and the Franco-Prussian War of 1870–71.
14. *Living Age* 65 (November 14, 1914): 432–33.
15. Charles Eliot to Jacob Schiff, December 3, 1914, reprinted in *New York Times Current History* 1 (1915); 467.
16. John Allison, "Who Wanted and Was Prepared for War in Europe in 1914," November 15, 1914, Tennessee State Library and Archives, Nashville, Ac. No. 90–037.
17. "What Americans Say to Europe," *New York Times Current History* 1 (1915); 430.
18. *Literary Digest* 49 (August 15, 1914): 253–54.
19. *Life*, August 20, 1914, 300.
20. *Living Age* 65 (November 7, 1914): 329.
21. Richard Harding Davis, *With the Allies* (New York: Scribner's, 1914), 3, 31.
22. "Ruler—Protem," Chicago *Defender*, August 15, 1914, 8.
23. Willa Cather, *One of Ours* (New York: Knopf, 1922), 76–77, 85. My thanks to Edward Gutiérrez for calling my attention to this book.
24. *Review of Reviews* 50, no. 3 (September 1914): 265.
25. *Life*, October 29, 1914, 759.
26. Oswald Villard, *Germany Embattled: An American Interpretation* (New York: Scribner's, 1915), 12–13, 27.

27. William Roscoe Thayer, *Germany vs. Civilization: Notes on the Atrocious War* (Boston: Houghton Mifflin, 1916), 21–22.

28. The arguments of Isabel Hull, *Absolute Destruction: Military Culture and the Practices of War in Imperial Germany* (Ithaca: Cornell University Press, 2006), are well worth considering here.

29. "What Americans Say to Europe," 430.

30. Cather, *One of Ours*, 78.

31. Villard, *Germany Embattled*, 24, 28.

32. Ray Stannard Baker, *American Chronicle* (New York: Scribner's, 1945), 103–7.

33. Henry Stimson and McGeorge Bundy, *On Active Service in Peace and War* (New York: Harper and Brothers, 1948), 83.

34. See Michael S. Neiberg, *Dance of the Furies: Europe and the Outbreak of World War I* (Cambridge, Mass.: Harvard University Press, 2011), 40–43.

35. *Life*, September 17, 1914, 530, 520.

36. *New Republic* 1, no. 2 (November 14, 1914): 6.

37. See, for example, Ima Hogg, Diary 1914, "Travel Diaries," Box 4Zg86, Ima Hogg Papers, Briscoe Center for American History, University of Texas at Austin. She arrived in Europe just days after the assassination of Franz Ferdinand. She wrote two paragraphs about Bernhardi in her diary. My thanks to Virginia Bernhard for making it available to me.

38. Friedrich von Bernhardi, *Germany and the Next War* (New York: Longmans, Green, and Company, 1914), 288.

39. *Living Age* 65 (October 31, 1914): 314.

40. *Life*, September 10, 1914, 438.

41. Thayer, *Germany vs. Civilization*, 110.

42. *Life*, October 29, 1914, 772.

43. Bernhardi, *Germany Embattled*, 26.

44. "Self-Defense and Self-Delusion," *New Republic* 1, no. 2 (November 14, 1914): 25. The book itself can be found at https://archive.org/details/desdeutschenreic00frob.

45. Andrew C. McLaughlin, "The Great War from Spectator to Participant," Pennsylvania State Library and Archives, Harrisburg, PV 1890, 4–5.

46. "The Present European Conflict," Philadelphia *Tribune*, August 15, 1914, 4.

47. "War Is Hell: Where We Stand," Chicago *Defender*, August 15, 1914, 8.

48. Adriane Lentz-Smith, *Freedom Struggles: African Americans and World War I* (Cambridge, Mass.: Harvard University Press, 2009), 35.

49. *Life*, August 27, 1914, 345.

50. Davis, *With the Allies*, xi.

51. *Life*, August 27, 1914, 362.

52. *Life*, September 3, 1914, 391.

53. Watterson fought under Nathan Bedford Forrest in the Civil War, served two years in the House of Representatives, and received consideration for the vice presidency in 1892. He was quoted in the Philadelphia *Evening Ledger*, October 20, 1914, 8.

54. *New York Times Current History*, (April 1915); 97.
55. M. Ryan Floyd, *Abandoning Neutrality: Woodrow Wilson and the Beginnings of the Great War, August 1914–December 1915* (London: Macmillan, 2013), 8.
56. Edward Robb Ellis, *Echoes of a Distant Thunder: Life in the United States, 1914–1918* (New York: Kodansha International, 1996), 148.
57. McLaughlin, "The Great War from Spectator to Participant."
58. Baltimore *Afro-American*, August 1, 1914, 4.
59. Richard Gamble, *The War of Righteousness: Progressive Christianity, the Great War, and the Rise of the Messianic Nation* (Wilmington, Del.: ISI Books, 2003), 96–100.
60. *National Defence* 1, no. 5 (July–August, 1915): cover. The title is spelled correctly. It is unclear why the newsletter preferred the British spelling. The members of the National Security League that printed the newsletter were all American, not British or Canadian.
61. Herbert Croly, "The End of American Isolation," *New Republic* (November 7, 1914): 9–10.
62. "Europe at Armageddon," *North American Review* 200 (September 1914): 321.
63. Gamble, *War of Righteousness*, 108.
64. *Life*, August 13, 1914, 236.
65. *The Papers of Woodrow Wilson: 1914* (Princeton: Princeton University Press, 1979), 371.
66. *Life*, August 27, 1914, 344.
67. Newton D. Baker, *Why We Went to War* (New York: Harper and Brothers for Council on Foreign Relations, 1936), 20. In 1920, German ambassador to the United States Johann von Bernstorff noted that negative American attitudes toward Germany doomed efforts by German propagandists to present the German side of the story.
68. "Nellie Bly in Trenches," Washington *Herald*, December 8, 1914; and "Nellie Bly Describes War Horrors," New York *Evening Journal*, December 9, 1914.
69. Jan Cohn, *Improbable Fiction: The Life of Mary Roberts Rinehart* (Pittsburgh: University of Pittsburgh Press, 1980), 91. The nickname came in the 1920s, after Christie's career took off. In 1914, Rinehart was the far better known of the two, especially to American readers.
70. Mary Roberts Rinehart, *My Story* (New York: Farrar and Rinehart, 1931), 65, 145.
71. Irvin S. Cobb, *Paths of Glory: Impressions of War Written at or Near the Front* (New York: Grosset and Dunlap, 1918), chapter 3.
72. Cobb, *Paths of Glory*, 375.
73. Rinehart, *My Story*, 161.
74. *Review of Reviews* 50, no 3 (September 1914): 269, 282–83.

75. Although Russia, allied to Britain and France, had an autocratic government, few Americans saw the Russians as having made anything like the contributions to Western culture that the Germans had. Thus their sense of disappointment and even betrayal was far less acute.

76. Justus Doenecke, *Nothing Less than War: A New History of America's Entry into World War I* (Lexington: University Press of Kentucky, 2011), 28, 32; Hendrick, *Life and Letters*, 325.

77. Davis, *With the Allies*, 10, 15, 85.

78. Palmer, *My Year of the Great War*, 23.

79. http://digital.lib.uiowa.edu/cdm/printview/collection/ding/id/9296/singleitem.

80. Rinehart, *My Story*, 153.

81. *Life*, August 27, 1914, 385.

82. John Horne and Alan Kramer, *German Atrocities, 1914: A History of Denial* (New Haven: Yale University Press, 2001) should be the starting point for any discussion of Belgium. For more on the origins of German responses, see Hull, *Absolute Destruction*.

83. Davis, *With the Allies*. Of course, "concentration camp" in 1914 did not mean death camps in the World War II sense of the term. In this sense, it means something much more akin to refugee camps.

84. Philadelphia *Tribune*, August 29, 1914, 4; and Philadelphia *Evening Public Ledger*, November 10, 1914, 3.

85. Davis, *With the Allies,* 125, 132, 139.

86. "Bombardment of the Cathedral of Rheims," October 8, 1914, Spencer Cosby Papers, Box 1, Folder 18, United States Army Heritage and Education Center, Carlisle, Pa. Thanks to Louise Arnold-Friend for alerting me to these papers.

87. *Life*, November 19, 1914, 921.

88. *Life*, November 26, 1914, 946–47.

89. Philadelphia *Tribune*, August 29, 1914, 4.

90. Sarah McCulloh Lemmon, *North Carolina's Role in the First World War* (Raleigh: State Department of Archives and History, 1966), 6.

91. *Life*, October 8, 1914, 624, 657.

92. *New Republic*, 1, no. 5 (December 5, 1914): 8–9.

93. Richard Harding Davis, *With the French in France and Salonika* (New York: A. L. Burt, 1916), xii, 28–29, 62. The book is a compilation of his 1914 and early 1915 columns.

94. Edith Wharton, *Fighting France: From Dunkerque to Belfort* (New York: Scribner's, 1915).

95. Baker, *Why We Went to War*, 34, 36.

96. Doenecke, *Nothing Less than War*, 20.

97. Hugo Münsterberg, *The War and America* (New York: D. Appleton and Company, 1914), 110.

98. Corrine Bacon, ed., *Best Books on the War* (White Plains, N.Y.: H. W. Wilson, 1914).

99. "Second Day Battlefield of the Marne Now Picture of Devastation and Death," Washington *Evening Star*, September 19, 1914, 4.

100. Nelson Lloyd, *How We Went to War* (New York: Scribner's, 1919), 3.

101. *Life*, November 5, 1914, 851.

102. "Dr. Frissell on Causes of the Present European War," Baltimore *Afro-American*, February 6, 1915, 7.

103. Eric Ames, "The Impact of Culture—or What Münsterberg Saw in the Movies," in Lynne Tatlock and Matt Erlin, eds., *German Culture in 19th Century America* (Rochester, N.Y.: Camden House, 2005), 21–42.

104. Münsterberg, *The War and America*, 3–9, 28.

105. *Life*, October 29, 1914, 769.

106. Frederick Coburn to Hugo Münsterberg, August 5 and September 22, 1914, Boston Public Library MSS ACC 2499b (100a) and ACC 2499b (100C).

107. A. Lawrence Lowell to Hugo Münsterberg, September 25, 1914, Boston Public Library, MSS ACC 2499b (304a).

108. Alexander Waldenrath, "The German Language Newspapers in Pennsylvania During World War I," *Pennsylvania History* 42 (January 1975): 25–42.

109. Gilbert Vivian Seldes, *The United States and the War* (London: George Allen Unwin Ltd., 1917), 20.

110. Palmer, *My Year of the Great War*, vi, 125–26.

111. Washington *Evening Star*, September 28, 1914, 10.

112. Edward Rumely to Edwin Potter, June 10, 1915, in Rumely MSS, Box 6, June 9–21 folder, Lilly Library, Indiana University.

113. Frederick C. Luebke, *Bonds of Loyalty: German-Americans and World War I* (DeKalb: Northern Illinois University Press, 1974), 88–90.

114. Joseph Medill Patterson, *The Notebook of a Neutral* (New York: Duffield, 1916), 71, 87.

115. Chicago *Defender*, August 15, 1914, 8.

116. http://www.firstworldwar.com/source/usneutrality.htm.

117. Seldes, *The United States and the War*, 22.

118. Hendrick, *Life and Letters*, 361.

119. House quoted in Galen Jackson, "The Offshore Balancing Thesis Reconsidered: Realism, the Balance of Power in Europe, and America's Decision for War in 1917," *Security Studies* 21 (2012): 462. My thanks to Eugene Gholz for bringing this article to my attention.

120. Davis, *With the Allies*, xi–xiv.

121. J. N. Darling cartoons, Des Moines *Register*, August 5 and 6, 1914. Available at http://digital.lib.uiowa.edu/ding/.

Chapter 2

1. *Papers of Woodrow Wilson, 1914* (Princeton: Princeton University Press, 1979), 316.

2. Frederick Palmer, *Newton D. Baker: America at War*, vol. 1 (New York: Dodd, Mead, and Company, 1931), 36.

3. Columbia University Rare Books and Manuscript Library, World War I Collection, 1914–44, 1970 (UA #014), Box 17, Folder 1711.

4. "The End of American Isolation," *New Republic* 1, no. 1 (November 7, 1914): 9–10, 14.

5. "REPORT THOUSANDS KILLED. GERMANS DEFEATED IN BATTLE BY FRENCH," Washington *Times*, August 2, 1914, 1.

6. Irvin S. Cobb, *Paths of Glory: Impressions of War Written at or Near the Front* (New York: Grosset and Dunlap, 1918), 25.

7. Omaha *Daily Bee*, August 15, 1914, 3.

8. Burton Hendrick, ed., *The Life and Letters of Walter H. Page*, vol. 1 (Garden City, N.Y.: Doubleday, Page, and Company, 1922), 352–53.

9. Chicago *Defender*, August 29, 1914, 8.

10. US Department of State Newsletter, issues 105–16 (Washington: Bureau of Administration, 1970).

11. Ross Gregory, *The Origins of American Intervention in the First World War* (New York: W. W. Norton, 1971), 20. When later criticized for his performance at the Paris Peace Conference, David Lloyd George replied, "I think I did as well as might be expected, seated as I was between Jesus Christ [Wilson] and Napoleon [Clemenceau]."

12. Hendrick, *The Life and Letters of Walter H. Page*, 327–28.

13. Sarah McCulloh Lemmon, *North Carolina's Role in the First World War* (Raleigh: State Department of Archives and History, 1966), 3.

14. Gregory, *Origins of American Intervention*, 26; "Marooned in the European War District," Baltimore *Afro-American*, August 8, 1914.

15. Pittsburgh *Gazette-Times*, August 5, 1914, 1:5; and August 6, 1914, 3:1.

16. Gregory, *Origins of American Intervention*, 26. For a sense of the chaos of these days, see Eric Fisher Wood, *The Note-Book of an Attaché* (New York: The Century Company, 1915). Wood, then a young engineer living in Paris, volunteered to help the overwhelmed American embassy there. He went on to lead the Preparedness movement, join the British Army, help to form the American Legion, design Warren G. Harding's memorial, and rise to the rank of brigadier general in World War II.

17. Harvey O'Connor, *The Guggenheims: The Making of an American Dynasty* (New York: Covici-Friede, 1937), 341.

18. Woodrow Wilson eLibrary, ww2.dataformat.com, document number 32907; and Edward Robb Ellis, *Echoes of Distant Thunder: Life in the United States, 1914–1918* (New York: Kodansha International, 1996),

160–62. Another battleship, the *North Carolina*, tried to take gold to Turkey but turned back because the Ottoman government would not guarantee safe passage through the mines in the Dardanelles.

19. Ima Hogg, Diary 1914, "Travel Diaries," Box 4Zg86, Ima Hogg Papers, Briscoe Center for American History, University of Texas at Austin. Hogg was in Europe from June 30 to mid-September 1914.

20. Hendrick, *The Life and Letters of Walter H. Page*, 359.

21. Francis William O'Brien, ed., *The Hoover-Wilson Wartime Correspondence, September 24, 1914 to November 11, 1918* (Ames: Iowa State University, 1974).

22. Margaret R. Higgonet, ed., *Letters and Photographs from the Battle Country: The World War I Memoir of Margaret Hall* (Charlottesville: University of Virginia Press, 2014), 1.

23. Borden published a well-regarded and controversial memoir of that experience as *The Forbidden Zone* (Garden City, N.Y.: Doubleday, 1929).

24. *Life*, October 15, 1914, 670.

25. The plight of war-torn and typhus-ravaged Serbia came to Americans through the reporting of John Reed, who later rose to fame for his sympathetic portrayal of the Bolshevik Revolution, *Ten Days That Shook the World* (New York: Boni and Liveright, 1919). His Serbia reporting appeared as part of his popular book *The War in Eastern Europe* (New York: Scribner's, 1916). Warren Beatty played him in the 1981 movie *Reds*.

26. New York *American*, October 21, 1914, in Columbia University Rare Books and Manuscript Library, World War I Collection, 1914–44, 1970 (UA #014), Box 17, Folder 1711; and "The Story of Louvain" in Columbia University Rare Books and Manuscript Library, World War I Collection, 1914–44, 1970 (UA #014), Box 16, Folder 1615.

27. *Philadelphia in the World War* (New York: Wynkoop Hallenbeck Crawford, 1922), 21.

28. They may not have all had pure motives. Joseph Rogers, one of those American volunteers to the Canadian Army, noted that "many of my companions were murderers, jail birds, safe crackers, bank robbers, and whatnot. I soon learned from their conversation that the police were hot on their trail so they joined up." Joseph Rogers Papers, Folder 1. United States Army Heritage and Education Center, Carlisle, Pa.

29. Edwin Morse, *The Vanguard of American Volunteers: In the Fighting Lines and in Humanitarian Service, August, 1914–April, 1917* (New York: Scribner's, 1922), 15.

30. Paul Ayers Rockwell, *American Fighters in the Foreign Legion, 1914–1918* (Boston: Houghton Mifflin, 1930), 53.

31. "The Reminiscences of Miss Caroline King Duer," p. 18, Caroline King Duer Papers, Barnard College Archives, BC 20.20, Box 2, Folder 3.1. Duer went on to become the first female editor of *Vogue*.

32. "Bringing the War Home," Chicago *Defender*, February 27, 1915, 4.

33. Chicago *Defender*, August 8, 1914, 1; and August 29, 1914, 1. In World War I slang, a "Jack Johnson" was a heavy-hitting German 15cm artillery shell.

34. Newton D. Baker, *Why We Went to War* (New York: Harper and Brothers for Council on Foreign Relations, 1936), 111.

35. M. Ryan Floyd, *Abandoning Neutrality: Woodrow Wilson and the Beginning of the Great War, August 1914–December 1915* (London: Palgrave Macmillan, 2013), 16.

36. Nicholas Lambert, *Planning Armageddon: British Economic Warfare and the First World War* (Cambridge, Mass.: Harvard University Press, 2012); and William Silber, *When Washington Shut Down Wall Street: The Great Financial Crisis of 1914 and the Origins of America's Monetary Supremacy* (Princeton: Princeton University Press, 2007).

37. Woodrow Wilson eLibrary, ww12.dataformat.com, document number 27314.

38. Des Moines *Homestead*, April 22, 1915, 2.

39. "European War Will Take Thousands of Immigrants from U. S.," Chicago *Defender*, August 15, 1914, 1.

40. *Philadelphia in the World War*, 361, 418, 422.

41. Lane to John Crawford Burns, March 3, 1915, in *The Letters of Franklin K. Lane, Personal and Political*, ed. Anne Wintermute Lane and Louise Hendrick Wall (Boston: Houghton Mifflin, 1922), 166–67.

42. The Des Moines *Capital* reprinted and endorsed the *Tribune*'s editorial in its April 30, 1915, edition.

43. Lloyd, *Abandoning Neutrality*, 57.

44. Mary Roberts Rinehart, *My Story* (New York: Farrar and Rinehart, 1931), 198.

45. Jay N. Darling, "Just How Sorry Are We for Those at War? Try This on Yourself," Des Moines *Register*, December 12, 1914.

46. Des Moines *Capital*, April 16, 1915, 10.

47. Quoted in Silber, *When Washington Shut Down Wall Street*, 1.

48. Iowa *Homestead*, January 21, 1915, 3.

49. Pittsburgh *Gazette-Times*, August 1, 1914, 1:4.

50. National Bank of Commerce to E. Lutz, January 9, 1916, Box 23, Folder N, German-American Lumber Company Records, MSS 86–27, Florida State University Special Collections. The League explicitly encouraged German-Americans to participate, showing that it saw no contradiction between German ethnicity and profit.

51. "Farmers Vitally Concerned in Railroads: What the European War Means to the American Farmer," Iowa *Homestead*, January 28, 1915, 30.

52. Silber, *When Washington Shut Down Wall Street*, 135.

53. *Life*, October 15, 1914, 670.

54. New York *Times*, September 21, 1914, in Columbia University Rare Books and Manuscript Library, World War I Collection, 1914–44, 1970 (UA #014), Box 17, Folder 1711; and "The Response of Our Universities" in Columbia University Rare Books and Manuscript Library, World War I Collection, 1914–44, 1970 (UA #014), Box 16, Folder 1615.

55. A. R. Smith to E. A. Rumely, January 8, 1916, in Rumely MSS, Box 6, January 1–14 folder, Lilly Library, Indiana University.

56. Lane and Wall, *Letters of Franklin K. Lane*, 164.
57. Alice Roosevelt Longworth, *Crowded Hours* (New York: Scribner's, 1935), 236.
58. http://wwi.lib.byu.edu/index.php/Manifesto_of_the_Ninety-Three_German_Intellectuals.
59. *New Republic* 1, no. 7 (December 19, 1914): 17–18.
60. William Roscoe Thayer, *Germany vs. Civilization: Notes on the Atrocious War* (Boston: Houghton Mifflin, 1916), 159–60.
61. New York *Tribune*, April 25, 1915, 8.
62. *New Republic* 1, no. 7 (December 19, 1914): 17–18.
63. *Life*, December 24, 1914, 1197.
64. Baker, *Why We Went to War*, 24.
65. Stanley Washburn, *On the Russian Front in World War I: Memoirs of an American War Correspondent* 25.
66. Quoted in Thayer, *Germany vs. Civilization*, 164.
67. Alan Cywar, "John Dewey in World War I: Patriotism and International Progressivism," *American Quarterly* 21, no. 3 (Autumn 1969): 584.
68. Andrew Preston, *Sword of the Spirit, Shield of the Faith: Religion in American War and Diplomacy* (New York: Alfred A. Knopf, 2012), 245.
69. Hugo Münsterberg, *The War and America* (New York: Appleton and Company, 1914), 54, 139, 160.
70. Elizabeth Williams, *Pittsburgh in World War I: Arsenal of the Allies* (Charleston, S.C.: The History Press, 2013), 72–73.
71. Baker, *Why We Went to War*, 101–2.
72. Pittsburgh *Gazette-Times*, August 3, 1914, 3.
73. Ellis, *Echoes of Distant Thunder*, 166.
74. Ellis, *Echoes of Distant Thunder*, 168–72.
75. Jules Witcover, *Sabotage at Black Tom: Imperial Germany's Secret War in America, 1914–1917* (Chapel Hill: Algonquin, 1989), 59–61.
76. Henry Landau, *The Enemy Within: The Inside Story of German Sabotage in America* (New York: G. P. Putnam's Sons, 1937), 14–17.
77. In today's parlance, we would call them lone wolves.
78. Thomas J. Tunney, as told to Paul Merrick Hollister, *Throttled! The Detection of the German and Anarchist Bomb Plotters* (Boston: Small, Maynard, and Company, 1919), 9–13.
79. Preston, *Sword of the Spirit*, 241.
80. Frederick C. Luebke, *Bonds of Loyalty: German-Americans and World War I* (DeKalb: Northern Illinois University Press, 1974), 121–23.
81. *Life*, November 5, 1914, 806.
82. Malcolm Campbell, *Ireland's New Worlds* (Madison: University of Wisconsin Press, 2008), 164.
83. Edward Cuddy, "Irish-Americans and the 1916 Election: An Episode in Immigrant Adjustment," *American Quarterly* 21, no. 2 (Summer 1916): 233.
84. Campbell, *Ireland's New Worlds*, 163.

85. Thomas Rowland, "The American Catholic Press and the Easter Rebellion," *Catholic Historical Review* 81, no. 1 (January 1995), accessed via EBSCOHost.

86. Joe Doyle, "Striking for Ireland on the New York Docks," in *The New York Irish*, ed. Ronald Bayor and Timothy Meagher (Baltimore: Johns Hopkins University Press, 1996), 359.

87. Joseph Rappaport, "The American Yiddish Press and the European Conflict in 1914," *Jewish Social Studies* 19 (1957): 116.

88. *Literatur un Lebn* quoted in Rappaport, "American Yiddish Press," 123.

89. David Laskin, *The Long Way Home: An American Journey from Ellis Island to the Great War* (New York: Harper Collins, 2010), 91–92.

90. Rappaport, "American Yiddish Press," 115.

91. Thayer, *Germany vs. Civilization*, 7.

92. Longworth, *Crowded Hours*, 237.

93. Rinehart, *My Story*, 192.

94. Hendrick, *The Life and Letters of Walter H. Page*, 436.

Chapter 3

1. The incident nearly set off an Anglo-American diplomatic dispute when the British government unwisely responded to the *Falaba* sinking by vastly increasing the amount of goods it defined as contraband. The new contraband list, which included food, threatened American free trade and struck most American officials as much too harsh a response.

2. Erik Larson, *Dead Wake: The Last Crossing of the Lusitania* (New York: Crown, 2015), 8.

3. Diana Preston, *Lusitania: An Epic Tragedy* (New York: Berkley, 2002), 183.

4. Forman had written a play called *The Hyphen*, which, ironically enough, was sympathetic to the plight of German- and Irish-Americans. It flopped on Broadway; Forman was headed to London on the *Lusitania* in the hopes that somehow he could make the play a success in the West End. His body was never recovered. "Over Here: World War I and the Fight for the American Mind," Exhibit at the New York Public Library.

5. The largest riots were in Victoria, Winnipeg, and Montreal, all cities where prominent citizens had died in the sinking. My thanks to Matt Pollard and Chandar Sundaram for their discussion of the Victoria riot with me and for taking me to dinner across the street from what was then the Kaiserhof Hotel where the riot began. It is today the Rialto.

6. Edward Robb Ellis, *Echoes of Distant Thunder: Life in the United States, 1914–1918* (New York: Kodansha International, 1975), 203.

7. *Life*, July 29, 1915.

8. *Literary Digest*, May 22, 1915, 1198.

9. Herbert T. Ezekiel and Gaston Lichtenstein, *The History of the Jews of Richmond from 1769 to 1917* (Richmond: Herbert T. Ezekiel, 1917), 381. The

mere existence of the book shows the desires of Virginia's Jews to demonstrate their unwavering loyalty to the United States in its hour of need.

10. "About Men and Things," *Jewish Exponent*, June 18, 1915, 4.

11. "Editorial: A Time to Be Calm," *American Hebrew and Jewish Messenger*, May 14, 1915.

12. Philadelphia *Tribune*, May 22, 1915, 4.

13. *Afro-American*, May 15, 1915, 7.

14. See Phillip Gonzales and Ann Massmann, "Loyalty Questioned: Nuevomexicanos in the Great War," *Pacific History Review* 75, no. 4 (2006): 633–35.

15. David Laskin, *The Long Way Home: An American Journey from Ellis Island to the Great War* (New York: Harper Collins, 2010), 103.

16. Note the contrast to the Second World War, when Italy was a member of the Axis. Salvatore J. LaGomina, *The Immigrants Speak: Italian-Americans Tell Their Story* (New York: Center for Migration Studies, 1979), 55, 114, 187.

17. Christopher Sterba, " 'Your Country Wants You': New Haven's Italian Machine Gun Company Enters World War I," *New England Quarterly* 74, no. 2 (June 2001): 181.

18. *American Israelite* May 13, 1915, 4; and June 17, 1915, 4.

19. Jan Cohn, *Improbable Fiction: The Life of Mary Roberts Rinehart* (Pittsburgh: University of Pittsburgh Press, 1980), 93.

20. Robert J. Menner, "The Kaiser and Germany in Popular Opinion," *South Atlantic Quarterly* 15, no. 2 (April 1916): 101–12.

21. Arthur Gleason, *Our Part in the Great War* (New York: Frederick A. Stokes, 1917), 83. More information on Gleason can be found at http://lcweb2.loc.gov/service/mss/eadxmlmss/eadpdfmss/2009/ms009002.pdf.

22. Rabbi Samuel Price Papers, Box 1, 1915 diary entry for May 7. American Jewish Historical Society, New York, New York.

23. Manon *Sentinel*, May 13, 1915, 4.

24. Charles Seymour, ed., *The Intimate Papers of Colonel House*, vol. 2 (New York: Houghton Mifflin Company, 1926), 1.

25. See http://wwi.lib.byu.edu/index.php/Wilson's_First_Lusitania_Note_to_Germany.

26. Wilson later told Galt that he had said the words because he had had his mind on her, not on foreign policy. She finally agreed to marry him on June 29. See Larson, *Dead Wake*, 331.

27. Theodore Roosevelt to O. K. Davis, June 23, 1915, Gilder-Lehrman Collection, New-York Historical Society, GLC 08003.

28. "The German Attitude: 'Anything' for America," *North American Review* 202 (October 1915): 481–504.

29. See Ellis, *Echoes of Distant Thunder*, 214.

30. Henry Bourne Joy, "Millions for Tribute, Not One Cent for Defense: A Reply to Henry Ford," written August 28, 1915. https://archive.org/details/millionsfortribu00joyhiala.

31. David Woodward, *The American Army and the First World War* (Cambridge: Cambridge University Press, 2014), 19. Just a few weeks later, Pershing lost his wife and three daughters in a fire at the family's home at the Presidio in San Francisco. Pershing had been at Fort Bliss, Texas, preparing to relocate his family there when the fire broke out.

32. Gleason, *Our Part in the Great War*, 33; Charles F. Thwing, *The American Colleges and Universities in the Great War* (New York: Macmillan, 1920), 21.

33. Richard Harding Davis, *With the French in France and Salonika* (New York: A. L. Burt, 1916), 26–27.

34. Justus Doenecke, *Nothing Less than War: A New History of America's Entry into World War I* (Lexington: University Press of Kentucky, 2011), 84.

35. Theodore Roosevelt to "My Dear Castle," November 13, 1915, Gilder-Lehrman Collection, New-York Historical Society, GLC 00782.19.

36. John Patrick Finnegan, *Against the Specter of a Dragon: The Campaign for American Preparedness, 1914–1917* (Westport, Conn.: Greenwood, 1974), 37. Emphasis in original.

37. *New York Times Current History* 1 (1915); 517.

38. Ross Gregory, *The Origins of American Intervention in the First World War*, (New York: W. W. Norton, 1971), 66–67.

39. Frederick C. Luebke, *Bonds of Loyalty: German-Americans and World War I*, (DeKalb: Northern Illinois University Press, 1974), 131.

40. Richard Gamble, *The War of Righteousness: Progressive Christianity, the Great War, and the Rise of the Messianic Nation* (Wilmington, Del.: ISI Books, 2003), 112–15, 118.

41. Ellis, *Distant Echoes of Thunder*, 205.

42. Des Moines *Register*, January 15, 1916, available at http://digital.lib.uiowa.edu/cdm/singleitem/collection/ding/id/321/rec/2.

43. Harding remains the only cartoonist to win Pulitzer Prizes in consecutive years. Kirby won three Pulitzers for editorial cartoons, including the first such prize given in 1922. Some of their work can be seen in the Rudolph Franz scrapbook of World War I editorial cartoons in the Milton S. Eisenhower Library Special Collections Department at Johns Hopkins University. Darling, Clifford Beryman, and John T. McCutcheon all won the award as well at some point in their careers.

44. Woodward, *The American Army and the First World War*, 18.

45. *New York Times Current History*, (June 1915); 445–46.

46. "Why?" *North American Review* 201 (May 1915): 676–82.

47. Douglas Bukowski, *Big Bill Thompson, Chicago, and the Politics of Image* (Urbana: University of Illinois Press, 1998), 27.

48. Ellis, *Echoes of Distant Thunder*, 203.

49. William Mulligan, *The Great War for Peace* (New Haven: Yale University Press, 2014), 6.

50. This version of the story comes from Jules Witcover, *Sabotage at Black Tom: Imperial Germany's Secret War in America, 1914–1917* (Chapel Hill:

Algonquin, 1989), 120–21. The cloak-and-dagger details of the incident vary from story to story, but the basic facts do not.

51. Ellis, *Echoes of Distant Thunder*, 178.

52. Albert went on to become the *Reichsschatzminister* (director of the budget) for the Weimar government and then became its minister for reconstruction. He left government service in 1923 and later became the chairman of the board of the Ford Motor Company in Germany from 1937 to 1945.

53. Luebke, *Bonds of Loyalty*, 140.

54. The documents themselves are in "Austrian and German Papers Found in Possession of Mr. James F. J. Archibald," Falmouth, August 30, 1915, Newberry Library, Chicago, F 1009.37 v. 1, miscellaneous papers no. 16.

55. Henry Landau, *The Enemy Within: The Inside Story of German Sabotage in America* (New York: G. P. Putnam's Sons, 1937), 25.

56. My thanks to my friend and Dickinson College chemistry professor Cindy Samet for her help.

57. Howard Blum, *Dark Invasion, 1915: Germany's Secret War and the Hunt for the First Terrorist Cell in America* (New York: Harper, 2014), 228–29, 332–33; Landau, *Enemy Within*, 42–48.

58. Thomas J. Tunney, *Throttled! The Detection of the German and Anarchist Bomb Plotters* (Boston: Small, Maynard, and Co., 1919), 148–69.

59. Blum, *Dark Invasion*, 390.

60. The full speech is available at http://www.presidency.ucsb.edu/ws/?pid=29556.

61. http://avalon.law.yale.edu/20th_century/brycere.asp.

62. Ellis, *Echoes of Distant Thunder*, 230.

63. My thanks to Robert Cozzolino, curator of paintings at the Minneapolis Institute of Art, for calling my attention to the Bellows painting. It can be seen at http://www.hvallison.com/datatool/images/large/1918-002a.jpg.

64. Gregory, *Origins of American Intervention*, 11.

65. Tunney, *Throttled*, 191–212.

66. For a sense of her arguments, see Jane Addams, "Revolt Against War," *The Survey*, July 17, 1915.

67. Louise W. Knight, *Jane Addams: Spirit in Action* (New York: W. W. Norton, 2010), 204.

68. Luebke, *Bonds of Loyalty*, 134.

69. The series included *The Battle for New York* and *At the Defense of Pittsburgh*, which envisioned a German invasion of the United States in 1920–21. Both published in 1916, they aimed primarily at an adolescent and young adult audience.

70. Germanistic Society of Chicago 1907–16, Midwest MS 157, Newberry Library, Chicago.

71. "Austrian and German Papers," p. 17, document 13.

72. Luebke, *Bonds of Loyalty*, 131.

73. Alexander Waldenrath, "The German Language Newspapers in Pennsylvania During World War I," *Pennsylvania History* 42, no. 1 (January 1975): 33.

74. Any more, of course, than a modern-day air traveler knows what his or her airplane has in its cargo hold.

75. Waldenrath, "German Language Newspapers," 35.

76. Laskin, *Long Way Home*, 100.

77. "Address to Catholics of German Descent," September 24, 1916, in George Mundelein, *Two Crowded Years* (Chicago: Extension Press, 1918), 107.

78. Willa Cather, *One of Ours* (New York: Knopf, 1922), 78, 97.

79. Luebke, *Bonds of Loyalty*, 132.

80. Frederick Palmer, *Newton D. Baker: America at War* (New York: Dodd, Mead, and Company, 1931), 44.

81. See the reports in the Ogden *Standard*, May 6, 1915, 10; and the New York *Tribune*, April 24, 1915, 1.

82. Francis William O'Brien, ed., *The Hoover-Wilson Wartime Correspondence, September 24, 1914 to November 11, 1918* (Ames: Iowa State University Press, 1974), 7–9, 11.

83. Speech of Hon. Albert B. Cummins (R-Iowa), January 19, 1916, Tennessee State Library and Archives, Governor Tom Rye Papers, 1915–18, Box 44, Folder 6.

84. Alice Roosevelt Longworth, *Crowded Hours* (New York: Scribner's, 1935), 238.

85. Robert Lansing, *War Memoirs of Robert Lansing, Secretary of State* (Indianapolis: Bobbs-Merrill, 1935), 23.

86. Lansing, *War Memoirs*, 34–35.

87. Gregory, *Origins of American Intervention*, 72.

88. *Literary Digest*, September 4, 1915, 455–56.

89. *Literary Digest*, September 11, 1915, 509–11.

90. O'Brien, *Hoover-Wilson Correspondence*, 13.

91. *Literary Digest*, September 11, 1915, 510.

92. *Literary Digest*, October 9, 1915, 762–63.

93. Anne Wintermute Lane and Louise Herrick Wall, eds., *The Letters of Franklin K. Lane, Personal and Political* (Boston: Houghton Mifflin, 1922), 176–77.

94. Gleason, *Our Part in the Great War*, 38, 85.

95. Frederick Palmer, *My Year of the Great War* (New York: Dodd, Mead, and Company, 1915), 351.

96. *Literary Digest*, December 18, 1915, 1415.

97. Nelson Lloyd, *How We Went to War* (New York: Scribner's, 1919), 5.

98. Washington *Herald*, July 28, 1915, 1; and Chicago *Day Book*, August 3, 1915, 9.

99. On July 30, the *Tribune*'s editorial cartoonist depicted the devil in front of a 1915 calendar with the words *The World War, The Lusitania, The Eastland, The Weather, Mexican Conditions*, and *Strikes*. The devil mischievously rubs

his hands and says "Well! Let's See What I Can Do Next?" John T. McCutcheon Papers, Newberry Library, Chicago.

100. William Roscoe Thayer, *Germany vs. Civilization: Notes on the Atrocious War* (Boston: Houghton Mifflin, 1916), 172, 188.

101. Lane and Wall, *Letters of Franklin Lane*, 175–76.

102. Lansing, *War Memoirs of Robert Lansing*, 19–21. Emphasis in original. See also Willis Fletcher Johnson, "The Story of the Danish Islands," *North American Review* 204 (September 1916): 381–90. The United States also agreed to renounce all outstanding claims to Greenland.

103. Edward Gibbons and Floyd Gibbons, *Floyd Gibbons, Your Headline Hunter: A Biography* (New York: Exposition Press, 1953), 59. Gibbons later survived the German sinking of the *Laconia* in 1917, lost an eye while covering the exploits of the US Marine Corps at the Battle of Belleau Wood, and received a star on the Hollywood Walk of Fame.

104. Luebcke, *Bonds of Loyalty*, 144.

105. *Literary Digest*, November 6, 1915, 994, 1208–9.

106. Samuel Taylor Moore, *America and the World War: A Narrative of the Part Played by the United States from the Outbreak to Peace* (New York: Greenberg, 1937), 4, 13, 42.

Chapter 4

1. Washington *Times*, September 29, 1918, 24–25. I am consciously avoiding the use of the word *genocide* here because people in 1915 and 1916 did not use it. I am instead using the word they used most frequently, *massacres*. Eugene Rogan, *The Fall of the Ottomans: The Great War in the Middle East* (New York: Basic, 2015), 168–72, gives a good general background of the events at Van. Ronald Grigor Suny's article on the Armenian genocide at http://encyclopedia.1914-1918-online.net/home/, which provides an excellent starting point to this complex topic.

2. Clarence D. Ussher, *An American Physician in Turkey* (Boston: Houghton Mifflin, 1917, 2002 [reprint]), 118, 141–42, 149, 178.

3. "Mr. Roosevelt Blames Pacifists Here for Armenian Atrocities" and "Turks' Cruelty to Armenians Is Growing," from Eva Stotesbury World War I Scrapbook, Reel 17, Box A63, November 25 to December 2, 1915, Library of Congress Manuscript Division.

4. Anderson (South Carolina) *Intelligencer*, December 12, 1915, 15. The language of martyrdom came easily to Americans discussing Armenia. The Washington *Herald*, for example, used it in a December 12, 1915, article that discussed "the tragic story of the oldest Christian people" on earth.

5. Chicago *Day Book*, December 29, 1915, 5.

6. Gibran went on to great fame as a result of his 1923 book, *The Prophet*. By some accounts he is the third most-read poet in history behind only William Shakespeare and Laozi.

7. New York *Tribune*, October 14, 1915, 6.

8. New York *Tribune*, October 11, 1915, 6. Emphasis mine.

9. Arizona *Republic*, December 22, 1916, 1.

10. "Ours Not a Peace Christ Would Have" and "Miss Anne Morgan Says America Cannot Escape Its Duty to France," from Eva Stotesbury World War I Scrapbook, Reel 25, Box A95, October 20 to November 5, 1916, Library of Congress Manuscript Division.

11. Edward Rumely to George Odell, September 23, 1915, in Rumely MSS, Box 6, September 15–23 folder, Lilly Library, Indiana University.

12. José Antonio Montero, "Neutrality and Leadership: The United States, Spain, and World War I," Undefended Neutrality Conference, Seville, Spain, November 27, 2014. I am grateful to José Antonio for his willingness to share his findings with me.

13. "Coming Our Way: The Money Center of the World," Chicago *Tribune* April 19, 1915, Newberry Library, John T. McCutcheon Papers, Box 8; and "The Prosperity That Depends on the Suffering of Others," Chicago *Tribune*, October 21, 1916, Newberry Library, John T. McCutcheon Papers, Box 9.

14. Blaisdell Pencil Company of Philadelphia, for example, saw an exponential rise in business after 1914, in large part because its German competitors stopped exporting pencils and crayons. *Philadelphia in the World War* (New York: Wynkoop Hallenbeck Crawford, 1922), 425.

15. "Sermon Preached at the First Presbyterian Church by Dr. James Vance," October 1, 1916, Tennessee State Library and Archives, Records of the First and Downtown Presbyterian Churches in Nashville, 1827–1996, Box 6, Folder 9, p. 6; "Bible Business Boomed by War" and "America to Supply France After War," from Eva Stotesbury World War I Scrapbook, Reel 17, Box A63, November 25 to December 2, 1915.

16. Ray Stannard Baker, *American Chronicle* (New York: Scribner's, 1945), 300–301. The Hudson Guild still exists as part of the Chelsea-Elliot housing project on West 25th Street between 9th and 10th Avenues in Manhattan.

17. Irvin S. Cobb, *Paths of Glory: Impressions of War Written at or Near the Front* (New York: Grosset and Dunlap, 1918), 427.

18. *Life*, February 10, 1916, cover image.

19. Lawrence Sondhaus, *The Great War at Sea: A Naval History of the First World War* (Cambridge: Cambridge University Press, 2014), 26–27, 85; Shusuke Takahara, "The Wilson Administration and the Mandate Question in the Pacific," in *The Decade of the Great War: Japan and the Wider World in the 1910s*, ed. Tosh Minohara, Tze-ki Hon, and Evan Dawley (Leiden: Brill Academic Publishing, 2015), 149–67.

20. Richard Walden Hale, *Letters of Warwick Greene, 1915–1928* (Boston: Houghton Mifflin, 1931), 5.

21. Chicago *Day Book*, March 7, 1916, 25.

22. See Justus Doenecke, *Nothing Less than War: A New History of America's Entry into World War I* (Lexington: University Press of Kentucky, 2014), 160–66.

23. Yes, dear readers, that really was his name.
24. Keokuk (Iowa) *Daily Gate City*, March 26, 1916, 1.
25. David F. Houston, *Eight Years with Wilson's Cabinet*, vol. 1 (Garden City, N.Y.: Doubleday, Page, and Company, 1926), 152–54.
26. Claudius O. Johnson, *Borah of Idaho* (Seattle: University of Washington Press, 1936), 199.
27. Edward Rumely to Prof. von Schulze-Gaevernitz, April 21, 1916, in Rumely MSS, Box 7, April 21–30 folder, Lilly Library, Indiana University.
28. *America's Attitude Toward the War* (New York: Bankers Trust, 1917), 59, 65.
29. The Germans did pay an indemnity to the family of Enrique Granados.
30. *Life*, April 13, 1916.
31. *Life*, April 27, 1916.
32. The full note can be found at http://www.firstworldwar.com/source/uboat1916_usultimatum.htm.
33. Price Papers, P–95, 1913–62, Box 1: diary entries for April 20 and 22, 1916.
34. "Kaiser to Defy United States as His Answer," Philadelphia *Tribune*, May 15, 1915, 1.
35. Washington *Post*, May 6, 1916, 3.
36. Massillon (Ohio) *Evening Independent*, April 20, 1916, 4.
37. Walter Lippmann, "The World Conflict in Its Relation to American Democracy," *Annals of the American Academy of Political and Social Science* 72 (July 1917): 1–2, 5.
38. Price Diary, May 5, 1916.
39. Houston, *Eight Years*, 157.
40. The survey of opinion appeared in the Galveston *Daily News*, May 15, 1915, 4. A small handful of German-language newspapers dissented from the majority. The Indianapolis *German Telegraph-Tribune*, for example, called Wilson's diplomacy "extravagant" and "a palp able injustice" to Germany.
41. John Patrick Finnegan, *Against the Specter of a Dragon: The Campaign for American Military Preparedness* (Westport, Conn.: Greenwood, 1974), 149, 151.
42. Gilbert Vivian Seldes, *The United States and the War* (London: George Allen and Unwin, Ltd., 1917), 93.
43. Franklin Martin, *The Joy of Living: An Autobiography* (Garden City, N.Y.: Doubleday, Doran, 1933), 43, 58.
44. Alice Roosevelt Longworth, *Crowded Hours* (New York: Scribner's, 1935), 238.
45. Mary Roberts Rinehart, *My Story* (New York: Farrar and Rinehart, 1931), 215.
46. *Philadelphia in the World War*, 81.
47. Paul Ayers Rockwell, *American Fighters in the Foreign Legion, 1914–1918* (Boston: Houghton Mifflin, 1930), 211–12.

48. Washington *Evening Star*, November 4, 1917, 20.
49. Anna Murray Vail to Mrs. [Mariana] Schuyler Van Rennselear, August 12, 1916, American Fund for French Wounded Records, New York Public Library, Box 1, Folder 1.
50. New York *Sun*, July 23, 1916, 1.
51. New York *Sun*, October 1, 1916, 2. Starr's father rushed out a book in his son's honor, Louis Starr, *The War Story of Dillwyn Parrish Starr* (New York: G. P. Putnam's Sons, 1917).
52. For Britain, see Axel Jansen, "Heroes or Citizens? The 1916 Debate on Harvard Volunteers in the 'European War'," in *War Volunteering Modern Times: From the French Revolution to the Second World War*, ed. Christine Krüger and Sonja Levsen (London: Palgrave MacMillan, 2011), 150. The number of Americans in the Canadian Army is still unclear, but may be as high as eighty thousand. Jonathan Vance, Keynote Address, *The Great War's Shadow: New Perspectives on the First World War*, Calgary, Alberta, September 25, 2014.
53. Edwin Morse, *The Vanguard of American Volunteers in the Fighting Lines and in Humanitarian Service, August, 1914 to April, 1917* (New York: Scribner's, 1919), 132.
54. C. Earl Baker, *Doughboy's Diary* (Shippensburg, Penn.: Burd Street Press, 1998), 1.
55. Paul J. Ferguson and Michael Neiberg, "America's Expatriate Aviators," *Military History Quarterly* 14 (Summer 2002): 58–63.
56. Morse, *Vanguard of American Volunteers*, 241.
57. See, for example, Theodore Roosevelt, "Lafayettes of the Air," *Collier's* 57 (July 29, 1916): 16.
58. "Americans in the French Army," May 9, 1916, in Spencer Cosby Collection, Box 4, Folder 7, United States Army Heritage and Education Center, Carlisle, Pa.
59. Quoted in Ferguson and Neiberg, "America's Expatriate Aviators," 60.
60. New York *Evening World*, November 21, 1916, 12; and Lincoln Ayer, "American Airmen Drop Three Germans in Day's Battles," in Stotesbury World War I Scrapbook, Reel 25, Box A96.
61. Sarah McCulloh Lemmon, *North Carolina in the First World War* (Raleigh: State Department of Archives and History, 1966), 8–10.
62. Even a newspaper as tiny and, one presumes, as focused on local affairs as the Keowee (SC) *Courier* put Rockwell's death on the front page of its September 27, 1916, edition.
63. Alexandre Millerand, *L'Effort Charitable des États-Unis* (Paris: Blunt and Gay, 1917), 17.
64. Anna Murray Vail to Mrs. [Mariana] Schuyler Van Rennselear, August 5, 1916, American Fund for French Wounded Records, New York Public Library, Box 1, Folder 1.
65. Photo from Stotesbury World War I Scrapbook, Reel 25, Box A96.

66. Richard Gamble, *The War of Righteousness: Progressive Christianity, the Great War, and the Rise of the Messianic Nation* (Wilmington, Del.: ISI Books, 2003), 133, 137.

67. Richard Harding Davis, *With the French in France and Salonika* (New York: A. L. Burt, 1916), 223.

68. "Workers Here Rush Winter War Relief," in Stotesbury Scrapbook, Reel 17, Box A63; and "Club in New York Pledges $500,000 for Belgian Relief," in Stotesbury Scrapbook, Reel 27, Box A103.

69. National Allied Relief Committee, April 3, 1916, Tennessee State Library and Archives, Governor Tom Rye Papers, 1915–18, Box 28, Folder 13.

70. The program can be found at: https://ia700401.us.archive.org/22/items/theenslavementof00newy/theenslavementof00newy.pdf.

71. Robert J. Menner, "The Kaiser and Germany in Popular Opinion," *South Atlantic Quarterly* 15, no. 2 (April 1916): 101, 107–8, 110.

72. Peter Connolly-Smith, *Translating America: An Immigrant Press Visualizes American Popular Culture, 1895–1918* (Washington: Smithsonian Books, 2004), 199.

73. "Political Degeneracy of Modern Germany" and "Germany's Great Lost Cause," in Stotesbury Scrapbook, Reel 25, Box A95, October 20 to November 5, 1916.

74. Herbert Bayard Swope, "Conditions Under Which Germany Would Make Peace at This Time," in Stotesbury Scrapbook, Reel 25, Box A95; and Swope, "9,000,000 Here Are Ready to Do Her Bidding to Make Kultur Rule World," in Stotesbury Scrapbook, Reel 25, Box A96, November 7 to 19, 1916. The book appeared as *Inside the German Empire* (New York: Century Company, 1917), with an introduction from American ambassador to Germany James Gerard.

75. Andrew Preston, *Sword of the Spirit, Shield of the Faith: Religion in American War and Diplomacy* (New York: Alfred A. Knopf, 2012), 240.

76. Edward Clark, *Something Doing Every Minute: Memoirs of the Professional Life* (New York: Exposition Press, 1964), 16.

77. "The Great Conspiracy Exposed," *Fatherland* 4, no. 7 (March 22, 1916): 1–4, Tennessee State Library and Archives, Gov. Tom Rye Papers (GP37), Box 44, Folder 6.

78. "The War from All Sides: Books of Absorbing Interest on the Greatest War of All Times," *Confederate Veteran* 23, no. 11 (November 1915): 528.

79. "The Bomb Plot Thickens," *Literary Digest*, April 29, 1916, 1205.

80. The full address is reprinted in *Issues and Events* 4, no. 18 (April 29, 1916): 310; and in the April 17, 1916, issue of the New York *Times*.

81. Anna Murray Vail to Mrs. [Mariana] Schuyler Van Rennselear, January 1, 1916, American Fund for French Wounded Records, New York Public Library, Box 1, Folder 1.

82. Anna Murray Vail to Mrs. [Mariana] Schuyler Van Rennselear, January 31, 1916, American Fund for French Wounded Records, New York Public Library, Box 1, Folder 1. Emphasis in original.

83. Seldes, *The United States and the War*, 132–38.

84. Chapter 7 of Steven H. Jaffe, *New York at War: Four Centuries of Combat, Fear, and Intrigue in Gotham* (New York: Basic, 2012), provides a good account of the background to the Black Tom incident.

85. "Munitions Explosions Cause Loss of $20,000,000," New York *Times*, July 31, 1916; and "One More Warrant in Munitions Blast," New York *Sun*, n.d., from Stotesbury Scrapbook, Reel 23, Box A88.

86. "Cause of New York Blast, with Its Toll of Millions, Sought. German Plot Seen," Philadelphia *Evening-Ledger*, July 31, 1916, 1.

87. "Two Held as Plotters in Munitions Fire," Washington *Times*, August 10, 1916, 1.

88. Jules Whitcover, *Sabotage at Black Tom: Imperial Germany's Secret War in America, 1914–1917* (Chapel Hill: Algonquin, 1989). See also Michael Neiberg, "World War I Intrigue: German Spies in New York!" in *Military History Quarterly*, available online at http://www.historynet.com/world-war-i-intrigue-german-spies-in-new-york.htm. Today the Black Tom site is home to the lovely Liberty State Park in Jersey City, New Jersey. Only one small, poorly written sign in a lonely corner of the park by the old piers tells visitors what happened there in 1916.

89. Henry Landau, *The Enemy Within: The Inside Story of German Sabotage in America* (New York: G. P. Putnam's Sons, 1937), 85.

90. Harvey O'Connor, *The Guggenheims: The Making of an American Dynasty* (New York: Covici-Friede, 1937), 359.

91. *Confederate Veteran* 23, no. 10 (October 1915): 438.

92. William Glasson, "Some Effects of the European War upon American Industries," *South Atlantic Quarterly* 14, no. 2 (April 1915): 108. The author was an economist at Trinity College in Hartford, Connecticut.

93. Francis Jones, Over-Seas Club of New York, to Governor Thomas Rye, January 8, 1916, Tennessee State Library and Archives, Gov. Tom Rye Papers, 1915–18, Box 28, Folder 13.

94. As Jennifer Keene notes, the Kansas wheat sacks were not "an isolated example" as similar expressions of thanks could be found all over the United States. See her article "Americans Respond: Perspectives on the Global War, 1914–1917," *Geschichte und Gesellschaft* 40 (2014): 271–72. Some of the flour sacks can be seen online at http://www.kshs.org/kansapedia/cool-things-embroidered-flour-sacks/16791.

95. "War Prosperity Pudding," Chicago *Tribune*, August 18, 1916, Newberry Library, John T. McCutcheon Papers, Box 9.

96. Des Moines *Register*, October 21, 1916.

97. See Andrew Lambert, *Planning Armageddon: British Economic Warfare and the First World War* (Cambridge, Mass.: Harvard University Press, 2012), 470–75.

98. Frederic Paxson, *American Democracy and the World War: Prewar Years, 1913–1917* (Boston: Houghton-Mifflin, 1936), 308.

99. Ross Gregory, *The Origins of American Intervention* (New York: W. W. Norton, 1971), 109. For more on the drift in Anglo-American

relations, see Ross Gregory, "The Superfluous Ambassador: Walter Hines Page's Return to Washington, 1916," *The Historian* 28, no. 3 (1966): 389–404.

100. "The Apathy of America," *Literary Digest*, October 21, 1916, 1025–26.
101. See Galen Jackson, "The Offshore Balancing Thesis Reconsidered: Realism, the Balance of Power in Europe, and America's Decision for War in 1917," *Security Studies* 21 (2012): 455–89.

Chapter 5

1. "Armament and Disarmament," June 14, 1915, Tennessee State Library and Archives, Jacob McGavock Dickinson Papers, Box 65.
2. New York *Tribune*, February 21, 1915, 6.
3. Quoted in William Mulligan, *The Great War for Peace* (New Haven: Yale University Press, 2014), 1.
4. Cedar Rapids *Republican*, August 26, 1915, 1.
5. Newell Dwight Hillis, "The Verdict of the American People," *New York Times Current History* 1 (1915); 574–75.
6. David Woodward, *The American Army and the First World War* (Cambridge: Cambridge University Press, 2014), 17.
7. Anne Cipriano Venzon, ed., *The United States in the First World War* (New York: Garland, 1995), 412.
8. H. W. Brands, *Woodrow Wilson: The American Presidents Series, the 28th President, 1913–1921* (New York: Macmillan, 2003), ii.
9. Frederic Paxson, *American Democracy and the World War: Prewar Years, 1913–1917* (Boston: Houghton Mifflin, 1936), 9.
10. Navy legend has it that the phrase "cup of Joe" in reference to coffee has its origins in navy sarcasm at the prohibitionist ban Daniels imposed.
11. Frederick Palmer, *Newton D. Baker, America at War*, vol. 1 (New York: Dodd, Mead, and Company, 1931), 40–41.
12. *Literary Digest*, May 22, 1915, 1199.
13. Robert Lansing, *War Memoirs of Robert Lansing, Secretary of State* (Indianapolis: Bobbs-Merrill, 1935), 40. Lansing wanted to have the flexibility to threaten war with Germany as a diplomatic tool, but he knew that that, too, would be mostly bluff.
14. Anne Wintermute Lane and Louise Herrick Wall, eds., *The Letters of Franklin K. Lane, Personal and Political* (Boston: Houghton Mifflin, 1922), 180.
15. Perry Belmont, *An American Democrat* (New York: AMS Press, 1967), 553.
16. Denton (Texas) *Record Chronicle*, February 11, 1916, 2. The survey was conducted by the Dallas *News*.
17. Charles Nagel to Edward Rumely, March 9, 1917, in Rumely MSS, Box 8, March 8–12 folder, Lilly Library, Indiana University.

18. Timothy J. Meagher, *Inventing Irish America: Generation, Class, and Ethnic Identity in a New England City, 1880–1928* (Notre Dame: Notre Dame University Press, 2001), 351.

19. "National Preparedness an Unrealizable Dream Under Existing Iron and Steel Conditions," *Manufacturer's Record*, October 28, 1915.

20. Powell Evans, "Communication on National Defense," Philadelphia, Pa., April 1916, in Tennessee State Library and Archives, Governor Tom Rye Papers, 1915–18, Box 44, Folder 6.

21. The quotation comes from the "eminent naturalist, explorer, and traveler" William T. Hornaday, then the head of the New York (now Bronx) Zoo. *National Defence* 1, no. 2 (April 1915): 6. The newsletter noted that he "needs no introduction to the American public."

22. "Nations Are like Individuals," Chicago *Tribune*, November 3, 1916, John T. McCutcheon Papers, Newberry Library, Box 9, Folder 251.

23. Harrisburg *Telegraph*, June 17, 1915, 1.

24. James A. Montgomery, "The Right of the Christian to Fight: Being a Sermon Preached in St. Peter's Church in Philadelphia, May 7, 1916 at a Service in Commemoration of the Victims on Board the *Lusitania* Killed May 7, 1915," Pennsylvania State Library, Harrisburg, Pamphlet PV 1186.

25. "Mrs. Catt on Women's Part in War," from Eva Stotesbury World War I Scrapbook, Reel 25, Box A95, October 20 to November 5, 1916, Library of Congress Manuscript Division.

26. "Speech at Orchestra Hall," Chicago, October 12, 1915, Tennessee State Library and Archives, Jacob McGavock Dickinson Papers, Box 65.

27. *Life*, October 15, 1914, 703.

28. John Patrick Finnegan, *Against the Specter of a Dragon: The Campaign for American Military Preparedness* (Westport, Conn.: Greenwood, 1974), 22, 24; Washington *Herald*, January 5, 1915, 2.

29. *National Defence* 1, no. 1 (March 1915): 18, 30.

30. "Shortage of Munitions of War for Field Army," *National Defence* 1, no. 2 (April 1915): 31.

31. New York *Evening World*, September 29, 1915, 1.

32. "How France Cares for Her Blind Heroes," Washington *Sunday Star*, July 25, 1915, part 4, 2.

33. Caroline King Duer Papers, Box 2, Folder 3.15, Barnard College Archives, BC 20.20.

34. *National Defence* 1, no. 1 (March 1915): 13–14, 39–40.

35. Theodore Roosevelt to "My Dear Castle," November 13, 1915, Gilder-Lehrman Collection, New-York Historical Society, GLC 00782.19.

36. Finnegan, *Against the Specter of a Dragon*, 13, 53.

37. Woodward, *The American Army and the First World War*, 22.

38. Speech of Hon. Albert B. Cummins, January 19, 1916, 7, Tennessee State Library and Archives, Gov. Tom Rye Papers, 1915–18, Box 44, Folder 6.

39. See Robert Miraldi, *The Pen Is Mightier: The Muckraking Life of Charles Edward Russell* (New York: Palgrave Macmillan, 2003), chapter 13.

40. Muscatine (Iowa) *Journal*, September 7, 1915.

41. Cummins speech, 2.

42. *Literary Digest*, March 20, 1915, 600.

43. Richard Franklin Bensel, *Passion and Preferences: William Jennings Bryan and the 1896 Democratic National Convention* (Cambridge: Cambridge University Press, 2008), 224–25.

44. Chicago *Day Book*, March 5, 1915, 11.

45. "Bryan Spurns the President's Plan for National Defense," *Current Opinion* 59, no. 6 (December 1915): 379. Although less harsh than the *World*, *Current Opinion* noted that Bryan's views were clearly in the minority.

46. "Greater Forts Seen Here by Calder," from Stotesbury Scrapbook, Reel 17, Box A63, November 25 to December 2, 1915, Library of Congress Manuscript Division.

47. "Incomes and Autos to Pay for Preparedness," from Stotesbury Scrapbook, Reel 17, Box A63, November 25 to December 2, 1915.

48. Mulligan, *Great War for Peace*, 129.

49. Paxson, *American Democracy and the World War*, 289. This is not the same American Legion that exists today as a veterans' organization.

50. *Philadelphia in the World War* (New York: Wynkoop Hallenbeck Crawford, 1922), 79.

51. Raymond Chamberlain, *The Only Thing for a Man to Do* (Boston: Privately published, 1921), United States Army Heritage and Education Center, Carlisle, Pa., D640.C515. Chamberlain was killed in action in September 1918 in France (see the conclusion).

52. Edward Clark, *Something Doing Every Minute: Memoirs of the Professional Life* (New York: Exposition Press, 1964), 11–12.

53. Finnegan, *Against the Specter of a Dragon*, 31–39.

54. *National Defence* 1, nos. 3 and 4 (May–June 1915): 61–62, 65.

55. "Canvass of Business Men Shows Nearly All Are for National Preparedness," Stotesbury Scrapbook, Reel 17, Box A63.

56. Henry Joy, "Millions for Tribute, Not One Cent for Defense: A Reply to Henry Ford," August 28, 1915, Hathi Digital Trust, http://catalog.hathitrust.org/Record/001588679.

57. "Great War Ends Christmas Day," New York *Tribune*, November 25, 1915, 6, from Stotesbury Scrapbook, Reel 17, Box A63.

58. Preston William Slosson, *The Great Crusade and After, 1914–1928* (New York: Macmillan, 1931), 9.

59. Arizona *Republic*, July 3, 1919, 2.

60. "Grotesque Says J. R. Day," from Stotesbury Scrapbook, Reel 17, Box A63.

61. Franklin Martin, *The Joy of Living: An Autobiography* (Garden City, N.Y.: Doubleday, 1933), 39; and "Edison's Plan for Preparedness," New York *Times Magazine*, May 30, 1915.

62. The ad can be seen in *Current Opinion* 55, no. 3 (March 1916): 217.

63. Columbia University Rare Books and Manuscript Library, World War I Collection, 1914–44, 1970 (UA #014), Box 16, Folder 1611.

64. Alfred Lloyd, "Expediency of an Academic Call to Arms," New York *Times*, November 25, 1915; "Greater Forts Seen Here by Calder," from Stotesbury Scrapbook, Reel 17, Box A63, November 25 to December 2, 1915 and "Columbia Men Indorse [*sic*] Defense," and "Columbia Students Oppose Militarism," New York *Times*, January 16, 1915, in Columbia University Rare Books and Manuscript Library, World War I Collection, 1914–44, 1970 (UA #014), Box 17, Folder 1711. Mitchel died on July 6, 1918, in an aviation accident while training to be a pilot for the US Army.

65. "US Urged to Arm in Many Sermons," from Stotesbury Scrapbook, Reel 17, Box A63.

66. "There's a Reason," *National Defence* 1, nos. 3 and 4 (May–June, 1915): 92.

67. The official was Lyman Gage, "The Sage of San Diego," who served as secretary of the Treasury. *National Defence* 2, no. 4 (December 1915): 132.

68. Arthur Gleason, *Our Part in the Great War* (New York: Frederick Stokes Co., 1917), 3, 119.

69. *National Defence* 3, no. 4 (February 1915): 183.

70. *The Monthly Bulletin of the Carnegie Library of Pittsburgh* 24, no. 2 (February 1919): 82.

71. David Laskin, *The Long Way Home: An American Journey from Ellis Island to the Great War* (New York: Harper Collins, 2010), 101.

72. Harrisburg *Telegraph*, October 18, 1915, 8.

73. *Literary Digest*, May 22, 1915, 1199.

74. Theodore Roosevelt to Charles Evans Hughes, September 18, 1916, in Rumely MSS, Box 7, September 26–30 folder, Lilly Library, Indiana University.

75. "A Plea for Peace," Tennessee State Library and Archives, Governor Tom Rye Papers, 1915–18, Box 44, Folder 9.

76. "Eliminating the Hyphen," St. Paul *Appeal*, July 17, 1915, 2.

77. "Neutrality and Public Opinion," address by Charles Nagel, delivered under the auspices of the Deutsche Gesellschaft of St. Louis, January 23, 1915, National Library of Ireland, Dublin, P1006.

78. "The Nation's Stand," Philadelphia *Jewish Exponent*, May 21, 1915.

79. William Roscoe Thayer, *Germany vs. Civilization: Notes on the Atrocious War* (Boston: Houghton-Mifflin, 1916), 192, 196, 199.

80. John Bernard Walker, *America Fallen! The Sequel to the European War* (New York: Dodd, Mead, and Co., 1915), 15, 182.

81. H. Irving Hancock, *At the Defense of Pittsburgh* (Philadelphia: Henry Altemus Company, 1916), 149.

82. Thayer, *Germany vs. Civilization*, 232, 235.

83. New York *Times Current History* 1 (1915); 454.

84. H. Nelson Gay to William Roscoe Thayer, June 22, 1915, New York Public Library MSSCOL 1124.

85. Theodore Roosevelt to "My Dear Castle."

Chapter 6

1. The best short explanation of the election is Nicole M. Phelps, "The Election of 1916," in *A Companion to Woodrow Wilson*, ed. Ross A. Kennedy (Chichester, West Sussex: John Wiley and Sons, 2013), 173–89.

2. Ogden *Standard*, January 20, 1916, 1.

3. For example, Wilson won 76 percent of the popular vote in Alabama; 80 percent in Georgia; 86 percent in Louisiana; 93 percent in Mississippi; and 97 percent in South Carolina.

4. "Difference in Our Disputes with Germany and Great Britain," *Current Opinion* 55, no. 6 (June 1916): 382.

5. See, for example, Oakland *Tribune*, February 10, 1916, 1, which featured a large-type headline that read "SECRETARY OF WAR GARRISON RESIGNS."

6. "Why the War College Asks for a Million Soldiers," *Current Opinion* 55, no. 1 (January 1916): 1e. The report itself is *Statement of a Proper Military Policy for the United States*, available at the United States Army Heritage and Education Center, US23.155.S73. The report is insightful and well researched. It includes this observation from volume 1, page 9: "The safeguard of isolation no longer exists. The oceans, once barriers, are now easy avenues of approach." American defense policy is characterized by the "erroneous conclusion drawn by the people from our past experiences in war. In developing such a policy victory is often a less trustworthy guide than defeat. We have been plunged into many wars and have ultimately emerged successful from each of them. The general public points to these experiences as an indication that our military policy has been, and continues to be, sound. That this is not really the belief of those in authority is shown by the fact that each war of importance has been followed by an official investigation of our military system and the policy under which it operated. The reports of these investigations give a startling picture of faulty leadership, needless waste of lives and property, costly overhead charges augmented by payment of bounties to keep up voluntary enlistments, undue prolongation of all these wars, and finally reckless expenditure of public funds."

7. "Secretary of War Garrison's Explanation of the Military Policy Recommended by Him," n.d. (but almost surely January or February 1916), Tennessee State Library and Archives, Governor Tom Rye Papers, Box 44, Folder 6.

8. Chicago *Day Book*, January 6, 1916, 4.

9. Boston *Transcript*, quoted in *Current Opinion* 55, no. 5 (May 1916): 309.

10. David F. Houston, *Eight Years with Wilson's Cabinet*, vol. 1 (Garden City, N.Y.: Doubleday, Page, and Company, 1926), 160–62.

11. Waterloo (Iowa) *Evening Courier*, May 26, 1916, 4. Gerald Linderman argues that these local links proved critical to the cohesion of the American system during the Civil War. See his *Embattled Courage: The Experience of Combat in the American Civil War* (New York: Free Press, 1987).

12. Lawrence Cress, *Citizens in Arms: The Army and Militia in American Society to the War of 1812* (Chapel Hill: University of North Carolina Press, 1982).

13. Of course, making fun of the militia also has a long history. See, for example, the satirical cartoons in the possession of the University of Michigan's Clements Library, http://theclementslibrary.blogspot .com/2014/10/recent-acquisition-fantastical-militias.html.

14. Waterloo (Iowa) *Evening Courier*, December 1, 1916, 4.

15. John Patrick Finnegan, *Against the Specter of a Dragon: The Campaign for American Military Preparedness* (Westport, Conn.: Greenwood, 1974), 86.

16. Ft. Wayne (Indiana) *Journal-Gazette*, January 21, 1916, 8; and Luddington (Michigan) *Daily News*, February 27, 1916, 4.

17. Finnegan, *Against the Specter of a Dragon*, 78.

18. George Herring, "James Hay and the Preparedness Controversy, 1915–1916," *Journal of Southern History* 30, no. 3 (November 1964): 396.

19. Philadelphia *Tribune*, February 26, 1916, 4.

20. Chicago *Defender*, March 18, 1916, 3.

21. Quoted in a letter from Theodore Roosevelt to Edward Rumely, September 28, 1915, in Rumely MSS, Box 7, September 18–25 folder, Lilly Library, Indiana University. The dates are correct. The letter must be in the wrong file.

22. "Lindley M. Garrison Quits Post as President Wilson's Secretary of War," Bisbee (Arizona) *Daily Review*, February 11, 1916, 1.

23. Frederick Palmer, *Bliss, Peacemaker: The Life and Letters of Tasker H. Bliss* (New York: Dodd, Mead, and Company, 1934), 111. Baker himself did not want the job, telling his friend Thomas Howells that he lacked the requisite knowledge of military matters to do it. See Newton D. Baker to Thomas Howells, February 13, 1916, New York Public Library, Manuscripts and Archives Division, Newton Diehl Baker Letters, Box 1. Howells apparently talked him into taking it.

24. *Current Opinion* 55, no. 1 (January 1916): 1d.

25. Michael S. Neiberg, *Making Citizen-Soldiers: ROTC and the Ideology of American Military Service* (Cambridge, Mass.: Harvard University Press, 2000), 23–24.

26. Herring, "James Hay and the Preparedness Controversy," 395.

27. Oakland *Tribune*, February 10, 1916, 1.

28. *National Defence* 2, no. 6 (February 1916): 211.

29. "A Letter from Colonel Roosevelt," *National Defence* 2, no. 4 (December 1915): 133.

30. Finnegan, *Against the Specter of a Dragon*, 84.

31. *National Defence* 3, no. 5 (July 1916): 241.

32. "History as It May Be," *Life*, February 10, 1916, 241, 244.

33. Also, of course, a reflection of abiding anti-Asian racism, especially on the West Coast.

34. Reprinted as "Disarmed" in *Current Opinion* 55, no. 6 (June 1916): 382.

35. Sarah McCulloh Lemmon, *North Carolina's Role in the First World War* (Raleigh: State Department of Archives and History, 1966), 13.

36. "Preparedness and the South," *Current Opinion* 55, no. 3 (March 1916): 208.

37. "The Perilous Road of Neutrality," *Current Opinion* 55, no. 3 (March 1916): 153; and "American National Spirit Aroused," *Current Opinion* 55, no. 4 (April 1916): 235.

38. Houston, *Eight Years with Wilson's Cabinet*, 195–97.

39. "Effect of the President's Appeals to the People for National Defense," *Current Opinion* 55, no. 3 (March 1916), 148.

40. Mary Roberts Rinehart, *My Story* (New York: Farrar and Rinehart, 1931), 213.

41. Caroline King Duer to Alice Duer, February 17, 1916, Caroline King Duer Papers, Barnard College Archives BC 20.20, Box 3, Folder 1.

42. Pearl Marshall, secretary to Chancellor McCormick, to Edward Rumely, October 15, 1916, in Rumely MSS, Box 8, October 14–19 folder, Lilly Library, Indiana University.

43. Philadelphia *Tribune*, October 21, 1916, 1.

44. Caroline King Duer Papers, Barnard College Archives BC 20.20, Box 2, Folder 3.15.

45. Clarence H. Cramer, *Newton D. Baker: A Biography* (Cleveland: World, 1961), 88. Baker was among those who disliked the slogan.

46. Díaz is credited with the evocative saying "Poor Mexico, so far from God, so close to the United States."

47. Alan Dawley, *Changing the World: American Progressives in War and Revolution* (Princeton: Princeton University Press, 2003), 79.

48. "Huerta Now Called a Mere German Agent" and "German Plot in Guns Held in Cuba," from Eva Stotesbury World War I Scrapbook, Reel 17, Box A63, November 25 to December 2, 1915, Library of Congress Manuscript Division.

49. Although the American press then and the American people now tend to see Villa as a bandit, he was instead a powerful political figure whom many American officials at one time wanted to support. In August 1914, during the period of good relations between Villa and the United States, he met with John Pershing at Ft. Bliss, Texas. Pershing later led the ill-starred expedition to find Villa and bring him to justice. See John T. Greenwood,

ed., *My Life Before the World War, 1860–1917: General of the Armies, John J. Pershing, a Memoir* (Lexington: University Press of Kentucky, 2013), 337.

50. Justin Kaplan, *Lincoln Steffens: A Biography* (New York: Simon and Schuster, 1974), 211–12; Edward Gibbons, *Floyd Gibbons: Your Headline Hunter, a Biography* (New York: Exposition, 1953), 55–57.

51. Edward Rumely to C. K. Warren, September 17, 1915, in Rumely MSS, Box 6, September 18–25 folder, Lilly Library, Indiana University.

52. N. G. Levin, *Woodrow Wilson and World Politics: America's Response to War and Revolution* (New York: Oxford University Press, 1968), 311.

53. "Mexican Bandits Send the Blood to Uncle Sam's Head," *Current Opinion* 55, no. 2 (February 1916): 73–74.

54. "Mexican Bandits Send the Blood to Uncle Sam's Head," 75.

55. Quoted in "Villa's Raid Secures the Right of Way for Defense Measures," *Current Opinion* 55, no. 5 (May 1916): 306.

56. Finnegan, *Against the Specter of a Dragon*, 166–71.

57. Palmer, *Bliss, Peacemaker*, 117.

58. C. Earl Baker, *Doughboy's Diary* (Shippensburg, Pa.: Burd Street, 1998), viii.

59. Thomas Boghardt, "Chasing Ghosts in Mexico: The Columbus Raid and the Politicization of U. S. Intelligence During World War I," *Army History* (Fall 2013): 11–15.

60. Anne Wintermute Lane and Louise Herrick Wall, eds., *The Letters of Franklin K. Lane, Personal and Political* (Boston: Houghton Mifflin, 1922), 207.

61. *The War Record of the Chicago Tribune*, vols. 1–2 (1919), 1:16.

62. *National Defence* 1, no. 1 (March 1915): cover.

63. Joseph Medill Patterson, *The Notebook of a Neutral* (New York: Duffield, 1916), 89–95.

64. Theodore Roosevelt to O. K. Davis, June 23, 1915, Gilder-Lehrman Collection, New-York Historical Society, GLC 08003.

65. Patterson, *The Notebook of a Neutral*, 89–95. His plan had little chance of success, as Britain already had a naval alliance with Japan that served its interests in the Pacific quite well.

66. Gilbert Vivian Seldes, *The United States and the War* (London: George Allen and Unwin, Ltd., 1917), 103.

67. Gibbons, *Floyd Gibbons*, 53.

68. "Villa's Raid Secures the Right of Way for National Defense Measures," 306–7.

69. Richard Gamble, *The War of Righteousness: Progressive Christianity, the Great War, and the Rise of the Messianic Nation* (Wilmington, Del.: ISI Books, 2003), 139.

70. Nimrod T. Frazer, *Send the Alabamians: World War I Fighters in the Rainbow Division* (Tuscaloosa: University of Alabama Press, 2014), 11.

71. Finnegan, *Against the Specter of a Dragon*, 107.

72. W. M. Hanson to J. A. Robertson, January 12, 1916, in Rumely MSS, Box 7, January 1–14 folder, Lilly Library, Indiana University.

73. *Literary Digest*, April 29, 1916, 1207.

74. Rinehart, *My Story*, 211.

75. His papers at the Manuscript Division of the Library of Congress, for example, make almost no mention of the war before American entry.

76. Justus Doenecke, *Nothing Less than War: A New History of America's Entry into World War I* (Lexington: University Press of Kentucky, 2014), 211.

77. Rinehart, *My Story*, 213.

78. "A Fight for the Soul of the Republican Party," *Current Opinion* 55, no. 6 (June 1916): 382.

79. The editorial was reprinted in Salt Lake City's *Goodwin's Weekly*, July 22, 1916, 1.

80. See, for example, the cartoon in Frederick C. Luebke, *Bonds of Loyalty: German-Americans and World War I*, (DeKalb: Northern Illinois University Press, 1974), 170, which showed the kaiser pasting a poster in support of Hughes that read, "Gott Strafe Wilson."

81. Luebke, *Bonds of Loyalty*, 168.

82. Alice Roosevelt Longworth, *Crowded Hours* (New York: Scribner's, 1935), 241.

83. Seldes, *The United States and the War*, 30.

84. Ross Gregory, *The Origins of American Intervention in the First World War* (New York: W. W. Norton, 1971), 102.

85. Sean Dennis Cashman, *America in the Age of the Titans: The Progressive Era and World War I* (New York: New York University Press, 1998), 479.

86. Edward Cuddy, "Irish-Americans and the 1916 Election: An Episode in Immigrant Adjustment," *American Quarterly* 21, no. 2 (Summer 1969): 237.

87. Luebke, *Bonds of Loyalty*, 181.

88. Charles Nagel to Edward Rumely, March 9, 1917, in Rumely MSS, Box 8, March 8–12 folder, Lilly Library, Indiana University.

89. "Hughes Explains About Lusitania," "The Attempt to 'Punish' the President," "For Hughes and the Allies," "Mr. Hughes and the Allied Blockade," and "Hughes Against Embargo on War Supplies," from Stotesbury Scrapbook, Reel 25, Box A95. There was a lot riding on Hughes in Youngstown, as he had first made a national name for himself in a speech he delivered there in 1908.

90. Henry Stimson and McGeorge Bundy, *On Active Service in Peace and War* (New York: Harper and Brothers, 1948), 87–88.

91. "What Hangs in the Balance" and "German-American Vote Much as It Was Before the War," Stotesbury World War I Scrapbook, Reel 25, Box A95.

92. Frederick Palmer, Newton D. Baker, *America at War, vol. 1*, (New York: Dodd, Mead, and Company, 1931), 73.

93. William Mulligan, *The Great War for Peace* (New Haven: Yale University Press, 2014), 174; Frederic Paxson, *American Democracy and the World War: Prewar Years, 1913–1917* (Boston: Houghton Mifflin, 1936), 365.

94. Edward Rumely to Mr. Vanderlip, October 14, 1916, in Rumely MSS, Box 8, October 14–19 folder, Lilly Library, Indiana University.

95. Eric T. Bradley Papers, Folder 1, pp. 147–52, United States Army Heritage and Education Center, Carlisle, Pa. Wilcox is best known today for the poem that contains the line "Laugh, and the world laughs with you/Weep, and you weep alone," for which she earned five dollars.

96. Seldes, *The United States and the War*, 34–35, 131–32.

97. Edward Clark, *Something Doing Every Minute: Memoirs of the Professional Life* (New York: Exposition, 1964), 16–17.

98. Palmer, *Newton D. Baker*, 82.

99. Seldes, *The United States and the War*, 9–10, 23.

100. Arthur Gleason, *Our Part in the Great War* (New York: Frederick Stockes, 1917), 128.

101. "Have We a Moral Right to Our Present Prosperity?" *Current Opinion* 60, no. 1 (January 1916), 1f.

Chapter 7

1. Timothy Meagher, quoted in Sara Goek, "The Big Picture," *Dublin Review of Books* 68 (June 2015), accessed online. My thanks to Róisín Healy for bringing the article to my attention.

2. Randolph Bourne, "Trans-National America," *Atlantic Monthly* (July 1916), 86–97.

3. In his case study of Worcester, Massachusetts, Timothy Meagher found that Irish-Americans "displayed little interest in the cause of their homeland" even during the Easter Rising. Timothy Meagher, *Inventing Irish America: Generation, Class, and Ethnic Identity in a New England City, 1880–1928* (Notre Dame: Notre Dame University Press, 2001), 359.

4. Of course, in this context, there is no connection between Irish Republicanism and the American Republican Party. See Jay P. Dolan, *The Irish-Americans: A History* (New York: Bloomsbury, 2008); and Joseph O'Grady, *How the Irish Became Americans* (New York: Twayne, 1973), for more background.

5. See, for example, the Thomas Nast cartoons at http://www.printmag.com/illustration/nast-irish; Chris McNickle, "When New York Was Irish, and After," in *The New York Irish*, ed. Ronald Bayer and Timothy Meagher (Baltimore: Johns Hopkins University Press, 1996), 350. The Fenian Raids featured five separate raids by Irish Republicans launched from American soil against Great Britain's Canadian possessions. The Fenian Brotherhood had hoped to use the raids to force Great Britain to give Ireland its independence. Few Americans supported the raids, especially given the

increase in tensions between the United States and Great Britain that resulted.

6. Noel Ignatiev takes a more complex view of this process in *How the Irish Became White* (London: Routledge Classics, 2008).

7. Frederick Palmer, *My Year of the Great War* (New York: Dodd, Mead, and Company, 1915), 248–49, 255.

8. The Easter Rising is too complex to deal with here. See Alvin Jackson, *Ireland, 1978–1998: War, Peace, and Beyond* (Chichester, West Sussex: John Wiley and Sons, 2010), chapter 5.

9. Thomas Rowland, "The American Catholic Press and the Easter Rebellion," *Catholic Historical Review* 81, no. 1 (January 1995): n.p., accessed via internet April 11, 2014.

10. David M. Tucker, "Some American Responses to the Easter Rebellion, 1916," *The Historian* 29, no. 4 (August 1967): 612, 617.

11. Charles Townshend, *Easter 1916: The Irish Rebellion* (London: Penguin, 2006), 105–6. Townshend argues that German support for the rebellion was so "ham-fisted" that perhaps Germany had meant for it to fail all along. For more see Christine Strotmann, "The Revolutionary Program of the German Empire: The Case of Ireland," in *Small Nations and Colonial Peripheries in World War I*, ed. Gearóid Barry, Enrico Del Lago, and Róisín Healy (Leiden: Brill Academic Publishers, 2016).

12. *Current Opinion* 55, no. 6 (June 1916): 391, 393.

13. "Message of Cheer Sent Out by the Rebels," *Irish Times*, May 20, 1916, 7.

14. Goek, "The Big Picture."

15. Reprinted in "German Plot for Armed Rising in America," *Irish Times*, May 24, 1916, 7.

16. Kilmer was killed on the Western Front in July 1918.

17. Townshend, *Easter, 1916*, 312.

18. David Brundage, "In Time of Peace, Prepare for War: Key Themes in the Social Thought of Irish Nationalists," in Bayer and Meagher, *The New York Irish*, 333.

19. Dolan, *The Irish-Americans*, 201–3.

20. Meagher, *Inventing Irish America*, 298.

21. Kentucky *Irish-American*, July 1, 1916, 1; and March 17, 1916, 3.

22. Malcolm Campbell, *Ireland's New Worlds* (Madison: University of Wisconsin Press, 2008), 171, 172–73.

23. Andrew Preston, *Sword of the Spirit, Shield of the Faith: Religion in American War and Diplomacy* (New York: Alfred A. Knopf, 2012), 245. Gibbons's parents were born in County Mayo, Ireland.

24. David Laskin, *The Long Way Home: An American Journey from Ellis Island to the Great War* (New York: Harper Collins, 2010), 113. See also Arthur S. Link, *Wilson, Volume 5: Campaigns for Progressivism and Peace, 1916–1917* (Princeton: Princeton University Press, 1965), 104–5.

25. Edward Cuddy, "Irish-Americans and the 1916 Election: An Episode in Immigrant Adjustment," *American Quarterly* 21, no. 2 (Summer 1969): 240.

26. Rowland, "The American Catholic Press and the Easter Rebellion," 30.

27. "Applies Wilson's Speech to Ireland," from Eva Stotesbury World War I Scrapbook, Reel 27, Box A103, October January 19 to 31, 1917, Library of Congress Manuscript Division.

28. John Duffy Ibson, *Will The World Break Your Heart? Dimensions and Consequences of Irish-American Assimilation* (New York: Garland, 1990), 83.

29. Rowland, "The American Catholic Press," n.p.

30. McNickle, "When New York Was Irish," 350.

31. Tammy Proctor, "Patriotic Enemies: Germans in the Americas, 1914–1920"; in *Germans as Minorities During the First World War: A Global Comparative Perspective*, ed. Panikos Panayi (Burlington, Vt.: Ashgate, 2014), 214–15.

32. Peter Connolly-Smith, *Translating America: An Immigrant Press Visualizes American Popular Culture, 1895–1918* (Washington: Smithsonian Books, 2004), 14.

33. George Mundelein, "Address to Catholics of German Descent," in Mundelein, *Two Crowded Years* (Chicago: Extension Press, 1918), 106.

34. Gilbert Vivian Seldes, *The United States and the War* (London: George Allen and Unwin, 1917), 132.

35. Connolly-Smith, *Translating America*, 129.

36. Frederick C. Luebke, *Bonds of Loyalty: German-Americans and World War I* (DeKalb: Northern Illinois University Press, 1974), 191.

37. Otto H. Kahn, "Prussianized Germany: Americans of Foreign Descent and America's Cause," lecture given at the Harrisburg Chamber of Commerce, September 26, 1917. National Library of Ireland, Dublin, P1001, 3, pp. 4, 9.

38. Otto Kahn, "Americans of German Origin and the War," n.d. (but certainly in early 1917), National Library of Ireland, Dublin, P1003, 22, p. 7.

39. C. Kotzenabe, "Americans of German Origin and the War." I have thus far found the letter reprinted in newspapers in a dozen states. All of them offered fulsome praise. The Aberdeen (Washington) *Herald* ran the letter under a headline reading "True German-Americanism," May 8, 1917, 1. The paper also noted that the letter was written before the American declaration of war.

40. Charles Nagel to Edward Rumely, March 9, 1917, in Rumely MSS, Box 8, March 8–12 folder, Lilly Library, Indiana University.

41. Edward Rumely to John Burgess, October 18, 1916, in Rumely MSS, Box 8, October 14–19 folder, Lilly Library, Indiana University.

42. Mundelein, "Address to Catholics of German Descent," 106–7.

43. "Says Germans Fail to Uplift America;" from Stotesbury Scrapbook, Reel 25, Box A95, October 20 to November 5.

44. "T. R. a Very Devil, Viereck Thinks," New York *Tribune*, April 29, 1916, 5.

45. "Münsterberg Sees Kultur Worldwide" and "Asks Ejection of Dr. Münsterberg"; in Eva Stotesbury Scrapbook, Reel 25, Box A95.

46. Alexander Waldenrath, "The German Language Newspapers in Pennsylvania During World War I," *Pennsylvania History* 42, no. 1 (January 1975), 34–35.

47. Newell Dwight Hillis, "The Verdict of the American People," *New York Times Current History* 1 (1915); 578.

48. "German-Americans," Chicago *Day Book*, May 3, 1916, 1.

49. New Ulm (Minnesota) *Review*, November 1, 1916, 4. New Ulm was founded by immigrants from Bavaria.

50. Rickenbacker's family emigrated from Switzerland and often spoke German at home.

51. Preston, *Sword of the Spirit*, 244.

52. "Pope Asked to Try for Peace," Tulsa *World*, December 13, 1916, 1. The Allies dismissed German efforts as insincere and cynical, though they did lead to a Papal Peace Note from Benedict XV in August 1917. See http://www.firstworldwar.com/source/papalpeacenote.htm.

53. George Mundelein, "Address at the Catholic Charities of Chicago," April 10, 1917, in Mundelein, *Two Crowded Years*, 147.

54. New Ulm (Minnesota) *Review*, November 1, 1916, 4.

55. Wilson did later veto the Volstead Act which provided for federal enforcement of Prohibition. The Republican Congress overrode his veto.

56. Ray Stannard Baker, *American Chronicle* (New York: Scribner's, 1945), 303.

57. Nagel to Rumely, March 9, 1917.

58. Christopher M. Sterba, *Good Americans: Italian and Jewish Immigrants During the First World War* (New York: Oxford University Press, 2003), 26.

59. The manufactured nostalgia for the Old World came much later with the 1964 Broadway phenomenon *Fiddler on the Roof.*

60. H. G. Enelow, "Russia and the Jews," n.d. (but certainly early 1917), in *The Allied Countries and the Jews*, sermons delivered at the Temple Emanu-El, American Jewish Historical Society, New York City.

61. Laskin, *Long Way Home*, 94, 99.

62. They also included the German-born Julius Kahn, a member of the House of Representatives from California who helped to draft the 1916 National Defense Act.

63. *Life*, February 10, 1916, 248.

64. "An Appeal to Patriotism," August 1916, Rabbi Samuel Price Scrapbook, P–95, Box 7, American Jewish Historical Society, New York City.

65. American Jewish Congress, I–77, Box 8, Folder 1, American Jewish Historical Society, New York City.

66. Rabbi Samuel Price Papers, P–95, 1913–62, Box 1, diary entry for November 28, 1914, American Jewish Historical Society, New York City.

67. Isaac Siegel, *European War Zone Conditions* (Washington: Government Printing Office, 1916), 9.

68. For more, see Jesse Kauffman, *Elusive Alliance: The German Occupation of Poland in World War I* (Cambridge, Mass.: Harvard University Press, 2015), 124–34.

69. See Abraham Duker, *Jews in the World War: A Brief Historical Sketch* (New York: American Jewish Committee, 1939), 11, 15. For more on the *Judenzählung*, see http://encyclopedia.1914-1918-online.net/article/wild_von_hohenborn_adolf.

70. Tamas Stark, "The 'Ostjuden' Question in Hungary During World War I: How Galician Jewish Refugees Became Hungary's 'Number One Enemies,'" paper delivered at *Representing World War I: Perspectives at the Centenary* conference, Toronto, October 31, 2014.

71. Ben Altheimer, "Aspects of the Anti-Semitic Movement in Germany," *American Hebrew and Jewish Messenger*, August 18, 1916, 456.

72. "Dull Misery," *Jewish Advocate*, January 11, 1917, 8.

73. "Among Our Brethren Abroad: Anti-Semitism in Germany," *American Hebrew and Jewish Messenger*, January 26, 1917, 377.

74. Price Papers, diary entry for November 7, 1914. He reiterated the promise of the Allies "that, in case they win, they will give Palestine to the Jews" in his January 2, 1915, diary entry.

75. Israel Zangwill, *The War for the World* (New York: Macmillan, 1916); and "Zangwill on the Jews as a Factor in the War—And After the War," *Richmond Times-Dispatch*, February 20, 1916, n.p. Zangwill favored a Jewish homeland, but did not care if it was in Palestine or somewhere else.

76. H. G. Enelow, "France and the Jews," n.d. (but certainly early 1917), in *The Allied Countries and the Jews*, sermons delivered at the Temple Emanu-El, American Jewish Historical Society, New York City.

77. H. G. Enelow, "England and the Jews," n.d. (but certainly early 1917), in *The Allied Countries and the Jews*, sermons delivered at the Temple Emanu-El, American Jewish Historical Society, New York City.

78. "Israel's Future in America," Rabbi Samuel Price Scrapbook, P–95, Box 7, American Jewish Historical Society, New York City.

79. The *American Hebrew and Jewish Messenger* reprinted the editorial with favorable comments in its March 16, 1917, issue.

80. Price Papers, diary entry for March 17, 1917. Emphasis in original.

81. "What It Means to Us," *American Israelite*, March 22, 1916, 4.

82. Enelow, "Russia and the Jews," 41, 47.

83. "Russia-Germany-America," *American Israelite*, March 29, 1917, 4.

84. http://www.gutenberg.org/files/19179/19179-8.txt.

85. *Iowa State Bystander*, September 4, 1914, 2; and May 21, 1915, 2.

86. Jennifer D. Keene, "Americans Respond: Perspectives on the Global War, 1914–1917," *Geschichte und Gesellschaft* 40 (2014): 274.

87. W. E. Burghardt Du Bois, "The African Roots of War," *Atlantic Monthly* 115 (May 1915): 707–14. See also "Lusitania," *The Crisis* 10 (June 1915), cited in chapter 3.

88. Keene, "Americans Respond," 275–76.

89. Chad L. Williams, *Torchbearers of Democracy: African American Soldiers in the World War I Era* (Chapel Hill: University of North Carolina Press, 2010), 13; "Five Negroes Lynched by a Florida Mob," High Point (North Carolina) *Review*, August 24, 1916, 2.

90. The numbers are compiled from a Tuskegee Institute study and are at http://law2.umkc.edu/faculty/projects/ftrials/shipp/lynchingyear.html. See also William Jordan, *Black Newspapers and America's War for Democracy, 1914–1920* (Chapel Hill: University of North Carolina Press, 2001), 43, who cites the number of fifty lynchings of African-Americans in 1915 and thirty-nine in 1916. There was also the notable lynching of the Jewish Leo Frank, the president of the Atlanta B'nai B'rith, in 1915 in Marietta, Georgia, although the numbers of white lynching victims was far smaller than the number of black victims.

91. Williams, *Torchbearers of Democracy*, 23–24.

92. Jordan, *Black Newspapers*, 41–42.

93. Jordan, *Black Newspapers*, 42, 45.

94. For more, see http://encyclopedia.1914-1918-online.net/article/colonial_military_participation_in_europe_africa.

95. See Isabel Hull, *Absolute Destruction: Military Culture and the Practices of War in Imperial Germany* (Ithaca, N.Y.: Cornell University Press, 2004), chapters 1–3.

96. For an excellent study of the many complexities of French racial attitudes, see Richard S. Fogarty, *Race and War in France: Colonial Subjects in the French Army, 1914–1918* (Baltimore: Johns Hopkins University Press, 2008).

97. Adriane Lentz-Smith, *Freedom Struggles: African-Americans and World War I* (Cambridge, Mass.: Harvard University Press, 2009), 17.

98. Jordan, *Black Newspapers*, 63.

99. Lentz-Smith, *Freedom Struggles*, 38, 40.

100. "Break Ground for New 8th Regiment Armory," Chicago *Defender*, August 8, 1914, 4.

101. "Telegraph Tips," Washington *Herald*, October 1, 1916, 1.

102. Fish's grandfather was secretary of state under President Grant, his father was speaker of the New York state assembly, and Fish himself went on to serve twenty-five years in the United States House of Representatives.

103. Peter N. Nelson, *A More Unbending Battle: The Harlem Hellfighters' Struggle for Freedom in World War I and Equality at Home* (New York: BasicCivitas, 2009), 7–8, 13.

104. Cedar Falls (Iowa) *Record*, June 1, 1916, 4.

105. Atlanta *Constitution*, June 23, 1916, 48.

106. Some of those soldiers, men of the 10th Cavalry Regiment, fought at the Battle of Carrizal.

107. "Down on the Mexican Border," Kansas City *Sun*, May 6, 1916, 1. Upon American entry into the war, the War Department, under pressure from both Wilson and Mississippi senator John Sharp Williams, put Young, then a colonel, on the retired list. They alleged that he was too ill for overseas service, but the move really came in order to prevent an African-American officer from rising to the rank of brigadier general. To prove how ludicrous the charge of ill health was, Young rode on horseback from Ohio to Washington, D.C., to protest his retirement in person, but to no avail. See Williams, *Torchbearers of Democracy*, 46–49.

108. Arizona *Evening World*, June 28, 1916, 2. The same issue of the paper supported war with Mexico if it did not return all prisoners of war from the Carrizal skirmish, black and white. Mexico eventually did so.

109. "Is the Clock Striking the Hour?" Chicago *Defender*, May 15, 1915, 8. Emphasis in original.

110. Philadelphia *Tribune*, July 8, 1916, 4.

111. *Afro-American,* February 12, 1916, 4.

112. Jordan, *Black Newspapers*, 62.

113. Jordan, *Black Newspapers*, 66. Emphasis in original.

114. Kevin M. Schultz, *Tri-Faith America: How Catholics and Jews Held Postwar America to Its Protestant Promise* (New York: Oxford University Press, 2011). My thanks to Andrew Preston for his discussion with me about this book.

115. For a case study, see Steven Wrede, "The Americanization of Scott County, 1914–1918," *Annals of Iowa* 44 (1979): 627–38.

Chapter 8

1. Other than perhaps Pope Benedict XV, who made peace efforts of his own. For more, see Ross Kennedy, "Peace Initiatives," in http://encyclopedia.1914-1918-online.net/article/peace_initiatives.

2. "To Make Peace Permanent," *Cooper's International Journal* 26, no. 12 (December 1916): 599.

3. The Treaty of Bucharest, in Elke Bornemann's words, reduced Romania to "the position of a vassal state of Germany, with its sovereignty a mere shadow," quoted in Vejas Liulevicius, "German Occupied Eastern Europe," in *A Companion to World War I*, ed. John Horne (Malden, Mass.: Wiley-Blackwell, 2010), 456. The Treaty of Brest-Litovsk, which the Germans imposed on Russia, seized one million square miles, sixty-two million people, and enormous quantities of oil, grain, and other resources.

4. "The Progress of the World," *Review of Reviews* 55, no. 1 (January 1917): 4–7, 31.
5. *America's Attitude Toward the War* (New York: Bankers Trust, 1917), 71.
6. Washington *Evening Star*, January 13, 1917, 1.
7. "German Views Regarding Holland," *Review of Reviews* 55, no. 1 (January 1917): 90, reported that German officials had demanded the annexation of Holland, which the German officials said was "already fertilized by German blood, for the enlargement of their economic domain."
8. *Literary Digest* 54, no. 1 (January 6, 1917): 2; and 54, no. 3 (January 20): 109.
9. "Peace Hopes Fade in Washington," New York *Times*, January 19, 1917; "Prussians Demand Ruthless War"; and Associated Press, "1,000 Submarines Being Built for Starvation War," from Eva Stotesbury World War I Scrapbook, Reel 27, Box A103, January 19 to 31, 1917, Library of Congress Manuscript Division.
10. "What Newspapers of This Country Say Regarding President's Speech" and "The President's Peace Terms," from Eva Stotesbury World War I Scrapbook, Reel 27, Box A103, January 19 to 31, 1917, Library of Congress Manuscript Division.
11. "Warns Nation Its Neutrality May Bring War Here," from Stotesbury Scrapbook, Reel 27, Box A103.
12. Woodbridge N. Ferris to Edward Rumely, October 31, 1916, in Rumely MSS, Box 8, October 20–31 folder, Lilly Library, Indiana University.
13. Stewart Paton, "Psychology of Neutrality," from Stotesbury Scrapbook, Reel 27, Box A103.
14. *Literary Digest* 54, no. 2 (January 13, 1917): 51.
15. "The Progress of the World," *Review of Reviews* 55, no. 3 (March 1917): 227. The problem would have been multiplied many times over had Americans been able to see into the future and know about the millions of people killed by the 1918–19 influenza epidemic, itself at least partly a product of the reduced health conditions, crowding of people at the front and at home, and the global movements of people and animals that the war created.
16. "The Progress of the World," *Review of Reviews* 55, no. 3 (March 1917): 238.
17. Samuel Dutton, "The United States and the War," *Annals of the American Academy of Political and Social Science* 72 (July 1917): 14. The essays in this volume come from the academy's March meeting.
18. Winston Churchill, *A Traveler in Wartime* (New York: Macmillan, 1918), 9. There is no relation to the more famous British politician of the same name. This Winston Churchill was born in St. Louis.
19. Andrew McLaughlin, "The Great War from Spectator to Participant," Pennsylvania State Library, Harrisburg, pamphlet PV 1890, 9–10.
20. Walter Lippmann, "The World Conflict in Its Relation to American Democracy," *Annals of the American Academy of Political and Social Science* 72 (July 1917): 4.

21. *Review of Reviews* 55, no. 4 (April 1917): 375.
22. Columbia University to American Ambassador in Petrograd, April 13, 1917, in Columbia University Rare Books and Manuscript Library, World War I Collection, 1914–44, 1970 (UA #014), Box 16, Folder 1613.
23. "The Progress of the World," *Review of Reviews* 55, no. 4 (April 1917): 340–41.
24. "The Progress of the World," *Review of Reviews* 55, no. 4 (April 1917): 346.
25. Lippmann, "The World Conflict," 3.
26. "Press of Country Thinks Break Sure," and "Comments of This Morning's Newspapers on the German Note," from Stotesbury Scrapbook, Reel 27, Box A103.
27. *Literary Digest* 54, no. 6 (February 10, 1917): 321–23.
28. Sarah McCulloh Lemmon, *North Carolina's Role in the First World War* (Raleigh: State Department of Archives and History, 1966), 15.
29. Preston William Slosson, *The Great Crusade and After, 1914–1928* (New York: Macmillan, 1931), 28.
30. Justus Doenecke, *Nothing Less than War: A New History of America's Entry into World War I* (Lexington: University Press of Kentucky, 2014), 252–61.
31. John Patrick Finnegan, *Against the Specter of a Dragon: The Campaign for American Military Preparedness, 1914–1917* (Westport, Conn.: Greenwood, 1974), 185.
32. Newton D. Baker, *Why We Went to War* (New York: Harper and Brothers for Council on Foreign Relations, 1936), 93–94.
33. Baker, *Why We Went to War*, 95.
34. Anne Wintermute Lane and Louise Herrick Wall, eds., *The Letters of Franklin K. Lane, Personal and Political* (Boston: Houghton Mifflin, 1922), 233.
35. Rabbi Samuel Price Papers, P–95, 1913–62, Box 1, diary entries for February 2 and 4, 1917, American Jewish Historical Society, New York City.
36. *America's Attitude Toward the War*, 99.
37. See, for example, the Chicago *Day Book* of February 7, 1917.
38. Henry Landau, *The Enemy Within: The Inside Story of German Sabotage in America* (New York: G. P. Putnam's Sons, 1937), 92–94.
39. *Literary Digest* 54, no. 4 (January 27, 1917): 177.
40. "Is It Armageddon?" *Jewish Advocate*, February 8, 1917, 8.
41. Samuel Taylor Moore, *America and the World War* (New York: Greenberg, 1937), 57. The Senate did not then have a rule on the length of filibusters or a way to end them. This debate led to the first cloture vote in Senate history. Lodge, at least, was partly motivated by his deep personal hatred for Wilson. As he told Theodore Roosevelt, he "never expected to hate anyone in politics with the hatred I feel toward Wilson." See Anne Cipriano Venzon, *The United States and the First World War: An Encyclopedia* (New York: Garland, 1995), 350.

42. Lemmon, *North Carolina's Role in the First World War*, 15; and "Senate to Uphold Wagner," New York *Sun*, April 4, 1917, 5.

43. Floyd Gibbons, *And They Thought We Wouldn't Fight*, ed. Michael S. Neiberg (Chicago: Lakeside, 2014), 30.

44. http://www.archives.gov/education/lessons/zimmermann/.

45. See Thomas Boghardt, *The Zimmermann Telegram: Intelligence, Diplomacy, and America's Entry into World War I* (Annapolis: United States Naval Institute Press, 2012), for the full story.

46. These fears gave Wilson some pause, as he worried that Americans suspicious of British motives might not believe such a transparent German act of aggression. Zimmermann admitted to the telegram knowing that the British could prove its authenticity in any case. He also may have hoped that he could negotiate with Mexico and Japan openly.

47. Phillip Gonzales and Ann Massmann, "Loyalty Questioned: Nuevomexicanos in the Great War," *Pacific Historical Review* 75, no. 4 (December 2006): 641.

48. *Review of Reviews* 55, no. 4 (April 1917): 355–56.

49. Roy V. Myers, *Notes on the World's War*, 2, United States Army Heritage and Education Center, Carlisle, Pa.

50. Price Papers, P–95, 1913–62, Box 1, diary entry for March 1, 1917.

51. "Questions," S. Stephen Da Costa Papers, Folder 1, United States Army Heritage and Education Center, Carlisle, Pa.

52. *Review of Reviews* 55, no. 3 (March 1917): 255.

53. "The Crisis," *Jewish Exponent*, February 9, 1917, 4.

54. Lemmon, *North Carolina's Role in the First World War*, 16.

55. Frederick Palmer, *Bliss, Peacemaker: The Life and Letters of Tasker H. Bliss* (New York: Dodd, Mead, and Company, 1934).

56. Richard Gamble, *The War of Righteousness: Progressive Christianity, the Great War, and the Rise of the Messianic Nation* (Wilmington, Del.: ISI Books, 2003), 142–48.

57. McLaughlin, "The Great War from Spectator to Participant," 14–16.

58. John Sharp Williams, "War to Stop War," *Annals of the American Academy of Political and Social Science* 72 (July 1917): 178–81.

59. Franklin Lane to George Lane, April 1, 1917, in Lane and Wall, *Letters of Franklin Lane*, 243.

60. Margaret R. Higgonet, ed., *Letters and Photographs from the Battle Country: The World War I Memoir of Margaret Hall* (Charlottesville: University of Virginia Press, 2014), 3. The colleges were Barnard, Bryn Mawr, Goucher, Mt. Holyoke, Radcliffe, Smith, Vassar, and Wellesley.

61. Howard Gray, *The Mind of America* (London: Darling and Son, 1918), 10.

62. The speech was reprinted as A. W. Ricker, *Why We Acquiesce: To Win the War. Where the Socialists Stand Now* (San Francisco: People's Library, 1918).

63. Alan Cywar, "John Dewey in World War I: Patriotism and International Progressivism," *American Quarterly* 21, no. 3 (Autumn 1969): 580–84.

64. *Literary Digest* 54, no. 7 (February 17, 1917): 388.

65. Charles Nagel to Edward Rumely, March 9, 1917, in Rumely MSS, Box 8, March 8–12 folder, Lilly Library, Indiana University; *Review of Reviews* 55, no. 3 (March 1917): 259; and Tammy Proctor, "'Patriotic Enemies': Germans in the Americas, 1914–1920," in *Germans as Minorities During the First World War: A Global Comparative Perspective,* ed. Panikos Panayi (Burlington, Vt.: Ashgate, 2014).

66. Franklin Lane to George Lane, February 20, 1917, in Lane and Wall, *Letters of Franklin Lane,* 238. These letters are a terrific source for the frustration many of Wilson's advisors felt toward him in these crucial weeks.

67. Newton Baker to Thomas Howells, February 25, 1917, Newton Diehl Baker Letters, New York Public Library Manuscripts and Archives Division.

68. "Address Delivered by Hon. Jacob M. Dickinson, as Chairman of a Patriotic Meeting, at Auditorium Theater, Chicago, Saturday, March 31, 1917," Tennessee State Library and Archives, Jacob McGavock Dickinson Papers, Box 65, Folder 6.

69. Alice Roosevelt Longworth, *Crowded Hours* (New York: Scribner's, 1935), 243–44.

70. Doenecke, *Nothing Less than War,* 256.

71. Ross Gregory, *The Origins of American Intervention in the First World War* (New York: W. W. Norton, 1971), 125.

72. Lemmon, *North Carolina's Role in the First World War,* 15.

73. Price Papers, P–95, 1913–62, Box 1, diary entry for March 25, 1917.

74. Doenecke, *Nothing Less than War,* 281.

75. *Philadelphia in the World War* (New York: Wynkoop Hallenbeck Crawford, 1922), 27.

76. Correspondence Re: Offering Services to the Nation, Tennessee State Library and Archives, Nashville, Gov. Tom Rye Papers, 1915–18, Box 31, Folder 9.

77. Columbia University Rare Books and Manuscript Library, World War I Collection, 1914–44, 1970 (UA #014), Box 16, Folder 1611.

78. "The Progress of the World," *Review of Reviews* 54, no. 3 (March 1917): 230.

79. Mary Roberts Rinehart, "The Altar of Freedom," *Saturday Evening Post,* April 21, 1917, 6, 37.

80. "The Progress of the World," *Review of Reviews* 55, no. 3 (March 1917): 235.

81. Price Papers, P–95, 1913–62, Box 1, diary entry for April 6, 1917.

Conclusion

1. Quoted in Mark Harris, *Five Came Back: A Story of Hollywood and the Second World War* (New York: Penguin, 2014), 7. Alsop was a great-grandnephew of Theodore Roosevelt.

2. F. Scott Fitzgerald and Matthew J. Bruccoli, *The Short Stories of F. Scott Fitzgerald: A New Collection* (New York: Scribner's, 1995), 512. For more see

Edward Gutiérrez, *Doughboys on the Great War: How American Soldiers Viewed Their Experiences* (Lawrence: University Press of Kansas, 2014); G. Kurt Piehler, *Remembering War the American Way* (Washington: Smithsonian Institute Press, 2004); and Samuel Hynes, *The Soldier's Tale: Bearing Witness to a Modern War* (New York: Penguin, 1998).

3. F. Scott Fitzgerald, *The Great Gatsby* (New York: Scribner's, 1995 edition), 10–11. Of course, like so much else in the novel, Gatsby's medals could well have been an affectation designed to help him win the heart of Daisy Buchanan. See Maureen Corrigan, *So We Read On: How the Great Gatsby Came to Be and Why It Endures* (New York: Little, Brown and Company, 2014), 67–68.

4. Tom Brokaw, *The Greatest Generation* (New York: Random House, 2001).

5. There is a small memorial called Pershing Park at 14th and Pennsylvania Avenue but it has never served as a site of memory for the war. There is currently a plan to redesign Pershing Park, but it is highly unlikely that it will be even a fraction of the size of the World War II memorial. My thanks to industrial designer Louis Nelson, designer of the Korean War Memorial, for his insights on this process.

6. Eventually the National Parks Service did agree to take on the task of cleaning and repairing the monument, but only after private money was raised to pay for it. There was legislation pending to rededicate it as the National World War I Memorial, but given that only the names of men from Washington appear on it, that solution was always problematic, to say the least.

7. This is the phrase used on the official Army medals from the war.

8. Its website is www.theworldwar.org. I would like to thank Lora Vogt, Matt Naylor, Jon Casey, Doran Cart, and everyone at the museum for their help and hospitality on many visits there.

9. The historian is Mark Levitch. See http://www.centenarynews.com/article?id=1650. Fittingly enough, the first United Nations conference was held at the San Francisco Opera House in 1945.

10. Lisa W. Foderaro, "Defaced World War I Memorial in Brooklyn Is Rebuilt," *New York Times*, September 11, 2004, A20.

11. Pittsburgh's hippest and most rapidly gentrifying neighborhood, Lawrenceville, has chosen as its emblem of resurgence a silhouette of the Doughboy Statue in the heart of the neighborhood at Butler Street and Penn Avenue. Although few of the people who come there today will know it, the Lafayette Escadrille's Billy Thaw is buried just a short stroll away in Allegheny Cemetery.

12. See, for example, Sean Kirst, "Ultimate Sacrifice, Communal Memory: Long After World War I, Appreciating Solvay's Forgotten Son," *Syracuse Post-Standard*, May 18, 2014, available at http://www.syracuse.com/kirst/index.ssf/2014/05/ultimate_sacrifice_communal_memory_almost_a_century_after_world_war_i_solvay_hon.html.

13. Studs Terkel, *The Good War: An Oral History of World War II* (New York: Ballantine, 1985).

14. Paul Fussell, a veteran of the war, offered a scathing critique of American memory in his *Wartime: Understanding and Behavior in the Second World War* (New York: Oxford University Press, 1990). See also John Bodnar, *The Good War in American Memory* (Baltimore: Johns Hopkins University Press, 2010).

15. Private Alexander Clay, 33rd (US) Infantry Division, 131st Regiment, Veterans Survey, USAHEC.

16. For more see my *Potsdam: The End of the Second World War and Remaking of Europe* (New York: Basic, 2015).

17. For a current example, see David Stockman, "The Epochal Consequences of Woodrow Wilson's War," available at http://davidstockmanscontracorner .com/the-epochal-consequences-of-woodrow-wilsons-war/. By contrast, Newton Baker noted in his memoirs that he never once spoke to a banker during his time as secretary of war. Wilson, moreover, was unpopular with Wall Street, which overwhelmingly backed Charles Evans Hughes in 1916. Wilson's advisor Edward House even moved far uptown when he came to New York City to avoid being anywhere near the solidly Republican Wall Street community. Newton D. Baker, *Why We Went to War* (New York: Harper and Brothers for Council on Foreign Relations, 1936), 119.

18. New York *Tribune*, October 22, 1916, 1.

19. These scholars include Christopher Capozzola, Julia Irwin, Jennifer Keene, Erez Manela, Chad Williams, Edward Gutiérrez, and many more.

20. Raymond Chamberlain, *The Only Thing for a Man to Do* (Boston: Privately Published, 1921), v, 12. Available at the United States Army Heritage and Education Center, Carlisle, Pa.

INDEX

Abbott, Lyman, 75, 222
Aberdeen Herald, letter supporting
  US entry into war, 275n39
Acculturation and assimilation
  of German-Americans, 187, 190
  of immigrants, 179–180
  of Jewish-Americans, 194–195
  WWI's impact on, 205, 235
Adams, Charles Francis, 55
Addams, Jane, 84, 141
AFL (American Federation of Labor),
  84, 136, 223
African-American press. *See also*
  individual newspapers (e.g.,
  Chicago Defender)
  on Belgium, 29
  on black nurses in France, 46
  on Continental Army Plan,
    157–158
  on French Army, 47
  on *Lusitania* sinking, 68
African-Americans
  American identity of, 199–204
  Anti-Hyphenism among, 147
  economic opportunities for, 49
  in federal reserve, 157

lynchings of, 200, 204, 278n90
WWI, attitude toward, 5
Afro-American (Baltimore newspaper)
  on autocracies, end of, 23
  on *Lusitania* sinking, 68
  on Preparedness, black community
    and, 204
  on US, need for true democracy in,
    200, 201
Aid and charities during war, 44–47,
  112–113
Aid to Serbia Fund, 112–113
Airplanes, private financing for
  military use, 140
Albert, Heinrich, 78–79, 80, 256n52
Alexander, Moses, 194
Allies. *See also* Britain; France; Italy;
  Russia
  American volunteers for, 74, 109–112
  Jewish support for, 197
  Morgan's underwriting of loans to,
    98–99
  Ohioans' support for, 117
  proclamation supporting, 116
  trade with, 47, 49
  US, dependence on, 153, 215

287